The
ecstasy
of loving God

BOOKS BY JOHN CROWDER

Miracle Workers, Reformers, and the New Mystics

The Ecstasy of Loving God

AVAILABLE FROM DESTINY IMAGE PUBLISHERS

The
ecstasy
of loving God

Trances, Raptures,

and the

Supernatural Pleasures

of Jesus Christ

john crowder

DESTINY IMAGE® PUBLISHERS, INC.

P.O. Box 310, Shippensburg, PA 17257-0310

"Speaking to the Purposes of God for this Generation and for the Generations to Come."

This book and all other Destiny Image, Revival Press, Mercy Place, Fresh Bread, Destiny Image Fiction, and Treasure House books are available at Christian bookstores and distributors worldwide.

For a U.S. bookstore nearest you, call 1-800-722-6774.

For more information on foreign distributors, call 717-532-3040.

Or reach us on the Internet: www.destinyimage.com

ISBN 10: 0-7684-2742-8

ISBN 13: 978-0-7684-2742-4

For Worldwide Distribution, Printed in the U.S.A.

6 7 8 9 10 11 / 20 19 18 17

Dedication

I dedicate this work to my wife, Lily, who has stood by my side as a "co-pioneer" in this enthralling Kingdom adventure. Your heart for experimentation and your willingness as a radical risk-taker has brought freedom, life, and transformation to thousands of lives—and all this with four kids in tow. This book would not have been written without your enthusiastic sacrifice.

Acknowledgments

I acknowledge some very special people who made this work possible—first and foremost David Vaughan and Justin Abraham for their constant encouragement to press deeper into the mystical realms. Their total abandonment to the wildfire of God's Spirit and their inability to care about religious appeasement has been a stalwart support. As Henry Adams once said, "One friend in a lifetime is much; two are many; three are hardly possible." Thanks for being true friends.

I would like to recognize the contributions of my children. More than anyone else, perhaps, they have shared their father's time and energy with the church. They have provided regular inspiration during the writing of these chapters, and they are each very beautiful as individual gifts from God.

Our Sons of Thunder associates and staff have also been a huge encouragement during the writing of this book. Association with a fore-running ministry brings blessings, and at times, misunderstanding. Your hunger for the deeper things of Heaven and your boldness to forge ahead into new ground is a great delight. Heaven knows you. We run with the best.

Thanks to Benjamin and Stephanie Dunn for drinking deeply of the Spirit anywhere and everywhere, especially at the most inappropriate times and places. Your uninhibited example of carefree indulgence in the Gospel is a refreshing injection in the midst of empire-building ministry machines, boring meetings, and conference doldrums. Stay whacked.

There are a number of mystical theologians to whom I am likewise indebted for their research and collections of historical narratives. These include Montague Summers, R.P. Augustin Poulan, Albert Farges, Albert J. Hebert, Herbert Thurston, and Joan Carroll Cruz. The work of Ann Taves, Leigh Eric Schmidt, and William DeArteaga was also highly beneficial. On a personal note, I am grateful for the writings of C.S. Lewis, John Piper, and Mike Bickle, as well as the real-life example and writings of some of my favorite mystics, Teresa of Avila and Brother Lawrence.

Lily and I are also ever appreciative of the support of our parents. You are the best!

And last, thanks to Destiny Image for your thoughtful contributions to this work, as well as your venturesome willingness to expose the Church to supernatural, mystical Christianity in an age when unbelief has—for a short season—prevailed. We appreciate your support.

Endorsements

The Church has long been amiss in not understanding ecstasy, indeed nearly all our high experiences in our Lord's loving presence. We tend to revile what we don't understand (see Jude 10). We have often reacted to the word *ecstasy* as though it means some kind of off-kilter wildness that needs to be avoided in the name of common sense and balance. John Crowder's book dispels fear and gives historical understanding and wisdom, properly enticing all of us into loving encounters with our Lord. In this time, when the Holy Spirit is calling us all into intimacy with the Lord Jesus Christ, this book is greatly needed and should be welcomed by all Christians who seek His face.

JOHN SANDFORD
Cofounder, Elijah House Ministries

Combining a depth of historical research and passion for Jesus, John Crowder brings together a rare blend for an emerging generation voice. His writings inspire me, challenge me, and make me turn my head. His calling to take the historical orthodoxy of the Holy Spirit packaged into a "today's style" is an amazing work of art.

JAMES W. GOLL
Cofounder, Encounters Network and Prayer Storm Director

John Crowder is an inspiration to the emerging generation. He lives a supernatural lifestyle rooted in years of deep study of church history and the Word. He challenges the mindsets of our time to release us into the very fullness of Christ. His messages are stretching, revelatory, and revolutionary. We highly commend him to you and know that this book is a timely reve-lation of the intimate realm God is calling His end-time Church to embrace. Get ready to experience a deeper union with Jesus than you've known before and to see Him work great supernatural exploits through your life. You are part of the generation that creation has been groaning for. This is your time to arise and shine to see nations changed forever.

JUSTIN ABRAHAM
Cofounder, Emerge Wales

God is opening up to us the mystic realm like never before. I was like a child in a candy store reading John's last book, *Miracle Workers, Reformers, and the New Mystics.* It so resonated with what I saw God wanted to release to this generation. *The Ecstasy of Loving God* builds powerfully upon John's last publication and opens up to us even more in our day that which is ours by inheritance. After reading this book, you will be inspired to enjoy Him like never before and to press for greater dimensions of the Kingdom of God to manifest in your life. John and Lily Crowder are great friends and mentors to our family and are real pioneers of the new things that God is releasing in these days.

DAVID VAUGHAN
Cofounder, Emerge Wales

John Crowder is a revolutionary writer and speaker who carries a message of a heart overwhelmed and immersed with divine pleasure, and I am honored to call him a friend.

BENJAMIN DUNN
Joy Revolution

Human beings are hard-wired for pleasure. Our native habitat is Eden, Hebrew for *pleasure.* Outside of pleasure, we suffer the stress of an alien and painful environment—the world. Through the ages, mystics and prophets have escaped the system by passing through the veil into a state of holy love and boundless pleasure in God. Plunge into the joy of mystical communion! John's excellent scholarship and profound insights invite you into the pleasure-glory realms of God's love!

CHARLES STOCK
Senior Pastor, Life Center Ministries
Harrisburg, Pennsylvania

John Crowder has always been someone I have respected and loved. He is more than a public persona; he is a deep, sincere individual who genuinely wants the *real thing.* His previous book, *Miracle Workers, Reformers, and the New Mystics,* was truly groundbreaking, and I actually used it as a personal devotional, wanting to read it slowly, daily, as to not rush through it, but really absorb it. As with everything God does, we go from glory to glory. *The Ecstasy of Loving God* is no exception to that principle, and you will be blessed as you read it. Congratulations, John, on another pioneering work!

DAVID TOMBERLIN
David Tomberlin Ministries

Table of Contents

Foreword

John Crowder is a true revivalist. As a miracle worker, teacher, and author, John communicates like none other. Not only is John a friend of God, he is a friend of mine. I have witnessed his love for God and others over and over, and there is a solid consistency woven through his life.

This new book, *The Ecstasy of Loving God*, is an incredible must-read for all who hunger and thirst for the greater glory of God.

In every generation from age to age there have been forerunning believers, saints and mystics, who have risen up in their day and stepped past the so-called religious order of their time to release a higher reality and demonstration of the Kingdom of God. With mind-boggling power and consequence they have wonderfully manifested authority that reached beyond what most had ever seen or experienced. These forerunning saints were birthed out of an intimate relationship with Jesus Christ, and as lovesick slaves they crossed over the line of mediocrity to challenge the stagnant traditionalist mindset of the day. They drastically impacted the world around them as they released a true sign of what was to come in the Body of Christ. Each was unique in what they brought. Each was unique in what they contributed—and now this collective boiling pot of revelation and impartation is being released upon an end-time glory generation for world harvest. God will have a company of believers that will believe Him for the humanly impossible. He will have a people that will live supernaturally, acting as blood-bought sons and daughters—offspring of the living God.

This new rising glory generation is not satisfied with the status quo or the religious order of the day. This generation will not stop until they are walking in the full manifestation of the same power and glory of the early mystics, reformers, saints, and revivalists.

In John Crowder's book, *The Ecstasy of Loving God*, we're able to see fresh into the lives of many past saints and understand what fueled their passion and caused them to move in the awesome wonder of the bizarre miracles they displayed. We see their dedication and consecration to the Lord in communion and how it was maintained through a life of contemplative prayer and interior graces. These saints would literally lose sight of themselves being rapt in ecstatic, blissful communion with Jesus. Even the state of their physical bodies would be altered to manifest an outward light in appearance of a higher place in God revealing His glory.

As you read this book, be prepared to see the Christian life from a whole new perspective, and be challenged by saints whose lives of devotion have changed cities, states, regions, and impacted nations for the glory of God. We are shifting into a new place with God, but we must leave some of the old paradigms we are accustomed to in order to embrace the new. In order for us to shift we must be transformed inwardly. *The Ecstasy of Loving God* will bring helpful insight into becoming a Kingdom shaker and reveal helpful keys to rediscover realities of living a presence-filled life. You will be speechless as you read testimony after testimony of those who have given all and paid the ultimate price to keep their first love.

JEFF JANSEN
Global Fire Ministries

Preface

This book emerged from the womb of a broader work I began on the *Song of Solomon* several years ago. In seeking the common theme of the Canticles, I found a continual revelation of the *God of Bliss*—the idea that the pleasure of God is the very essence of the Gospel.

After much counsel with the Lord, I have decided to wait a few years more before releasing that volume on the Song. It will continue to mature (age as fine wine) for a season. But know that the pages of this book were also written and brewed in the wine cellar of holy love. The Church began in the drunken glory on Pentecost, and the Church age will end as we pop the cork on the best wine saved for last. This is bridal wine. The wine of His Spirit. First love intoxication.

My prayer is that you find the loving joy of Christ as your supreme pleasure in these pages, beyond any earthly substitute. As C.S. Lewis wrote, "I sometimes wonder whether all pleasures are not substitutes for joy."[1] It is impossible to pursue Christ without being overtaken by the benefit of His holy pleasure. Author and speaker John Piper notes that the very way we bring glory to God is by *enjoying* Him!

"To the extent we try to abandon the pursuit of our own pleasure, we fail to honor God and love people," says Piper. "Or, to put it positively: the pursuit of pleasure is a necessary part of all worship and virtue. That is, the chief end of man is to glorify God *by* enjoying Him forever."[2]

To separate pleasure from God is impossible. Follow happiness to its end and you will find God. The world endorses every route that leads to happiness. A lot of billboards promise happiness, but their end is death. He is the fountainhead of bliss. In Second Corinthians 12, we read of the apostle Paul being the subject of an "inexpressible ecstasy." This is beyond human explanation. The Gospel comes as a heartfelt revelation.

Many Christians have been conditioned to believe that the personal satisfaction they derive from God can become idolatrous. Even in the thought work of Lewis, he determined that the personal satisfaction of love was not *evil*, as long as it did not become an idol. But Piper takes Lewis' work to the next level, and more to the heart of Scripture. He says that our personal satisfaction in God is the very essence of true worship!

"The longing to be happy is a universal human experience, and it is good, not sinful. We should never try to deny or resist our longing to be happy, as though it were a bad impulse," writes Piper. "Instead, we should seek to intensify this longing and nourish it with whatever will provide the deepest and most enduring satisfaction. The deepest and most enduring happiness is found only in God."[3]

I hope to build on this theological framework of divine pleasure, laid by Lewis and Piper. And to it, we will add deep draughts of supernatural experience that will pull us from the pages of dusty books and into the tasting room of heavenly delights. To this, we will add a strong dose of the mystics and the bizarre miraculous exploits that accompany a life lost in translation.

Eden literally means "pleasure." You were made for it. What separates the Christian from every manmade religion on earth is our acceptance that *God came to us*, to give us what we could not earn for ourselves: access to bliss forevermore. He plugged us back into the pleasure of Himself. This is *good news*. This work is not a book of formulas, to help you climb an unseen ladder of experience. In Acts 10, we read that the apostle Peter "fell" into an ecstasy. No climbing involved. Just falling back and resting in the finished works of the Gospel. Let go into His arms until you find yourself obsessed on things divine.

Introduction

Ecstasy, in a general sense of the word, is a euphoric pleasure in God. A culmination of His infinite joy that affects us spirit, soul, and body. Be inspired as you read this book to drink deep from Heaven's wine room, as we lay claim to the daily practice of His presence.

Our aim in this work is simple. We hope to engage a lifestyle of bliss. A holy intoxication on the love of Jesus that can be the daily bread of all believers.

On a scholarly note, we will treat "ecstasy" in the traditional sense of the word. Not only as a form of delight, but also as a state of mystical prayer. Theologically, ecstasies are also known as *trances* or *raptures*. Since biblical times, trances have been marked by visions and spiritual encounters, as well as frenzied physical manifestations and miracles. In explaining ecstatic prayer, I will endeavor to blur the lines between everyday lifestyle and divine encounter. Not just as a form of prayer, but as a comprehensive way of living. Dwelling in unbroken union. Let your days become a fragrant song where Heaven and earth continually collide.

If the satisfaction you derive from God is mediocre, or at best lacking, I will make the case for a realm of happiness that is altogether transformative and otherworldly.

A large portion of this volume is dedicated to a study of mystical theology. I will pull from many of the church fathers to discuss the primary stages of interior or *contemplative* prayer. Ecstasy has long been considered the highest state of inner prayer. We will also cover a wide range of supernatural phenomena that have accompanied true life ecstatics: from physically floating right off the ground to glowing and walking through walls. The path of holy pleasure is unquestionably a path of marvels.

From Pentecost onward, the Book of Acts records trances in the lives of Peter, Paul, and the first apostles. From the early church to the Christian mystics of the Middle Ages—and the famous revivalists of the 18th century to present—God's movements on the earth have always been marked by these supernatural states. In this book, we will journey from Old Testament ecstatics like Samuel and Elijah, to those of the future who will usher in a massive wave of harvest glory on the streets in these last days. God has always wanted a people who live in the heavens, even as they walk on the earth. And the world is hungry for the demonstration of a Gospel of power and true pleasure. More than a state of mind, you will see how God's happiness is the very essence of true love. In this book, you will be encouraged to drink from the *river of His pleasure* (see Ps. 36:8)!

Understandably, for the modern reader not versed on the subject of contemplative prayer, the very topic of *trances* and *Christian mysticism* may sound strange, unorthodox, or scary. The fact that you have picked up this volume means you are either brave or hungry! From the onset, know we are simply talking about the practice of God's presence, where the grace gifts of the Holy Spirit pour freely to us through the cross of Jesus Christ. His finished work is the source of our bliss.

Consider this simple explanation of trances from the great revivalist John G. Lake:

> Now what is a trance? A trance is the Spirit taking predominance over the mind and body, and for the time being the control of the individual is by the Spirit; but our ignorance of the operations of God is such that even ministers of religion have been known to say it is the devil.[1]

In my previous book, *Miracle Workers, Reformers, and the New Mystics*, we sought to recover some lost terminology that originated within the church (*mystic*, for instance, was always a Christian term pertaining to "religious mysteries"). Likewise, trances and ecstasies are merely states of being overcome by God's Spirit. *Trances* should be Christianity 101. It is high time we recover the language and practice of contemplative prayer. There is little pre-packaged Charismatic jargon here. God is reawakening His church to the spiritual reality of His Kingdom. He is restoring supernatural, mystical Christianity in this hour.

Get ready for the messiest revival the world has ever seen! While ecstatic experience is biblically orthodox, it is far from tame or *ordinary* in its practical application. Ecstatics have always produced the most bizarre physical manifestations: falling over, fainting, shaking, trembling, uncontrollable laughter, running, shouting, and convulsing. Not to mention the signs, wonders, and miraculous phenomena that accompany them. Such strange outward behavior has marked the lives of many great saints and prophets. And these wild ecstatic contortions have been present in every great revival—at the birth of every mainstream denominational movement in church history. The inward working of God's goodness tends to produce an uncontrollable wildfire when He takes the helm of clinical, religious sobriety—when He turns our water into wine.

Overall, this is a book about joy. A book about pleasure. It is time we demonstrate to the world that true *ecstasy* is not a street drug but a Person.

The pleasures of God you experience in the closet are about to spill out to the streets in wild abandonment as the Holy Spirit ushers in the great end-time harvest.

Part I

created for pleasure

Chapter 1

a covenant of bliss

You were created for pleasure, and nothing else will do. There is a yearning inside every person to know the Source of all pleasure, who is ecstasy incarnate. At the core of all humankind is a desperate craving, formed by God Himself, which only He can satisfy. We are all born with a seeking heart crying out for ultimate fulfillment. There is a desperation inside that will settle for nothing less, because everything else is shakable, unreliable, and hollow. All else is *"vanity of vanities; all is vanity"* said King Solomon (Eccles. 1:2).

> *"...and I will shake all nations, and they shall come to the Desire of All Nations, and I will fill this temple with glory,"* says the Lord of hosts (Haggai 2:7).

Today the world is in birth pangs, being shaken from a natural perception of things observable and awakened to a heightened awareness of things unseen. We are being awakened to the *glory realm*—the atmosphere of God's tangible, manifest presence. The spiritual realm of Heaven is a *greater* reality than the known, material universe. One might say it is a meta-reality, for the spiritual always affects and overrides the physical. Things which are shifted in the spirit bring direct consequence to the natural realm.

These are exciting times as God shifts our concept of reality. He is preparing us for the phenomenal—angelic encounters, visitations of Jesus, bizarre miracles, and multitudes of souls coming into the Kingdom. The thing which most needs shifting today is *us*. God will not have an end-time church that is depressed, cynical, doubting, religious, or powerless. He will have a church that lives and breathes from a heavenly vantage point, even while their feet still touch the earth. This church will be filled with joy, faith, intimacy, and power like no previous generation.

In this day, God will not have for Himself a purpose-driven church, but a Spirit-driven church—an intimate bride who is moved and motivated by the cloud of His presence. He is looking for lovers, not do-gooders. A people who are enraptured by His fragrance and lost in the eternal weight of His goodness.

Like Adam, you were created to experience Heaven and earth simultaneously. God made Heaven and earth together in the beginning, so that Adam would explore them both in interwoven harmony. And on the cross of Calvary, the veil of Christ's flesh was torn, reopening the heavens and reversing the curse of fallen humanity. At the cross, He restored us to the perfect pleasure of Eden. Heaven on earth is our portion—as it was the very prayer of Jesus. A people are being *caught up* in the Spirit today, who have access back through the fiery seraphim who guard the Tree of Life.

This lifestyle of transcendence, between Heaven and earth, is the very inheritance for which Jacob wrestled the angel. Jesus is our Promised Land. He is the land of inheritance flowing with milk and honey. This land is a free gift of grace, but it must be taken and occupied. This is the way of the realm of the Spirit. *"The kingdom of heaven suffers violence, and the violent take it by force"* (Matt. 11:12). Yet even the taking of the Kingdom is a walk of grace.

In this volume, we will explore the ancient paths of Eden. This is nothing other than the very bliss of God. We will explore contemplative prayer—most specifically that state of prayer the Christian mystics called *ecstasy*. We will see the supernatural phenomena that accompany these ecstatic states. We will drink comprehensively of the new wine of God's Spirit—the wine of intimacy that intoxicates us, entrances us, and eventually possesses us until we are fully consumed agents of holy fire.

Many confuse the concept of contemplative prayer, assuming it is some system of mental assent into a spiritual state. There is no True Door into the heavenlies apart from Christ Himself. Contemplation is simply the unfolding of the free right of passage Christ has already given us into heavenly places. It is utterly and thoroughly a journey of grace.

This is no book of formulas. The way we drink of this wine is simple. We drink by faith. This is a journey into the ecstatic joy and love of God. We will look throughout the ages into the lives of men and women, revivals and movements where individuals and entire masses of people on the streets were swept away into the enchanting realms of His glory. These outbreaks of awakening should serve to inspire us. For the fire of passion in our own secret garden can ignite a mighty wildfire of revival in the nations today.

Releasers of the Glory

Everyone on earth is seeking the spiritual happiness that we as believers have to offer. All the nations of the earth are seeking bliss. Something in the heart of humankind remembers Eden. More than any new age philosophy, the church has true utopia—true nirvana—to offer a desperate, dying world. Our nirvana is Christ, the Desire of all nations! Our Kingdom of joy is right here at hand! It is no farther than a breath away (see Matt. 3:2).

You have something to offer the desperate world. We should be bread to the hungry and drink to the thirsty. If the world around us is falling to hell in a hand basket, it is the church's fault. We are the gates of Heaven: the very hands and feet of Jesus in the earth today. Jacob's ladder lives in our bellies! Jesus is not here; He left *us* here to get the job done with His Spirit. We are the salt and light of the world. If the world is getting sour, it is because we are not being salty enough. If it is dark, we are not shining brightly enough. The prophets of old learned not to be critics of the world around them, but rather to empathize, stand in the gap and acknowledge that *their sin is our sin*. They shared the blame for sleeping on the clock, and they impacted their respective generations. They were signposts of love and power that was altogether otherworldly. These men shifted cities, regions, and nations.

How much more will this latter company of prophets demonstrate a greater glory than their predecessors! The more of God's love we drink in, the more we will have to give away. We are only able to love God and the world to the degree we receive His love for ourselves! We only love Him *"because He first loved us"* (1 John 4:19). We must drink deeper so we can go much farther! We must run far beyond our fathers. Ours is now a covenant of ever-increasing glory. Our spiritual tools are sharper. Through the atoning sacrifice of Christ, we now have unprecedented access to the heavenly realms—we see and hear what the prophets of old longed to see and hear. This is a strategic time to shake off the slumber and become effective agents for change.

And change is coming. In fact, there is a revolution on the rise. God is in the process of changing the face of Christianity, and He will do it in one generation. The task at hand is to bring His Kingdom to earth. To become visible demonstrations of unseen realities. How can we lead the blind, if we are blind ourselves? His wine is coming to blur our vision, so that we can receive *His vision*.

Our role as releasers of the Kingdom must be subsidiary yet intrinsically connected to our role as lovers. If we stray from the bliss, the Kingdom we will miss. It is easy in this hour to be sidetracked by good things. Fasting, serving, healing the sick, and even prayer can sidetrack me from the glad presence of the Most High. As soon as we forget the euphoria of Jesus, we have missed the mark. If your prayer does not overwhelm you—get you "whacked" in His love—then pray differently. Don't fast from food if you aren't feasting on Heaven. When God shows up, you should be a happier person!

God wants a people addicted to His pleasure—a people who serve Him for no other reason than the delight they take in Him. This is the very heart of true worship. It is not self-centered. It is putting God at the very center of self, so that self cannot possibly be satisfied without Him.

With Christ in us, Christians become doors to Heaven in the earth. As we become addicted to Heaven, it spills out of us—over our thresholds and into the streets. What are we doing with this supernatural Kingdom we so glibly talk about, yet rarely access? If we claim to be "citizens of heaven" (Phil. 3:20), then why do we spend so much time here on earth? A prophetic generation of seers must emerge who live suspended between earth and sky. An Enoch company that is continually swept away, even though they still walk the streets.

The visionary realm is opening to such a degree that many will be caught away for weeks at a time on spiritual sojourns—whether in the body or out of it, they will not know. Open visions of Jesus are becoming commonplace. Followers of wicca, new age, and other occultist practices are being challenged in the streets in radical power encounters like Elijah on Mount Carmel. These are just the beginning stages of end-time harvest. Most Christians claim belief in angels, but have never seen one. The angelic is about to open up full scale, and encounter will be quite commonplace, as it already is in various places today. Where there is now no paradigm for this type of activity, there will soon be a framework. In fact, a significant percentage of the church is so ignorant regarding this topic alone; they literally believe that people *turn into angels* when they go to Heaven! I say this not to mock or criticize individuals; but we must sound a clarion call that it is high time to learn, grow up and get outfitted for war. God is birthing people into war zones right now, and it is no longer an option to get equipped in the supernatural.

As Heaven invades earth in our era, there is an exciting collision taking place. Its driving force will not be religious duty but an addiction to the tangible, manifest presence of God. Religion kills, but Jesus thrills.

The Coming Corporate Trance

There is literally coming a corporate *trance* that will be required to press into the areas God is calling His church. Our minds, emotions, and faculties must become caught away to such a degree that we are no longer constricted by natural restraints, legalistic structural mantras, or worldly thought processes. God is coming to brainwash us! He wants us to be transformed by the renewal of our minds (see Rom. 12:2). The seductive atmosphere of Heaven is calling us like a siren. Long before Jesus returns in the natural, His glory will return to the church *in the Spirit*. Why wait for His return—you can be *raptured* every day! God is transforming our mindsets and throwing off our tainted perceptions of reality. He is calling us to believe the Truth, and not live by the natural eye or ear. The more we believe in angels, the more we see them. The more we believe in God's healing power, the more healings take place. The more we believe God is present among us, the more we experience His love. *Faith* is our connector to heavenly glory. We must believe.

Jesus did not judge by what He saw with His natural eyes or ears. Rather, He lived out of the Secret Place, in intimacy with the Father. The

Scriptures say of Jesus that He was in Heaven, on earth at the same time. If you are a born-again believer, the same is true now of you! You have access to come boldly before His throne, and in fact—in Christ—you are seated there already (see Eph. 2:6). The more we grow in faith and love, the more we are established in that realm.

Right now the world is in a trance of its own. And many more seducing spirits are being unleashed in this hour. There is a drunkenness that the world offers. But the answer to combating the drunkenness of the world is not to embrace a religious, powerless sobriety. As believers, we are called to be Holy Ghost winebibbers! We are called to live an intoxicated lifestyle, inebriated on the presence of God to the point of full possession. The love of Christ elates us, for His *"love is better than wine"* (Song of Sol. 1:2). Perhaps more than any prophet, Joel speaks of this new wine of God's Spirit flowing—so copious is this wine that it flows from the mountaintops! Interestingly, the only sin Joel preaches against is the sin of drunkenness. We will either be drunk on the things of the world or drunk on the things of Heaven. The choice is ours. We will either be possessed by the demonic or possessed by the Spirit of God in the days ahead. There is an increasing clash between the light and darkness, and there will be no gray areas between.

For the most part, the church has been possessed by the same slumbering spirit that intoxicates the world. Possession by the Holy Spirit of God seems foreign to us, because we have only known the doping of the natural senses. But our definition of *normal* is often aberrant behavior in the eyes of God. Sadly, it seems normal for most Christians to fall into a trance-like state in front of a television set. Watching four hours of soft-porn advertisements, getting fed atheistic worldviews and prime-time blasphemy, with the kids present on the living room floor—this is considered ordinary. But laughing, shaking, and flailing on the ground for four hours under the power of God in divine ecstasy seems so foreign to mainstream Christianity! Some churches have yoga classes on Wednesdays, but would balk at holy drunkenness. Some Charismatics are OK with this, but even they have their limits. The wine of God is being poured without measure to the hungry and the thirsty right now. The result is a paradigm of divine trance—the bliss of Heaven—that changes us through and through to manifest our stature as a people of light.

God is releasing wholesale encounter today. More than any time in history, He is pouring out His Spirit on all flesh (see Acts 2:17). People are having visions, experiencing raptures, and moving prophetically more than ever before. In the meetings of revivalist Maria Woodworth-Etter in the early 20th century, tens of thousands would be carried away into trances and divine ecstasy simultaneously. Entire regions were changed as a result. This was but a prototype of what is to come in this final outpouring.

Believers are about to begin encountering the glory realm with such intensity that they will be taken up in the Spirit for weeks at a time—sometimes unable to eat or drink or even carry on a coherent conversation. Missionary Heidi Baker was wheeled around in a wheelchair for seven days when she was first struck with the drunken glory. Although she thought she was losing her mind at the time, she has now planted thousands and thousands of churches in Mozambique, completely intoxicated with the love of Christ!

We will read of other mystics and seers in church history who were lost in divine ecstasy for days, weeks, and even years at a time. Christians will be known for their bliss.

God is revealing Himself in this hour as the supreme Elation of the soul. True love of God is evident in those whose only pleasure is derived from drawing near to Him. In this season, He is preparing a bridal company. He will sweep corporately over masses of believers with a state of supernatural ecstasy that surpasses anything the world has to offer. Unless you've been locked away in Sunday school for the past 15 years, you know there is actually a drug on the street called "ecstasy" which is geared to heighten one's sensuality. Truly, the world is craving the Third Heaven ecstasy of the love of the Son of God. Hebrews 9:11 says that, *"Christ arrived as the high priest of the bliss that was to be..."* (James Moffatt Translation).[1] He is not offering us an ecstasy resulting from external means, but rather, in spite of them! You can drink your glee, even when the natural world is caving in on you. History gives us countless stories of martyrs who experienced unspeakable pleasure, even while their persecutors tortured them!

No longer will your outward circumstances dictate your emotions. You are about to plug into the heaviest hit Heaven has to offer.

Extasis

Interestingly, the English word *trance* is derived from *ecstasy*. Trances, ecstasies, and raptures are one in the same. A trance, in the Latin, is literally "extasis." In the Greek, the word for **trance** is translated from "ekstasis" in the Scriptures. The very term "ecstasy" is biblical; it originated in the church and belongs in the church! Peter fell into an ekstasis when he saw the vision of the net in Acts 10, which he further describes in Acts 11:5:

> *The next day, as they went on their journey and drew near the city, Peter went up on the housetop to pray, about the sixth hour. Then he became very hungry and wanted to eat; but while they made ready,* **he fell into a trance** *and saw heaven opened and an object like a great sheet bound at the four corners, descending to him and let down to the earth* (Acts 10:9-11).

> *But Peter explained it to them in order from the beginning, saying: "I was in the city of Joppa praying; and* **in a trance** *I saw a vision, an object descending like a great sheet, let down from heaven by four corners; and it came to me"* (Acts 11:4-5).

The trance is not a vision itself. Peter was in the trance when the vision came to him. A trance is a state of drunken sensory suspension where visions are likely to occur.

Paul was likewise praying in the temple when he fell into an ekstasis in Acts 22 and received strategy from the Lord:

> *Now it happened, when I* [Paul] *returned to Jerusalem and was praying in the temple, that* **I was in a trance** *and saw Him saying to me, "Make haste and get out of Jerusalem quickly, for they will not receive your testimony concerning Me"* (Acts 22:17-18).

The root word for *ecstasy* refers to a state of "amazement" in the Greek.

It is a condition of being carried away as by an overwhelmingly delightful emotion. Joseph Thayer translates the word as:

> A throwing of the mind out of its normal state...whether such as makes a lunatic or that of a man who by some sudden emotion is transported as it were out of himself, so that in this rapt condition, although he is awake, his mind is drawn off from all surrounding objects and wholly fixed on things divine that he sees nothing but the forms and images lying within, and thinks that he perceives with his bodily eyes and ears realities shown him by God.... thrown into a state of blended fear and wonderment.[2]

The state of ecstasy is a condition of "standing outside ourselves." We become so hungry for the Lord that we have to move into His realm! Throughout the following chapters we will trace the history of ecstatic experience in the church and investigate the dynamics of trances and the supernatural phenomena that accompany them. Where Peter and Paul describe a few singular ecstatic experiences, I believe God has reserved an even greater glory for this end-time church. I believe that many will live (and have already lived) entire ecstatic lifestyles, pulled away continually in the exhilaration of Heaven.

The word *ecstasy* refers to an intense, euphoric experience. It can be hard to define, as it refers both to a heightened state of spiritual consciousness, as well as an intensely pleasant experience. As one's concentration comes into a divinely heightened state of focus, our awareness of exterior senses and intellectual thoughts are often diminished. It is often accompanied by a cessation of voluntary physical mobility. The resulting "spiritual drunkenness" is what the early apostles experienced on Pentecost—what the priests of Solomon's temple experienced as they were unable to stand up under the glory cloud. It is what the Christian mystics encountered in the deep throes of inner prayer, and it is the Charismatic Christian practice which we call being "slain in the Spirit." It has accompanied the First and Second Great Awakening revivals in the Americas, and was present in the birthing of every significant new move of God or new denomination in church history. We have a clear scriptural basis from the writings and experiences of the apostles that the ecstatic trance is a valid New Testament state of consciousness afforded to believers for receiving revelatory spiritual communication, and moreover, experiencing intimacy with God through the Holy Spirit.

There is a corporate shift coming in which God is throwing our minds out of their normal state and catching us up into the visionary realm. I do not purport that everyone will have a simultaneous, physical manifestation of trembling or comatose-like experience. But the word *ecstasy* is appropriate, because of the elation and absolute enchantment being afforded to us. Open communion with Heaven. A lifestyle of feasting on Heaven today. The basic fact that our sins have been canceled and we now have open access to the God of the universe means we will *"relish and feast on the abundance of Your house; and You cause them to drink of the stream of Your pleasures"* (Ps. 36:8 AMP). The church is about to have a wholesale revelation that we can taste, touch, see, hear, and feel God today—that we don't have to wait for Heaven, because it is already here! The Kingdom is at hand. The eyes of our spirits are being enlightened in this hour. We speak recklessly about the forgiveness of sins, but few pause to consider the indulgent pleasure awarded to those who are in right standing before God. The greatest ecstasy, the greatest state of awe and wonder that has been extended to us is the offer to be fully cleansed and return to the sweet nectar in the bosom of all that God is.

> *Oh the bliss of him whose guilt is pardoned, and his sin forgiven! Oh the bliss of him whom the Eternal has absolved, whose spirit has made full confession!* (Psalm 32:1-2 Moffatt)

This supernatural delight is for right now! Not tomorrow. When John the Baptist said that the Kingdom of Heaven is close at hand, he meant that it is within fingers' reach. There will be a company of people who live their entire lives in varying degrees of this inebriated, trance-like state, more aware of the presence of Heaven than their natural surroundings. Imagine living in a transcendent state of *standing outside oneself.* A lifestyle of joy unspeakable. This is more than a corporate mindset shift that will happen in one generation. This is an entire generation moving beyond the mind altogether and apprehending the unimaginable.

The atonement—the very concept that God would forgive our sins—is much more offensive than we realize. The basic premise of the cross is that God opens us up to pure and holy pleasure—all the time! A free ticket to the rivers of Heaven's delight *in the now*. A pleasure we do not earn. Religious people secretly know there is divine pleasure, but in feeling they have to work for it or purify themselves, they miss it altogether. It comes by faith in Christ's finished work. Breathe deeply…relax. It's done!

Since forgiveness is a common theological principle in the Western world, we usually think little of it. Of course, we are thankful that our sins are forgiven: especially more so at the beginning of our walk. But we have scarcely explored all the appropriations it brings us. It is blissfully offensive to human reason! It means we become partakers of the divine nature. We enjoy the benefits of everything Heaven has to offer. We can stand outside of time itself and have productive, interactive encounters with the God of the universe.

> *This secret was not made known in other eras in the way it is now being revealed to God's special messengers by the Spirit. The revealed secret is simply that the outsiders are now insiders sharing in the inheritance, the family, and the promises which come from Christ's message of good news about God* (Ephesians 3:4-6 Ben Campbell Johnson Translation[3]).

In Christ, the atonement has opened up for us our entire inheritance. Jesus once asked a group of listeners, *what is easier to do, forgive sins or heal the sick?* He essentially said that the two things were one in the same. In fact, the word for salvation, *sozo*, is often used interchangeably for *salvation* (forgiveness of sins)*, healing, and deliverance* from demons. I would conjecture that it means even much more. It is the very substance and ability of Heaven that comes and brings life, liberty, and abundance. Jesus is our Sozo. After speaking on the forgiveness of sins in Luke 5, He healed a paralytic, and this was the crowd's response:

And overwhelming astonishment and ecstasy seized them all, and they recognized and praised and thanked God; and they were filled with and controlled by reverential fear and kept saying, We have seen wonderful and strange and incredible and unthinkable things today! (Luke 5:26 AMP)

Christ, the High Priest of our bliss, gives us now a foretaste of the pleasures and powers of the age to come. Most of us have lived a life of spiritual paralysis in comparison to what is being offered us. We have never once exercised the limbs of our spirit man to the degree they could be extended. But when the radical realization of the love of God comes—which obliterates our sin nature and fulfills our deepest cravings—we are infused with supernatural mobility. A slumbering, paralyzed church is about to be revived by the breath of God's euphoric, awakening winds.

What will revival look like? Will it look like the rapid spread of religious culture among the heathen? No. It will look like renaissance. It will be color and motion and ecstasy—humanity living out its evil-free existence.

Known for Your Bliss

We are called to a life of celebration. You have been grafted into a pleasure pact with God.

Whenever God cuts a covenant with humankind, it is always to our benefit. God never brings us into an agreement where a superior pleasure is traded for an inferior one. He would never pull you from the temporary enjoyment of sin in exchange for a lesser gratification. Whenever God made a deal with humankind, it was always a win-win situation for us. Let us take His covenant with Abraham for example. We call Abraham a "father," not merely for his mentorship in the faith, but because God made him who was impotent to be the father of nations and gave him *something from nothing*.

And he blessed him and said: "Blessed [favored with blessings, made blissful, joyful] *be Abram of God Most High, Possessor* [and Maker] *of heaven and earth"* (Genesis 14:19).

Abraham's barrenness was traded for ultimate fruitfulness and joy. This was both natural and spiritual. His son of promise was named Isaac, meaning *laughter*. When God cut an agreement with you at salvation, you exchanged your life for His. Your mediocrity was traded for explosions of joy. God never intended that you trade the pleasures of this life for stale, stoic religion. You have been invited into a covenant of experiential love through the intoxicating wine of Christ's blood and the heaven-rending, broken bread of His body. Your covenant, like that cut with Abraham, should bring others into envy at the prospect of your spiritual delights:

> *Said the Eternal to Abram, "Leave your country, leave your kindred, leave your father's house, for a land that I will show you; I will make a great nation of you and bless you and make you **famous for your bliss**; those who bless you, I will bless, and anyone who curses you I will curse, till all nations of the world seek bliss such as yours"* (Genesis 12:1-3 Moffatt).

Christ is the Desire of all nations. All crave Him, whether they realize it or not. All that we do to pursue vain pleasure in this life is merely an unrealized wandering for the forgotten paths of Eden. Those who meet the Source of pleasure begin to manifest this enthralling fragrance to the envy of all nations. You become known for your happiness. Few people care to know religion that brings death, but all of humanity longs to know the *true inheritance* that is yours in Christ.

> *Thou art what I obtain from life, O thou Eternal, thou thyself art my share; fair prospects are allotted me, a blissful heritage is mine. . .* (Psalm 16:6 Moffatt).

God holds nothing back from you. You are an insider. You have access to all His goodness. All of His treasures are now yours. All of His secrets are at your disposal, even as He held nothing back from Abraham:

> *Abraham went to escort them, and the Eternal thought, "Shall I hide from Abraham what I am going to do, seeing*

*that Abraham is to become a large and powerful nation,
and that all the nations of the world are to seek bliss like
his?"* (Genesis 18:17-18 Moffatt).

The covenant Christ has cut with you is absolutely ridiculous. It makes
no sense to the natural mind. The nations of the world will not be drawn
to your moral stance on the issues. It is not your right-wing politics that will
entice them, nor will they be lured by your ability to articulate doctrine.
The *bliss.* This is what will compel a sea of lost humanity. Supernatural
pleasures forevermore.

We need not wait for the sweet by and by to experience this otherworldly intoxication. The pact has already been made. We can eat our
fattened calf today in the sweet now and now.

*Happy is he whom thus Thou choosest to dwell in Thy
courts, close to Thee. Fain would we have our fill of this,
Thy house, Thy sacred shrine—it's bliss!* (Psalm 65:4
Moffatt)

Chapter 2

love God and do whatever

My one vocation: to consider You.

The Christian life is really not that complicated. If we can get the love part right, everything else will fall into place. St. Augustine said, "Love God and do whatever."

Unfortunately, our striving little souls even try to make a dead work out of loving God. Have you ever heard a grumpy old preacher tell you that "Love is not a feeling," and to do good things even when you don't feel like it? Sounds like stoicism to me.

I have a very big problem with the "love is not a feeling" emphasis found in many guilt-driven religious streams. Yes it is true that we move on faith rather than feeling, but such language is often used to quench emotive demonstrations of devotion. Whoever vilified feelings and equated them with the lusts of the flesh was grossly mistaken. When we try to surgically separate one's feeling and emotions from love in order to define it only as an esoteric, selfless serving verb, we've missed the point. The love of God should electrify us, push us to hunger, and stir a fiery passion in our bones that cannot be quenched. Consistent lack of emotion in our spiritual walk can often be defined in one simple word: *complacency.*

The definition of spiritual complacency has nothing to do with the absence of godly activity. But it has everything to do with substituting activity for an enthralling relationship. Many teach that after we have believed in Christ, we should do many things. But this is not true. According to the Scriptures, after we believe in Christ and receive His Spirit, we have to *love Him.*

Perhaps the apostle Paul put it best in First Corinthians 16:14: *Do everything in love.*

All of our acts should be immersed and flowing out of the love-trance of Heaven. John of the Cross said, "In the evening of life, we will be judged on love alone."[1]

It is natural that every aspect of you should hunger for God. This is really not a supernatural thing, but rather it is what you were created for. Your relationship with God is not some obscure issue relegated to the unseen realms of the spirit. Even for the uninitiated, it is not a spooky thing. Even your physical body was designed to be a host, a carrier of Him. He fits you like a glove. Your mind, your decision making processes, your emotional life and even your natural body yearn for the harmony that comes when the eternal God steps inside of you and wears you like a garment. In fact, Adam wore God like clothing! He didn't know he was naked in the Garden of Eden because he never was until sin entered. As we are clothed with His glory presence, we become lost in the divine. God rests inside of me, and I walk inside of Him—spirit, soul, and body. David said:

> *My soul longs, yes, even faints for the courts of the Lord;*
> *my heart and my flesh cry out for the living God* (Psalm
> 84:2).

Even David's physical body and soul were thirsty for experiential, emotive love. He says in Psalm 143:6, *"My soul thirsts... like a parched land"* (NIV).

Your physical body is not evil. The super-structure called the "sin nature" or the "lusts of the flesh" is evil, but Christ has eradicated that on the cross (see Col. 2, Rom. 6, and Gal. 2:20). God also created our feelings, and feelings themselves are not evil. The unrenewed mind does seek to pervert and manipulate the feelings—giving them outlet in a place where they do not belong. But feelings themselves are a gift from God.

"But be sure that human feelings can never be completely stifled. If they are forbidden their normal course, like a river they will cut another channel through the life and flow out to curse and ruin and destroy," writes

A.W. Tozer.[2] To some extent, we could view feelings as being *amoral*—they are neither good nor evil. It is what we do with those feelings, where they are directed and whether we choose to dwell in certain ones, which can result in a good or evil action. Feelings are also a beautiful, built-in thermostat, by which we gauge the spiritual climate and discern the atmosphere around us.

In many eras of history, it was those flakes, ecstatics and crazies—those troublers of Israel—who were accused of lunacy, often because they relied more on spiritual instinct than on common sense, manmade rules. Inside of them was a very evident passion for God that would sometimes produce aberrant behavior. Consider Ezekiel chopping up his hair to the wind (see Ezek. 5). Hosea marrying a prostitute (see Hos. 1). After their deaths, of course, they are recognized for possessing a true gift of discernment. But while they lived, these shock prophets were not in line with cultural norms. It takes a fiery zeal and an emotional life fully consumed by divine passion to pursue God in the radical fashion He desires.

We should not be ruled by our feelings, but neither should we ignore them. The apostle Paul showed us that he did not succumb to negative feelings:

> *Who is weak, and I do not feel weak? Who is led into sin,*
> *and I do not inwardly burn?* (2 Corinthians 11:29 NIV)

The key to resisting feelings of temptation is to become overwhelmed by God's delight. As we cultivate a lifestyle in the glory, we begin to feel what God feels. We begin to experience His rich and exotic emotional life. Our soul should be filled with wonder and awe. We do not become stoics, but instead, we truly become *alive*.

It is our addiction to the God of ecstasy that enables us to consistently prevail over sin. Sin does offer some pleasure for a season, but to those who have tasted and seen the true goodness of God, it does not hold a match to the superior pleasures of loving Him.

"God made us spiritually, physically and emotionally needy people. In the depths of our hearts we long for happiness. We desire it, and we yearn deeply for pleasure. We are designed by God to be pleasure seekers. This in itself is not sinful; finding our pleasure in unrighteousness is what is sinful," writes Mike Bickle in *The Pleasures of Loving God*.[3] "God does not call us to holiness to keep us from a life of pleasure. Holiness is not drudgery. Instead, God calls us to a holiness that fully releases infinite and perfect pleasure to us forever."

To reject all "feeling" in our Christian walk will only lead us dwell in bad ones. Frustration. Anxiety. Fear. Self-righteousness. Boredom. Anger. We live first by the truth, but emotional satisfaction and holy pleasure must surely be present. *"Nel vino la verita"* is an old Italian proverb that states, "The truth is in the wine."

The Truth is what sets us free to experience a full and abundant life. The Truth is that our old sinful self no longer exists—it was crucified together with Christ, and now we are new creatures, able to experience the joyous atmosphere of evil-free living. Our old anxious self is dead with Christ! We have freedom from hate, frustration, and anger. Our old, boring, religiously sober self is also crucified with Him! We are now free to experience His glad and exotic emotions.

Ours is a God of strong affections. The emotions of God are so vivid; we cannot begin to comprehend their complexity. Yet we can experience them. Song of Solomon 5:13 says, *"His cheeks are like a bed of spices, banks of scented herbs."* The cheeks represent the emotions. All of your emotions are visible on your cheeks. God's emotional life is rich and fiery. Finding your satisfaction in the God of ecstasy is the secret key to conquering sin. The exotic emotional life of God is so exhilarating and addictive that humankind is quite the boring creature in comparison. Those who worship a dull god of stoicism—though they call him by a Christian name—are really worshiping an idol. A mere shadow of the truth. It is one thing to worship the Son of God by name, but it is another thing to know His nature, worshiping Him both in Spirit and in truth.

We do not worship a dead god on the wall of a building who lacks feeling or sensory perception. It is for lack of feeling and senses that He mocks our lifeless idols:

> *Not to us, O Lord, not to us but to Your name be the glory, because of Your love and faithfulness. Why do the*

nations say, "Where is their God?" Our God is in heaven;
He does whatever pleases Him. But their idols are silver
and gold, made by the hands of men. They have mouths,
but cannot speak, eyes, but they cannot see; they have ears,
but cannot hear, noses, but they cannot smell; they have
hands, but cannot feel, feet, but they cannot walk; nor
can they utter a sound with their throats. Those who make
them will be like them, and so will all who trust in them
(Psalm 115:1-8 NIV).

Our God sees, hears, feels, and experiences deep emotion. Unfortunately, we often idolize a false perception of God—an emotionless, judgmental, or aloof being in the sky who leaves us to sort out our own problems. This deistic image is no more real than a statue of wood or silver. But God has called us to be like Him. To be *alive*. We are created in His image with sensory perception that enables us to fully taste and see His goodness. Anyone who looks full into the face and presence of God cannot help but be overcome in his emotions. In his advocacy for a complete and utter joy in the life of the believer, John Piper writes:

> Don't let the childlike awe and wonder be choked out by unbiblical views of virtue. Don't let the scenery and poetry and music of your relationship with God shrivel up and die. You have the capacities for joy which you can scarcely imagine.[4]

Our sensory capacities for joy require a supernatural transformation in order to be fully awakened. Your problem as a Christian will never be that you "feel too much," nor ever will it be that you are "too joyful." Your capacity for joy will forever be expanding. You have scarcely scratched the surface. Happiness is limitless in God. As it is now, we are still numb to the eternal depths of divine pleasure that have been offered us in the wine of Christ's new covenant. Anyone who has truly been filled with the Holy Spirit knows that this joy has nothing to do with bland, theological theory. Furthermore, Piper writes, "I have argued so far that disinterested benevolence toward God is evil. If you come to God dutifully offering him the reward of your fellowship instead of thirsting after the reward of His fellowship, then you exalt yourself above God as His benefactor and belittle Him as a needy beneficiary—and that is evil."[5]

Serving God in a non-affectionate manner is not a sign of spiritual endurance, faithfulness, or nobility. Serving God apart from a sense of pleasure is antichrist in nature. God wants nothing to do with your sacrifice, your prayers, or your attendance at His festivals apart from the fond attachment of your heart (see Isa. 1). Jesus quoted Isaiah when He said, *"These people honor Me with their lips, but their hearts are far from Me"* (Matt. 15:8). In other words, He does not want your money or your Sunday mornings if it does not come as an overflow of experiencing His bliss. Our lives are rooted in enjoying God and delighting ourselves in Him.

The Recovery of Passion

This call to rational duty, apart from tangible pleasure, is a manifestation of the *religious spirit*—it is gnostic in origin and crept into the church through Greek rationalism in the first century. The famous Greek philosopher Plato made a distinction between two parts of a man: the *reason* (the mind and its capacity for thinking) and *passion* (including the emotions). He concluded that the reason was the supreme part of our nature, which should subdue the lower parts: the feelings and emotions. Plato's ideas not only fueled gnostic/antichrist ideas that infiltrated the early church, but they also impacted many great thinkers throughout history.

René Descartes, another influential philosopher, believed that the emotions actually originated in the body as products of bodily organs. He bought into the same general belief of Plato—that the reason is our highest human mechanism—and believed that these "physical" emotional drives could overcome a person and override their rational control.

Scottish philosopher David Hume, in the 18th century, further resonated the ideas of Descartes, saying that emotions had their origins in the physical body.

Charles Darwin came on the scene, and he wrote that emotions were leftover remnants from ancient animalistic behaviors. Again, there was a higher appeal toward reason, and a call to quench the inferior, emotive "passions."

Sigmund Freud and other early psychologists followed this same theme of relegating emotions to a bodily origin, connected to the nervous system, thus they were lower and separate from the higher nature of reason.

In his book *Feel*, Christian writer Matthew Elliott points out how this negative view of emotions infiltrated New Testament scholarship. "These ideas about emotion were very much in line with what I had learned from pastors and writers and teachers in the Christian culture in which I'd grown up," writes Elliott. "Sure, preachers today are more modern than Descartes—they don't claim that emotions are generated from bodily organs or blood—yet they still view the emotions with some level of suspicion or concern."[6]

All of us have heard someone suggest that the joy of the Lord is not a feeling but an *attitude*. We've been told that love is "not merely an emotion, but a choice." We've been instructed that love has to do less with feeling, and more about volitional acts of the will.

Elliott began researching the titles of some of the most popular Christian books on the market today written about emotions. The titles themselves were very revealing, echoing more of Plato than the Bible:

Deadly Emotions
Managing Your Emotions: Instead of Your Emotions Managing You
A Woman's Forbidden Emotion
Emotions: Can You Trust Them?
Those Ugly Emotions
Winning Over Your Emotions

"The most common statement I read in these books was that the 'love' Jesus commanded was not a feeling. Yet, as I read on and on into what had been written by theologians—hundreds of books and articles, and finally a thousand—I could never find a single argument that rested on the Bible itself that said love or joy were not feelings. Mostly it was just stated as fact," adds Elliott. "It seemed to me as if many Christian teachers and preachers today were resorting to some extraordinary word tricks to avoid the suggestion that what the Bible says about love, joy, hope, and other emotions is really something we are supposed to feel."[7]

The church has taught us that emotions and feelings are unreliable as indicators of truth, and so we are conditioned to believe they are trivial and useless, if not outright dangerous. Immanuel Kant, the stoic philosopher, taught that doing the *action of love* was important, even if the feeling of love was not present. The rational intention reigned supreme. This is the same, unchristian worldview that is taught as a staple from pulpits all around the world. Even staid reformer John Calvin admitted, "Duties...are not fulfilled by the mere discharge of them, though none be omitted, unless it is done from a pure feeling of love."[8]

True Essence of Worship

A "hedonist" is one who lives for pleasure. John Piper believes that all are called to be *Christian hedonists*, those who live for the pleasure of God. After all, God is the highest pleasure. To be a true hedonist, one would logically have to follow pleasure to its greatest degree. Thus, he would have to become a Christian. Christ, in His endlessness, is the climax of our search for perfect gratification. Piper, in his book *Desiring God*, points out that the very core of the Catholic catechism says:

> "The chief end of man is to glorify God and to enjoy Him forever."

This is humankind's most biblical aim. But Piper clarifies this even further. He says, "The chief end of man is to glorify God *by* enjoying Him forever." The greatest way we can ever bring glory to God is by utterly appreciating Him at the core of our being. God does not seek our disinterested service, but longs to be the object of our enjoyment. Piper writes:

> I was converted to Christian Hedonism. In a matter of weeks I came to see that it is unbiblical and arrogant to try to worship God for any other reason than the pleasure to be had in Him.[9]

The problem is not that our feelings are invalid in the Christian walk. The problem is they are too limited to fully experience God. The love of God is so huge and intense that when He begins to pour over us, it is like plugging a million-volt charge through a five-volt fuse. We just can't handle the glory. Our lower senses are so shallow and incapable of handling such joy and beauty that they must often be crushed and reconfigured to handle a greater capacity of love and power. God is so infinitely beautiful that His gladness actually terrorizes us. The fear of the Lord is not based in His anger—the fear of the Lord is based in the awesomeness of His delight, which is beyond our capacity to handle as mere mortals. Our hearts must be expanded and softened to take it in.

Centuries ago, Albert the Great said it this way:

> This must be the intention, scope, and end of a spiritual man, that he may in this corruptible body deserve to possess an image of the future bliss, and begin even in this world as it were to have a foretaste of the pledge of that heavenly felicity, and of that conversation of glory.[10]

God has destined us to be containers of His presence, and so He is transforming us from glory to glory to exude a richer, thicker concentration of Himself here on earth. Just as Jesus modeled the manifest glory in His physical being when He transfigured on Mount Tabor in Luke 9—and as Moses and many other saints in the church age brilliantly beamed with rays of shekinah glory from their faces—there will literally be a people who shine like light bulbs with the manifest presence of God, this side of Heaven. Our hearts and souls must be expanded to handle this degree of manifest power. God actually wants to *expand* your capacity for pleasure, so you can handle more of Him! The problem is, our pleasure sensors get blocked when we cram them full of the *lesser pleasures* of the world.

"One reason the delights and pleasures of Heaven are at present denied us is that we are unable to avoid the excesses of legitimate joys and pleasures in our fallen condition and in this present world," notes Christian writer Lambert Dolphin.[11]

Matthew Elliott puts it this way:

> The great tragedy is that as the church stresses what not to feel and how not to feel, we will and do find other things to feel strongly about. We must find our emotional outlet somewhere. Sometimes, I think the reason people get addicted to stuff is because they have worked so hard not to feel the things they were made to feel and enjoy.[12]

Let us feel and enjoy God Himself. He is the Delight of Paradise forever. The more we find our sustenance from the fountain of His goodness, the more we lose our taste for lesser pleasures. Bernard of Clairvaux writes:

> *Jesus, Thou joy of loving hearts,*
> *Thou fount of life, Thou light of men,*
> *From the best bliss that earth imparts*
> *We turn unfilled to Thee again.*

Only God can truly fulfill us. Acknowledge your emotional dependency on God. Admit your need to be continually sustained by His pleasure. Confess your inability to serve Him apart from being fully absorbed in the pure exhilaration that fuels you. Confess your boredom, depression, and frustration apart from Him. Your dependency on the wine and joy of God's pleasure is the very thing that honors Him. Don't think that God wants anything more from you than this utter dependence on Him.

The ecstasies of God are not strictly about emotions, feelings, or the realm of soulish experience. But they are very much about walking in the intoxication of first love. Ultimately, our goal through the course of these chapters is to grow more in our love for God. This is, of course, the first and greatest commandment—to love Him with our entire being: *with all our heart and with all our soul and with all our mind and with all our strength* (see Mark 12:30).

Did you know that the thing from which you derive the most pleasure is the very thing you worship? For some people it is Prozac, the NFL, or pornography. It could be a wicked or a mundane thing. But ask yourself: where do you find the most irresistible pleasure? That is what you worship. We must worship and serve God for one reason alone: because we can't help ourselves. We are entranced.

> "Worship is basically adoration, and we adore only what delights us. There is no such thing as sad adoration or unhappy praise. We have a name for those who try to praise when they have no pleasure in the object. We call them hypocrites," writes Piper.[13]

God made you for His pleasure. And He made you intrinsically needy and dependent on His unspeakable joy. If you are struggling with sin or addiction, don't try to kill your appetite for pleasure. It is impossible. Just direct it to the true source of all pleasure. You will be amazed to find that He has perfectly and supernaturally designed you to have all your deepest needs met in Him.

What are your deepest desires?

In *The Seven Longings of the Human Heart,* Mike Bickle writes:

> God has placed deep longings in the heart of every human being. We all long for beauty, for greatness, for fascination, for intimacy. We all long to be enjoyed, to be whole-hearted, to make a lasting impact. Many of us have been taught to deny these longings. We've been told they are not of God. But the problem is not the longings—they are given of God and cannot be denied. Problems only arise when we attempt to fulfill godly, legitimate longings in ungodly, wrong ways. Only God can fulfill the longings He has given to us. Only God can truly satisfy the deepest longings of our hearts. When we realize our longings are godly and God wants to fulfill them, we find freedom and joy. We experience intimacy with God in ways we'd never thought possible. [14]

There is only one proper reason for pursuing God, and that is to find ultimate satisfaction in Him.

Possessed by Joy

I believe in the excess and overindulgence in the love of God. Did you know that the very purpose of the ministry of Jesus on the earth was to give you and Him a better buzz?

> *These things I have spoken to you, that My joy may remain in you, and that your joy may be full* (John 15:11).

This joy of Heaven is indescribable. Compared to our future state in Heaven, every one of us here on earth suffers severe clinical depression. You can never out-laugh God and your joy level will never be too extreme for Him. Jesus is a lot happier than you are, so don't think He is trying to dampen you down (see Heb. 1:8). There is no way you could ever get too happy for God. You could never be too wild for Him, never too spontaneous.

I have heard religious orators go so far as to say that joy and happiness are different, and that God brings only joy—*not happiness*. I haven't found that in the Bible yet, but I think there must be an institution called the *Seminary of Wet Blanket Theology* that cranks out this crock of stupidity.

God wants you *possessed* by joy!

> ...the ransomed of the Lord will return. They will enter Zion with singing; everlasting joy will crown their heads. **Gladness and joy will overtake them**, and sorrow and sighing will flee away (Isaiah 35:10 NIV).

To be overtaken by joy means to be "taken over" by joy! Get possessed by the joy of Jesus! Stop dictating your own joy level. Let Jesus do it for you, and see how happy He will let you get. Don't waste your life in a dry, boring church. You will be amazed at how little deference Jesus gives to starchy people who want to keep you sober and depressed. You are not called to pious moderation. At this heavenly feast, there is no limit to our intake. The great revivalist Jonathan Edwards once wrote, "There is no such thing as excess in our taking of this spiritual food. There is no such virtue as temperance in spiritual feasting."[15]

God is calling us not to a mere *mediocre* joy. The psalmist wrote, "I will go to the altar of God, to God my *exceeding joy*" (Ps. 43:4). We are permitted—even commanded—to a joy without limit. How can we have such excess of emotion, without it becoming idolatry? The answer is simple. God does not just give us joy as a gift. *God Himself is my exceeding joy.* He is both the Minister of the Drink and the Drink itself. Augustine wrote in his Confessions, "How sweet all at once it was for me to be rid of those fruitless joys which I had once feared to lose.... You drove them from me, you who are the true, the *sovereign joy*. You drove them from me and took their place, you who are sweeter than all pleasure...."[16]

God is bringing many sons and daughters to bliss! The Easton's 1897 Bible Dictionary[17] translates the *glory* as the "bliss of Heaven" in several verses. Consider the following Scriptures in this light:

> *I consider that our present sufferings are not worth comparing with the glory* [bliss] *that will be revealed in us* (Romans 8:18 NIV).

> *In bringing many sons to glory* [bliss], it was fitting that God, for whom and through whom everything exists, should make the author of their salvation perfect through suffering (Hebrews 2:10 NIV).

The glory of God is His very goodness. Moses prayed, "show me Your glory," and the Scriptures tell us that God's "goodness" passed by. The glory is God's goodness (see Exod. 33:18-19). God is good, not in some abstract, religious definition of the word "good." Not a "sit still, shut up and say your prayers" *good*. Not just "good for you" like cough medicine. God is really sweet, yummy to the tummy, delectable and exquisite—*taste and see that the Lord is good!*

The Radical Nature of Encounter

God's sheer goodness is so great that it is uncontainable. It goes far deeper than a surface manifestation of laughter, shaking, or bodily demonstration. In churches that are experiencing renewal, I often see people "fake" their joy in order to look spiritual—as if their laughter is a supernatural manifestation when it is not. This usually comes out of insecurity as people seek to find their identity behind a particular manifestation. *Just laugh! Don't hyper-spiritualize it.* This is a subtle thing, but nevertheless the work of a religious devil. Of course, there is no need to over-analyze every laugh, twitch, crunch, or yelp. As you will see in the following chapters, I am a stronger advocate for manifestation than just about anyone. Crazy is OK; just keep it real.

There is no need to recreate a past experience or feign your happiness. God wants to give true joy that is thorough and lasting. Manifestations are valid, and I am even a proponent for *daily encounter.* But truly encountering God should cause you to be *changed.* Don't tell me you've seen an angel, but you still look like hell! When God really shows up, you are not just twitching to look spiritual in front of your friends. You are undone.

When John the Beloved encountered the Lord on the isle of Patmos, the Scriptures say he was "in the Spirit on the Lord's Day" (Rev. 1:10). In the *Twentieth Century New Testament* translation, John literally says, "I fell into a trance."[18] The Moffatt translation reads: "I found myself rapt in the Spirit." And perhaps my favorite translation of this verse comes from the *Berkeley Version of the New Testament*: "I became *Spirit-possessed.*"[19]

However you read it, the Scripture is clear that John was pulled beyond himself in divine encounter. And how did he respond? His body was overcome and he *fell to the ground as though he was dead* (see Rev. 1:17). This was a radical encounter for John, and something shifted tremendously in his life. His body responded physically to the intensity of God's presence.

In a similar case, we should look at Saul's conversion on the road to Damascus in Acts 9. Saul, full of anger and hatred toward Christians, was on his way to persecute believers when the following encounter took place:

As he journeyed he came near Damascus, and suddenly a

light shone around him from heaven. Then he fell to the ground, and heard a voice saying to him, "Saul, Saul, why are you persecuting Me?" And he said, "Who are You, Lord?" Then the Lord said, "I am Jesus, whom you are persecuting. It is hard for you to kick against the goads." So he, trembling and astonished, said, "Lord, what do You want me to do?" (Acts 9:3-6)

Here, we see two separate ecstatic encounters with similar results. *Falling, trembling, astonishment,* and in Saul's case, complete transformation. Some would argue that God only moved in this way because these were unique experiences for two "special" people. I would disagree. This is not how God deals with two superheroes. *This is how God deals with humanity.*

Anytime the brilliant Person of the Living God intersects human flesh, there is shaking and baking that takes place. We react body, soul, and spirit. We become pulled outside of ourselves. We see things that others don't see. We lose control of ourselves. We collide with something new, fresh, and uncontainable. This is more than the familiar goose bump you had at last week's service.

When you ask God to possess you—to fully consume you in His love—this is a deep, uncontrollable, and even scary bliss that is simply too hot to handle.

Chapter 3

the house of wine

He has taken me to the banquet hall [lit., house of wine], *and His banner over me is love* (Song of Solomon 2:4 NIV).

There is a place in the Spirit, known as the House of Wine. It is the place of intimacy and delight. It is the place where God overshadows you with His banner of love. Bible translator James Moffatt calls this place the "chamber of joy." For all who believe, Jesus has taken you there already!

The first miracle in the ministry of Jesus was the changing of water into wine at the wedding banquet at Cana in Galilee. This was marital wine—the wine of intimacy. The joyous lifeblood of communion. Jesus started it all with wine—and before going to the cross, He concluded His earthly ministry with Passover wine. On Calvary, He became a drink offering, spilling Himself out for you and me.

Jesus did not just make a tea cup of unfermented grape juice at Cana. It was not a plastic thimbleful. He made six huge jars that held 180 gallons of intoxicating wine. Imagine how many people it would take to drink that much wine. Jesus knew how to throw a party. On top of it all, everyone was already wasted when He made it! The master of the banquet said:

Everyone brings out the choice wine first and then the cheaper wine after the guests have had too much to drink; but you have saved the best till now (John 2:10 NIV).

There is something we should recognize about the *excess* of loving God in this passage. Not a thimbleful. Not a flask or barrel. Not even a room of wine. An *entire house* of wine is ours in the Spirit! Wine always refers to Christ's love. There is never a limit to the amount of this love we can drink. Song of Solomon 5:1 encourages you to *"drink your fill, O lovers!"* (NIV).

After Cana, the next order of business recorded in John 2, is when Jesus went straight to the temple and cleared house of the money-changing filth. I have watched many a church service clear out when the new wine starts to flow freely. It interrupts our preconceived religious affairs. The problem with wine is that it does something to us: *we lose control.* Prophetic teacher Graham Cooke often says, "Jesus turned the water into wine 2,000 years ago, and the church has been trying to change it back ever since."

Jesus and His disciples did not sip on Kool-Aid or Welch's. Jesus drank the hard stuff. The religious order likes to water down this fact, because they are the same bunch who water down the offense of the Gospel itself. They know nothing of abandonment or the excess of joy. Jesus turns the water of the word into the wine of revelation and life. Theory and experience are made reality. Wine, unlike water, is actually *alive*. Every bottle of wine has live agents inside of it which, if not kept properly, turn to vinegar. In the same way, *"the life is in the blood"* (see Lev. 17:14).

Dead religion hates the wine of life.

One of the first miracles Jesus will ever perform for you is to make the water of His Word come alive.

Living in the Wine Cellar

I have met many who were deeply impacted through the ministries of Rodney Howard-Browne and the refreshing that came during the Toronto Renewal in the early 1990s. As God poured out His wine in those days, thousands of believers were getting plastered right in the middle of church, rolling on the floor, barking like dogs and roaring like lions, all the time howling with thunderous laughter as God broke off the dead, demonic restraints of manmade religious "order" and filled His people with *"joy unspeakable and full of glory"* (1 Pet. 1:8 KJV). As with any move of God, passions wane over time. And coupled with friendly-fire persecution from other less responsive believers, many who were sincerely touched in the wine room began to lose their fervor and intoxication over time. While they may look back fondly on those years, the same slap-happy intensity of those experiences has drifted, and many even make excuses for it.

For some, it was "just a season." Others have gone so far as to say it was good, but they have *matured* in some way since then. No longer overwhelmed by waves of drunken stupor, I have heard still others excuse their present lack of intensity by saying, "I have learned to *stand in the glory*" (in other words, "I have learned to hold my liquor").

I would have to disagree with all of the aforementioned theologies. Simply stated, if you can stand in the glory, it is time you encounter a *greater* glory! We have some pretty fantastic excuses for losing our first love and growing lukewarm. This may sound harsh, but the truth of the matter is that we do not have to wait for a dispensation from God before we drink! Don't blame your sobriety on the "seasons." I do not just visit the wine room occasionally; I have learned to *live* in the wine room!

Your salvation experience and all your spiritual gifts were appropriated by faith. So it is the same with drinking in the Spirit. It is important to realize that even as you are now seated with Christ in heavenly places, so also are you seated with Him at the banqueting table. So also do you have access to His wine cellar. Read as Madame Guyon, in the 17th century, describes the bride's encounter in the wine room:

> The beloved of the King, as the result of her delightful meetings with Him, appears to her companions to be intoxicated and beside herself. And truly she is in this state, for, having tasted of the finest wine of the Bridegroom at His banquet, she could not help being seized with the most extreme devotion.[1]

Here is a description of Guyon's own first encounter of getting whacked in the wine room:

The first time He made me a partaker of such singular grace I was so feeble that I would rather have preferred the sweetness of the divine breast to the strength of this excellent wine. Therefore, He was content to show me its effects, allowing me to drink only a little of it. But now that experience and His grace have rendered me wiser and stronger, I can no longer drink only a little. I have drunk so abundantly of His strong and pure wine, that His banner over me is love.[2]

God would never restrict you to just a sip. God would not tease me with the exceeding pleasures of His Spirit, and then yank away the experience. I believe that my Bible says we are moving from *"glory to glory"* (2 Cor. 3:18). From one mountaintop experience to the next, with ever-increasing intensity. God does not offer hollow promises of a good life, and then abandon you. Jesus said, "I will not leave you orphans" (John 14:18). It is actually an orphan mindset that would expect God to give you a teasing little drop of refreshment, then skip town.

> For [the Spirit which] you have now received [is] not a spirit of slavery to put you once more in bondage to fear, but you have received the Spirit of adoption [the Spirit producing sonship] in [the bliss of] which we cry, Abba (Father)! Father! (Romans 8:15 AMP).

Sonship is bliss. If you are in Christ, know that the Lord will not give you the key to this wine room, only to take it away again. Jesus saves His best wine until *last.* Your experience in the wine room should be getting better and better every day. I don't know what frequency you are tuning into, but the truth is, this ride of faith should be getting progressively better. I appreciate revivalist Todd Bentley's words: "If renewal was over, I would still be a closet drinker!" Jesus does not limit your intake of His Spirit. You can have as much of Him as you are willing to risk:

> *. . . drink your fill, O lovers* (Song of Solomon 5:1 NIV).

How thirsty are you? Theodoret of Cyrus, in the fifth century, comments on this single verse, saying:

> He commands these persons not merely to drink, but to be drunken; for there is a drunkenness that works temperance and not delirium—one that does not enfeeble the limbs but lends them strength.[3]

Drink Deeply

God has always used wine as a typology of His celebratory nature. He says in Ephesians 5:18:

> *And do not be drunk with wine, in which is dissipation; but be filled with the Spirit.*

This literally means "continually keep being filled" with the Spirit! Keep drinking! The *New Testament in Modern Speech* translation of this verse says to "drink deeply" of the Holy Spirit.[4] And *The Centenary Translation* also says to "drink deep in the Spirit."[5] Other versions tell us to "ever be filled" with the Spirit[6] and to "be getting filled in Spirit."[7] Needless to say, this is a continual, lifelong drink. Not a one-time event.

Bible commentator and translator C.S. Lovett paraphrases this portion of Paul's letter to the Ephesians as follows:

> *Don't look to wine for your stimulation. That leads only in the direction of ruin. Instead, be filled with the Spirit. Let Him exhilarate your soul and even the excess will be turned to joy in the Lord! Then as you speak to one another, the ecstasy will rise still higher. Your tongues will be loosed in psalms and hymns and spiritual songs, rather than carousing.*

Lovett comments further saying, "Be filled. The imperative Greek verb makes this a command. We are to find all our excitement in Christ, not in other stimulants, whether baseball or a bottle....Let a church move to sample this power, and the joy which follows can shake a city!"[8]

Bible commentator William Hendriksen notes:

> Intoxication is not the effective remedy for the cares and worries of this life. The so-called "uplift" it provides is not real. It is the devil's poor substitute for the "joy unspeakable and full of glory" which God provides. Satan is substituting the bad for the good. The real remedy for sinful inebriation is pointed out by Paul. The Ephesians are urged to seek a higher, far better, source of exhilaration. Instead of *getting drunk* let them *be filled*. What he is saying therefore is this: getting drunk on wine leads to nothing better than debauchery....On the other hand, being filled with the Spirit will enrich you with the precious treasures of lasting joy, deep insight, and inner satisfaction. It will sharpen your faculties for the perception of the divine will.[9]

One could argue that the same contrast Paul makes here—between drunkenness and being filled with the Spirit—is likewise paralleled in the life of John the Baptist. Of John it was prophesied in Luke 1:15 (ASV):

> *For he shall be great in the sight of the Lord, and **he shall drink no wine nor strong drink; and he shall be filled** with the Holy Spirit, even from his mother's womb.*

Rather than having wine or strong drink, John the Baptist would *be filled*. Bible Commentator Albert Barnes describes this "strong drink," saying, "The *strong drink* among the Jews was probably nothing more than fermented liquors, or a drink obtained from fermented dates, figs, and the juice of the palm, or the lees [dregs] of wine, mingled with sugar, and having the property of producing intoxication."[10] The "strong drink" was essentially a type of hard liquor.

Rather than imbibing liquor, John would be filled with the Holy Spirit.

Instead of vodka, he would drink "Godka"! Hendriksen says, "There are times when exhilaration of heart and mind is entirely proper....Exhilaration is wrong, however, when the method of inducing it is wrong." He points out that drunkenness was associated with pagan, Dionysiac orgies in New Testament days, and it was a means of worshiping false gods. But Paul was quick to contrast this overdose of natural wine with "the serene ecstasy and sweet fellowship with Christ which he himself was experiencing in the Spirit."[11]

I believe the early church understood this figurative language of "holy intoxication" quite clearly. An early Latin hymn stated:

> *May Christ be now the Bread we eat,*
> *Be simple Faith our potion sweet:*
> *Let our intoxication be*
> *The Spirit's calm sobriety*[12]

Other songs, dating as far back as the first century A.D., showed a tendency toward drinking deep of the Spirit. Some of these, as found in the Odes of Solomon, are thus translated:

> *And Speaking Waters touched my lips*
> *From the Lord's Spring, plenteously.*
> *And I drank and was intoxicated*
> *With the Living Water that does not die.*
> *But my intoxication caused no heedlessness:*
> *Rather, I abandoned selfhood,*
> *And turned towards the Most High, my God,*
> *And was enriched by His gift.*[13]

Again, we read of an uncontainable, unrestrainable river of intoxicating delight in the following Ode of Solomon from the same period:

> *For there went forth a Stream,*
> *And it became a river, great and broad;*
> *And it carried away and shattered everything,*

And it brought Water
To the Temple
And the barriers that were built by men
Were unable to restrain it,
Nor the art of them whose business it is to restrain it.
And it spread over the surface of all the earth,
And filled everything.
And all the thirsty upon the earth were given to drink of it,
And their thirst was relieved and quenched.
For from the Most High was the draught given.
Blessed, therefore, are the Ministers of that Drink,
Those who have been entrusted with His Water.[14]

Interestingly, the Holy Bible never lists even one prohibition against drinking *natural* wine if done in moderation. I say this not to endorse alcohol, but to show how temperance-minded we are in our observation of the Most High. God is not a moderate. He is an extremist.

At all of the major Jewish feasts, wine played a significant part throughout the entire community. We are called to a life of celebration. Wine was also poured in the Christian love feasts of the first centuries—and not just in a teaspoon with a cracker. These huge feasts were both meal and communion all in one.

The Love Feast

The love feast—or "agape"—was a time of meal and fellowship where the poor were invited. It was actually a hold-over from the old Jewish sacrificial system. An animal would often be butchered—obviously no longer for sacrificial means (Christ died once and for all), but perhaps it was a prophetic *reminder* of the cross—just as the ancient sacrificial system was a prophetic *foreshadowing* of the cross.

Relationship and community does not happen in the rows of a pew. It is in the conversations, the joys, the battles, and the mix of life. It happens over tables and in the mirth of celebration. The love feast was perhaps one of the greatest things we lost to the religious spirit. But it will be restored. God is reintroducing a holy "party spirit" back to the church in this hour, and setting us free from the dour pietism that robs our joy, creativity, and freedom.

As gnosticism crept into the early church, bolstering the "kill yourself" mentality of the religious order, many over-ascetic people began to despise the love feasts, largely because of the wine that was served. This became such a problem that the Council of Gangra in A.D. 355 actually anathematized these religious scoundrels who despised "the agapes based on faith." Unfortunately, this was dramatically reversed a few years later, and the love feasts were forbidden from being held in churches. Is it no wonder that this decision was rendered in Laodicea?

Many streams of the church found ways to recover a form of the love feast in their own respective eras. The Scottish Presbyterians, for instance, were known for their *holy fairs* from the 16th to 19th centuries. These were massive, multi-day communion celebrations that served as a precursor to American camp meetings, and later, modern revivalism.

"Sacramental occasions in Scotland were great festivals, an engaging combination of holy day and holiday....In them religion and culture, communion and community, piety and sociability commingled," writes Leigh Schmidt in his detailed historical work, *Holy Fairs*. "If these gatherings had the social excitement of fairs, they were also holy. People ate, drank, conversed, and courted, but they also prayed, meditated, and covenanted. The sacred and the social were inextricably combined at these events, and this combination was a critical part of their power. By comparison, the fairs of the worldly remained simple things—'poor, little, sensual, painted pleasures'—without the religious mystery and ultimacy that empowered these fair-days of the gospels."[15]

These communions were described as days of "Heaven upon earth" or seasons of "special intercourse with Heaven" with many accounts of ecstatic experience. The Eucharist was central to the power experienced in the revivalism of evangelical Presbyterians. Dating back to the Reformation itself, these feasts served as a type of transition between the large medieval Eucharistic festivals of Catholicism and the modern revivalism of today. The Scottish sacraments were long, protracted meetings with intense meditation at the communion tables. This would gradually be replaced by the "anxious benches" of the American frontier revivals, where people would sit for hours and agonize over their sins and pass through the birth canal of conversion. In later days, these extended times at the *seat of decision* would evolve into the modern-day "altar call" where converts would profess their decision to accept Christ.

Where people were once saved in a party, they now have a three-minute altar call.

These sacramental occasions eventually faded out of Presbyterianism itself, as "middle-class respectability, decorum, and self-control were incompatible with the fervor of these traditional sacraments."[16] The Victorian sense of prudence and temperance eventually drowned out the "festive" nature of these occasions with all their corresponding spiritual extravagance.

"In Scotland and in America the pressures were great to make certain that the Eucharist was not so much exhilarating or enlivening as it was safe and sobering," writes Schmidt. By the 1800s, Presbyterians were largely distancing themselves from the traditions of their forefathers. "From their perspective," he writes, "what had gone on during the old sacramental season came to look more like boisterous peasants at their cups than devout Christians at communion."[17]

The seasonal sacrament events gradually disappeared. It was in this era that fermented wine was also removed from communion, and the quantity of wine served was lessened. The communion service at the famous Cambuslang sacrament in Scotland, for instance, had required 112 bottles of wine, and at times, it was supplied by the gallon or the barrel for these events. Of course, there were up to 40,000 people in attendance, so that was not enough wine to get people drunk. Some holy fairs in the 18th century record an amount of wine equaling about four ounces per each communicant.[18] These changes caused great controversy from the 1830s onward, as the Victorian sense of propriety required drink and spirituality to be separated. But this went deeper than the use of mere alcohol. Enlightened critics sought to draw clear lines between faith and festival, between spirituality and sociability.

The social and jovial nature of these events could best be heard through the voice of their critics. "I have seen scenes that had much more of the fury of the bacchanalia, than the calm, serious, sincere devotion of a Christian sacrament," wrote an anonymous 18th century detractor. But in this, he was also speaking of the wild manifestations of ecstasy, travail, and enthusiastic spiritual contortions that accompanied these events.[19]

Expressions of celebration and emotion have been so repressed among many persons that they no longer feel comfortable in legitimately experiencing the joys and pleasures of life. In the times of Jesus, the Jews understood celebration. Passover and all the great feasts were truly festivals, full of worship, happiness, eating, drinking, and dance. They were a blend of the sacred and the secular, without divide. Community and intimacy thrived.

Of course, there is the potential for over-indulgence in the midst of such festivities. Paul even warns the Corinthian church of gluttony when they come together to feast (see 1 Cor. 11). However, Paul would never call for a clinical end to the feast simply because some bad apples are misguided or excessive with the *natural* pleasures. The spiritual joys of festive communion with one another are too valuable for that. The church, in fear, has repeatedly thrown out the baby with the bath water. Jesus was clear that we should allow the wheat and tares to grow up together. Legalistic "safety" and its overemphasis on rules, instead of relationship, often dampens the spirit of freedom, although it may appear to protect adherents from dangerous extremes. In essence, it causes us to "miss the party" and ignore the grand analogy of Heaven. C.S. Lewis writes:

> It is only in our "hours-off," only in our moments of permitted festivity, that we find an analogy. Dance and game are frivolous, unimportant down here; for "down here" is not their natural place. Here, they are a moment's rest from the life we are placed here to live. But in this world everything is upside down. That which, if it could be prolonged here, would be a truancy, is likest that which in a better country is the End of ends. Joy is the serious business of heaven.[20]

The love feast was indeed a party. Let me rephrase that: *church was indeed a party.* Church was never buildings and architecture and 40-day, seeker-sensitive programs in the early centuries. Church was a living organism of people who really, really enjoyed each other. They literally fed off the involvement they had with one another. The agapes were not sensual debaucheries that knitted them together, but a party *in the Spirit* where the new wine of liberty was shared.

> *You have filled my heart with greater joy than when their*
> *grain and new wine abound* (Psalm 4:7 NIV).

There is a great cloud of witnesses who have drunk of this deep river throughout the ages. Even Bernard of Clairvaux understood this state of supernatural drunkenness in the 1100s as he comments on the wine room of Heaven. "The bride is giddy when she returns to her friends.... She seems to be a little tipsy. This startles her friends. They ask what has happened. She explains it was her visit to the wine cellar," writes Bernard in his sermons on the Song of Songs.[21]

The prophet Jeremiah also made the analogy, writing: "I am like a drunken man, like a man overcome by wine, because of the Lord and His holy words" (Jer. 23:9 NIV).

The religious order has always sought to remove the living bliss from the lips of the people. But the love of God cannot be contained. The Lord has given us a cup that overflows. We need permission from no man to drink freely of the living fountain of life. You can drink from your overflowing cup in the grocery store. You can drink from your overflowing cup at Wal-Mart. I have been found regularly crawling under tables late at night in restaurants, or rolling on the floors of public places, so blitzed out of my skull from the new wine that I make a big spectacle. I don't even have to stop to "explain," and people still get saved!

Whenever we drink of the Spirit in public, it never fails that someone gets saved, prophetic words flow to the lost, or someone gets healed in the marketplace. People are attracted to true holiness. They are repulsed by religion. God wants to make *you* a sign and a wonder, and you can have fun in the process! You can even drink up in any church on any Sunday morning in any part of the world—whether they are legalists or not—and don't let the board of elders stop you! You have higher orders from a higher authority that says you can drink your fill, O lovers! You haven't learned to drink until you've been ousted from a few church services.

Public Drunkenness

The apostles of our faith gave us great precedent when they got whacked openly in public in Acts 2. Some of the crowd was perplexed and amazed, while others mocked, thinking the apostles were drunk with natural wine.

I have many great stories of successfully drinking in public. Once, right after a revival meeting in Maine, I was getting out of a van at the front of my hotel. I was so sloshed in the Spirit, I could hardly stand up. I was dropping pens and papers and water bottles, and just scrambling like a drunken fool. Standing there, just outside the hotel, was a large group of young adults who were frequenting a nearby bar. As they saw me bumbling about, I just looked at them and tipped back an imaginary wine bottle, as if I had been drinking too much. Several of them laughed, thinking I was just drunk on booze like they were. Then I walked over to them.

"Ever drank God?"

They were obviously thrown by the question, along with the fact that I was clearly more intoxicated than they were. They began to elbow one another, silently snickering, but they were too sloppy to be inconspicuous about it. It didn't matter to me that they thought I was crazy. They were listening, so I explained to them that God wanted to touch them with His Spirit and reveal Himself to them. In no time, I had a young man praying to receive the Lord into his life. If this were an isolated incident, one could attribute it to mere chance. But this type of thing happens quite frequently. The wine of God turns you into a magnet for new believers.

Spiritual wine drinking always produces fruit, as well as mighty acts of power. We will discuss this point later. But first understand what your overflowing cup is designed to do. Perhaps the Douay-Rheims English Translation of the Latin Vulgate puts it best:

> Thou hast prepared a table before me against them that afflict me. Thou hast anointed my head with oil; and *my*

chalice which inebreateth me, how goodly is it!
(Psalm 22:5 Vulgate D-R; Psalm 23:5 modern)

They shall be inebriated with the plenty of Thy house; and
Thou shalt make them drink of the torrent of Thy pleasure
(Psalm 35:9 Vulgate D-R; Psalm 36:8 modern).

Wine is a very critical symbol in understanding the nature of God. It reflects His merriment, the delights of Heaven and the transcendent nature of divine love. The Father uses the substance of wine to symbolize the most precious commodity in the universe: the blood of His own Son. Not only does it cleanse and cover us, but it gladdens our hearts and intoxicates us on the things of Heaven. It is the blood of a new covenant.

Come, all you who are thirsty, come to the waters; and you
who have no money, come, buy and eat! Come, buy wine and
milk without money and without cost (Isaiah 55:1 NIV).

The Bible clearly instructs us to be intoxicated on Heaven. Interestingly, the temperance movements in decades past, while having their positive effects on society, brought a strong vilification of natural wine to the American church. This sentiment has never been corporately shared by the church in Europe. Of course, I have nothing to gain by encouraging people to pop a cork of the bubbly—your decision to drink natural wine is between you and the Lord. However, some who have a problem talking about the "new wine" of the Spirit are the same who have dour demons of over-asceticism which order people *"to abstain from* [certain] *foods which God created to be received with thanksgiving by those who believe and who know the truth"* (1 Tim. 4:3).

As for the natural wine of the earth, the Lord has granted us freedom with this issue, so we should neither demonize it, nor force our beliefs about it onto others. Drunkenness is forbidden by Scriptures, but that is all:

Do not destroy the work of God for the sake of food. All things
indeed are pure, but it is evil for the man who eats with
offense (Romans 14:20).

Paradoxically, anyone who has abused alcohol probably did so because they have a strong calling to be filled with the Spirit. Without the *real*, we are predisposed to the counterfeit. Alcohol consumption is not worth a schism; however, it is worth addressing because it is typical of a larger spiritual dilemma: many Pharisaical devils try to draw hard lines where no hard lines exist. The Lord never said wine was bad in itself; He only discourages drunkenness (in the natural) while encouraging it in the Spirit.

"It is the abuse of wine that is forbidden, not the use," writes Bible commentator William Hendriksen, referring to natural wine. "That such abuse was a real danger in the early church, as it certainly is also today, appears from such restrictions as the following: 'The overseer therefore must be above reproach...not (one who lingers) beside (his) wine' (1 Tim. 3:3; cf. Titus 1:7); 'Deacons similarly (must be) dignified, not...addicted to much wine' (1 Tim. 3:8); and 'Urge aged women similarly (to be) reverent in demeanor...not enslaved to much wine' (Titus 2:3)."[22]

As we see, *excess* is the problem issue with natural alcohol. You are created for *excess in the Spirit*, but the natural pleasures of life (sex, drink, etc.) must always be moderated by the Word of God. There are many other verses touting the benefit of natural alcohol if used in moderation:

> *Wine...maketh glad the heart of man* (Psalm 104:15 ASV).

> *Give strong drink unto him that is ready to perish, and wine unto the bitter in soul* (Proverbs 31:6 ASV).

> *By the way, I should advise you to drink wine in moderation, instead of water. It will do your stomach good and help you to get over your frequent spells of illness* (1 Timothy 5:23, J.B. Phillips Translation).[23]

> *But the vine said to them, "Should I cease my new wine, which cheers both God and men...?"* (Judges 9:13)

> *Go, eat your food with gladness, and drink your wine*
> *with a joyful heart, for it is now that God favors what you*
> *do* (Ecclesiastes 9:7 NIV).

When the church adds its own little legalisms and restrictions—such as those which came through the temperance movement—these both amplify the drive to sin, and they portray something about the Lord's nature which is untrue. Jesus came feasting; He didn't come fasting. The early church father John Chrysostom writes, "Wine has been given us for cheerfulness, not for drunkenness."[24]

Here is an interesting quote from the apocryphal book of Sirach, which is of some value on the subject:

> *Wine is as good as life to a man, if it be drunk moder-*
> *ately: what life is then to a man that is without wine? For*
> *it was made to make men glad. Wine measurably drunk*
> *and in season bringeth gladness of the heart, and cheer-*
> *fulness of the mind: But wine drunken with excess maketh*
> *bitterness of the mind, with brawling and quarrelling.*
> *Drunkenness increaseth the rage of a fool till he offend: it*
> *diminisheth strength, and maketh wounds. Rebuke not*
> *thy neighbour at the wine, and despise him not in his*
> *mirth: give him no despiteful words, and press not upon*
> *him with urging him [to drink]* (Sirach 31:27-31).

Your position on natural wine should really be kept in the closet. As Paul said in Romans 14:22, "...*whatever you believe about these things keep between yourself and God*" (NIV). So why do I bring it up? I do so cautiously, but there are two main reasons. For one, God is not focused on natural wine, but He *is* a drinker. And second, if you do not learn to become intoxicated on Him, you *will* become intoxicated on the things of the world.

There may be a threshold of moderation for those who drink natural wine. But there is something innate within the core of every person that craves a drink without limit. Something that thirsts for a sea of endlessness. Jesus is the drink that lasts forever.

Come and quench your thirst on Jesus! Only He satisfies. Bernard of Clairvaux writes of the Bride and the eternal Bridegroom:

She loves. He is love. She is thirsty. He is a fountain.[25]

Part II

living in the bliss

Chapter 4

the God of play

One of the greatest mysteries of the ages is that our God's nature is revelry and play. Unless we become like little children, we will by no means enter the Kingdom of Heaven (see Matt. 18:3). He is not somber and fearsome because of His anger. He is fearsome because of the intensity of His gladness! He is not a bland puritan (despite what you've read in your history books, even puritans liked to play!). God is a God of color, beauty, and aesthetic wonder. Proverbs 8:30-31 reads:

> *Then I* [Wisdom] *was beside Him as a master craftsman; and I was daily His delight, rejoicing always before Him, rejoicing in His inhabited world, and my delight was with the sons of men.*

This passage speaks of the Spirit of Wisdom, who is the Holy Spirit, working alongside the Father at creation. Unfortunately, just about every translation butchers this passage—quite possibly because it rarely fits into the theology of its translators. It does not simply say that wisdom "rejoiced," though that is part of it. This word, *sachaq*, means "play."[1] It even means to joke or jest. It means to frolic. Holy Spirit was literally playing with the Father as God was *playing with His children at the dawn of creation.* Before you were created, God saw you, delighted in you, and played with you in the morning of the universe. Did you know that your Father wants to play with you? He does. He is not angry with you. He is neither aloof nor disinterested in the affairs of your life. Although He is a drinker, He is not an abusive one! He is the God of joy and mirth. He longs to spend time with you and show you the rivers of pleasure at His right hand.

We are living in a beautiful age when God is giving a revelation of His joy like never before to His children. I am utterly grateful for the move of God at Toronto, and the subsequent refreshing that continues to burn around the globe. Without the freedom to enjoy God's euphoric laughter and delight, our lives would truly not be worth the living. How precious that we should be alive in the generation that rediscovers Him as Daddy who plays with us!

Of course the ecstatic manifestation of *holy laughter* is not new to the church. Even revivalists John and Charles Wesley experienced this type of thing, though they didn't understand it. There is an account of the Wesley brothers taking a walk through a meadow, intending to sing psalms to God. But as they started to sing, Charles burst into noisy laughter. Next, John began to laugh uncontrollably: "Nor could we possibly refrain, though we were ready to tear ourselves in pieces, but we were forced to go home without singing another line," writes John. In his meetings, John's listeners were often taken "by such a spirit of laughter as they could in no wise resist."[2]

The German mystic and Dominican monk, Meister Eckhart, spoke of laughter at the very core of the Trinity. In a surprising passage he writes:

> ...the Father laughs at the Son and the Son at the Father,
> and the laughing brings forth pleasure, and the pleasure
> brings forth joy, and the joy brings forth love.[3]

God is truly a God of severity, but also a God of joy and play. It is difficult for many to reconcile the multifaceted nature of God on this level. How does one reconcile the play and severity of the Almighty? Before I share some wild encounters with this playful God of ours, I should lay a theological foundation for this question.

Three Levels of Progression

It is understandably difficult for one who has suffered tremendous loss or abuse to consider that God is supreme joy and pleasure. How can He be a God of playfulness, when there is so much suffering in the earth? Let us turn deeper for a moment to embrace a great mystery. For this rejoicing God of ours is not shallow or momentary like the temporal pleasures of this earth. His is a true and solid Kingdom of joy, which cannot be discerned apart from personal encounter.

Soren Kierkegaard, the great Christian theologian and father of postmodernism, points out that many Christian individuals must progress through three primary stages of existence in their maturation as believers. These stages are the *aesthetic*, the *ethical*, and the *religious* (meaning *spiritual*). As we progress through these three layers of spirituality, our perspective enables us to reconcile the paradox of the lightness and severity of God.

In the aesthetic stage—the most immature of the three phases—we only approach God on a surface level. If left in the aesthetic stage alone (think external beauty), people will live for the fleeting moment. Theirs is a shallow existence of satisfying their natural desires and living by physical, emotional, or intellectual impulses. They live for momentary happiness of career, social life, material possessions, entertainment, etc. Aesthetic persons always play, but they have no moral framework.

Aesthetic people may feel they are "unique," but those in the aesthetic stage always follow the thoughts and opinions of others. They are politically correct. Theirs is a religion of jumping on the social bandwagon and accepting what they are told. They never individuate through personal experience with the Divine to realize Truth on a private level. In today's terminology, we would consider such persons as "carnal Christians" or, at best, immature believers.

Those who progress on to the *ethical* stage, says Kierkegaard, understand that there is a moral duty to accept in this life, to put aside their own desires and take up responsibility. They understand that the external, aesthetic lifestyle leads only to bondage, and that true freedom is the freedom to pursue that which is of eternal value.

Unlike the aesthetic person, the ethical person could never spend a million bucks on a fine painting when considering the plight of AIDS orphans in Africa. Their hearts have been pricked by a higher sense of moral duty. The aesthetic life alone brings no true and lasting fulfillment. So the transition from the aesthetic to the ethical moves us to a higher moral aim. We learn perseverance, endurance, and moral clarity. Sacrifice for a greater purpose.

The ethical is not swayed by the opinions of others. It is compelled by a sense of right and wrong. It is here that a person learns to make commitments and determine his own course, rather than being motivated by the ups and downs of emotion. Moral duty. Principled responsibility. A willingness to go against the flow. This is the ethical stage. Many "faithful Christians" on your elder board live in this stage of progression.

Although the ethical sphere is quite admirable, Kierkegaard contends that man must go *further* to the place of true *spirituality*. Ultimately, the ethical sphere alone becomes self-reliant. Although the ethical stage has taught me to *deny self* for the greater good, I have also learned to rely on its moral constructs instead of the *person* of God. I have learned to rely on an ethical framework of right and wrong. I know the difference between good and evil—but I am not called to eat from the Tree of Knowledge of Good and Evil. Instead I am called to eat from the Tree of Life, which is the living person of Jesus. The law is not alive. Ethics cannot intoxicate me. We should not live for *goodness* in general, but we live for God. Many people like a system of *do-gooding*, but God Himself is left out of the picture.

Staying in the ethical, we can become legalistic. And so, one of the things God does is to present us with moral conflicts. These conflicts threaten the safety net we have built. For instance, life became complex for Abraham when God told him to kill Isaac. Imagine if one day God comes to you and says: *kill your son.* The moral dilemma is this: on the one hand he must obey the voice of God. But on the other hand, murder is intrinsically wrong. Amid the paradox of ethical conflict, we are pushed to *look beyond the question of right and wrong.* Paradoxes always push us past our existing paradigm, and up to a higher place. The next time you are caught in a paradox between black or white, God may be trying to open your eyes to Technicolor.

In the third and final sphere—the *spiritual* stage—we must look to God Himself, apart from an ethical system. Kierkegaard discusses the "teleological suspension of ethics," in which God suspends the law for a higher aim. Abraham had a choice to make: kill Isaac or disobey God. There was no legal paradigm for this, as both decisions seemed morally wrong. He did not simply reduce God to a system of moral law, but Abraham submitted even his own ethical paradigm to God by faith. *Faith* is the key word here, for there is no formula for navigating this realm. We have to step completely out of the boat and walk on water.

As Christians, we know that God is above ethics and law, and that Christ both transcends and fulfills the law. Ultimately, the spiritual sphere is beyond moral duty. Here, one is fully resigned to the living God, who is above and beyond systematics. In the ethical sphere, one is constantly faced with his or her own inability to fulfill religious obligation. But there is a place of faith and grace and intimate relationship with the Creator that lies beyond this realm.

Abraham submitted his ethical understanding *of God to God*. And somehow by faith, he believed that God, in His goodness, could even resurrect his son Isaac from the dead (see Heb. 11:17-19). This was not something he learned in the books. This was not something he could get from someone else. Faith of this sort only comes in the individual pursuit of God. Abraham trusted God.

The ethical stage, left by itself, results in a fear-based lifestyle. Deep inside, we all know we have failed our highest legal duties. But when we transcend to the spiritual sphere, one resigns everything to God, even his own attempts to transform himself. Kierkegaard hoped to awaken the church to an individual pursuit of a living God that people would not idolize and depend on a social and moral system of right and wrong. The ethical stage can become a religious system which substitutes itself for personal faith.

Kierkegaard aimed, "to keep people awake, in order that religion may not again become an indolent habit."

The brilliance of Kierkegaard is that he saw beyond ethics and morality to a living, interactive, interpersonal God. Many are so spiritually dull that they think Christianity and morality are the same thing. Church is not just a white-steepled community ethics club. It is not like the local Rotary or the soup kitchen. It is about a living, individual relationship with Jesus Christ. Religion can never intoxicate you. Only God can.

In our progression through the three stages—from aesthetic to ethical to spiritual—we are often prone to reject each lower sphere at the first glimpse of the higher. But that is not the way God works. God rarely ousts a thing altogether, but adds depth and substance to it when the new comes.

This is how He has always worked through church history. When a denominational stream of the church could not fulfill all that God wanted to do on earth, He never cut them off from the Body. He simply did a new thing, added a new tributary to the stream and helped everyone arrive at greater fullness. We can have the new and still keep the best parts of the old.

In the spiritual stage, a most wonderful thing happens: *God reconciles the aesthetic and the ethical stages at a higher plane of reality.* Suddenly there is no more conflict between the God of play and the God of sacrifice. Sacrifice only opens the door to a new dimension of play. Suffering only opens a door to greater glory, and the bloody cross becomes the most beautiful work of artistic symmetry in all of creation.

God is an *aesthetic* God. He is a God of music, a God of dance, and a God who longs to redeem the arts. He wants to bring financial provision to us and care for our external needs. He is a God of beauty, and all of creation gives voice to His handiwork. Yet the externals: arts, aesthetics, and money *in themselves* are frivolous. It would only make sense that the practical, ethical responsibilities of caring for orphans in Africa, solving the crisis of world hunger, and caring for war-zone widows would far outweigh the need for composing songs, building a fortune, and painting portraits. The ethical does, in fact, trump the aesthetic. But this does not negate the fact that God is an artist, that God has playful inclinations. God is the Creator, the Inventor of beauty. Just because God is ethical, does not negate His artistry.

God is a God of play. And He is serious about righteousness, justice, and morality. These two ends of the spectrum coexist in perfect harmony. At the stage of true spiritual individuation, we see how a God of pure play reconciles with a God of serious moral duty.

The Law Points to Pleasure

Joy is the serious business of Heaven. In the aesthetic stage, we are still seeking our joy apart from God. The need for joy is very real, but the need is for *real joy.* True pleasure is only found in the spiritual stage. After a while, the aesthetic man grows weary of the shallow pursuit of exterior pleasure, and he begins to grow ethical. He joins a church and starts trimming his hedges the way a Christian should. He is still looking for bliss, but he has grown up enough to realize that joy does not come from serving himself.

But the ethical man is still trying to earn his joy.

"Religious 'flesh' always wants to work for God (rather than humbling itself to realize God must work for it in free grace)," writes John Piper.[4] God, in His good grace, sees your striving little soul in the ethical stage, and He lovingly throws a monkey wrench into the works.

God is above the ethical stage, and on rare occasion, He may instruct you to do something that seemingly opposes established moral standards. He told Peter to eat unclean foods before Peter had an understanding that Christ had fulfilled the food ordinances on the cross. He told David to eat the showbread, which was against the law at the time. These are the tests God brings to confound our morality boxes. But God never throws ethics out the window; He only fulfills ethics at higher dimensions. The reason we can eat pork, for instance, is because Christ fulfilled the dietary laws on the cross—He never ordered Peter to "break" the food laws, only step into their fulfillment (see Acts 10).

God never espouses relaxed morality. For instance, in regards to sexual sin, murder, theft, and the like, I have never seen the "God told me to do it" excuse fly. Although God is above ethics, He is still impeccably ethical. Moral dilemmas should always point us to a higher level of revelation about God's nature. They should never denigrate the purity of God's right standards.

God's laws are like the physical law of gravity. If I choose to jump off a cliff, I will not break the law of gravity, I will only illustrate it. I will become a *splat* on the ground. God did not *hate me* by dropping me to the ground. I just chose to illustrate the impartial law of gravity. Anyone else who jumps off the cliff will encounter the same effects. The law of gravity is impartial. It applies to everyone.

In the same way, if I break God's moral laws, there is a penalty to be paid. Sexual immorality, greed, idolatry—these things all carry consequences. Not because God hates me as an individual, but because His laws have established ramifications. If I "jump off the cliff" by disobeying God's impartial law, I will go *splat*. Not because God hates me, but because His law is established the same for everyone. Homosexuality, abortion, racism—all of these sins have dire consequences, not because God hates the individuals who practice them, but because His impartial laws will cause anyone who commits them to go *splat.*

If we find pleasure in any of these things, and God says they are wrong, it does not mean He is against pleasure. He actually wants to *preserve our pleasure* by keeping it focused on Him, the source of true merriment. Sin will desensitize our pleasure receptors.

Whenever we choose sin, we are simply turning away from joy. Romans 3:23 says that "all have sinned and fall short of the glory...." This is because sin is a *glory deficit*. It robs you of ecstasy. The reason we obey God is for higher pleasure. Consider Isaiah 48:18:

> *If you would only listen to My orders, you would have bliss brimming like a river* (Moffatt).

Also, it is said of wayward or violent men that "They care not for what leads to bliss, their paths are void of justice; they take the crooked course, where bliss is all unknown" (Isa. 59:8 Moffatt).

Simply said, all the Lord's paths end in bliss. Other paths promise happiness but end in terror.

In Deuteronomy 28, God puts before the people a tremendous list of blessings that will happen if they obey Him, and a terrible list of curses that will follow if they don't. The choice is ours: unspeakable luxury or utter defeat. In this sense, the laws of God simply point us to Him, reminding us of where our sustenance comes from. Believe that God is for you! His laws are not about control, but the preservation of your happiness.

The Serious Business of Merry Making

Eventually, the ethical man will see that he is utterly incapable of doing all that the law demands. Since religion is unfulfilling, he will ultimately appeal to a higher court of grace. He will realize that his deepest longing is for the True Bliss, and paradoxically, only the bliss enables him to fulfill the moral law. There is serious ethical obligation and work to be done on the earth: souls to save, orphans and widows to feed, the list goes on. But without *something more*, he gets depressed and loses his joy.

Don't let the task overpower you! There is work to be done, but this does not negate the fact that God likes to party. In Kierkegaard's *spiritual* sphere, both the aesthetic God and the ethical God are reconciled into one. The amazing paradox is that God can make you most productive when you are doing the least amount of work, just coasting along plastered in His love!

His nature is that He is a God of rejoicing. The Love Feasts were wild. God loves a party, but He wants you to party with Him. Neither the prodigal son, nor the older brother understood this. The prodigal son was aesthetic. He loved to hit the club with the boys. The older brother was ethical, always hanging out with the amen corner. But neither of them was *spiritual*. They never understood that there's a party in Papa's house, and He's bringing the refreshments! You can be holy and hammered at the same time. This is, perhaps, the offense of the ages. It smacks too much of blending the sacred with the common.

It is quite an offensive suggestion to say that God wants you to be happy. Holy we can stomach. And a mild state of contentedness we can handle. But *happy?* Perhaps that would be OK as long as we are not *too* happy.

One of the primary strategies of the religious spirit against your life (the religious spirit is synonymous with the antichrist spirit) is to make you feel guilty about being a thoroughly happy person. The truth of the matter is that God sets blessings before the upright. Or better yet, He sets *bliss* before the upright.

> *For God the Eternal is a sun and shield, favour and honour He bestows; He never denies bliss to the upright* (Psalm 84:11 Moffatt).

You are upright because He made you upright! Bliss is your free gift.

> *O the* bliss *of those who have broken the law and been forgiven, whose sin has been put out of sight. O the* bliss *of the man whose sin is not debited against him by the Lord* (Romans 4:7-8, William Barclay Translation).[5]

One of the Greek words for "blessed" is *makarios*, meaning "to enlarge or prosper; *to make happy*."[6] Understand that we are not just talking about external "blessings" that necessarily come from an upright life. Not just material prosperity, health, or protection from calamity. All of that is yours too. But we are talking about a supernatural ecstasy that is afforded a person in Christ, thoroughly dribbling out of those who walk in the Spirit, which is beyond the scope of natural possibility. God does not just want to *bless* your natural, external life—He wants you internally *blissed* at infinite proportions. On your best day, you have yet to scratch the surface of Heaven's happiness for you right now.

Let us consider the beatitudes in Matthew chapter 5. Rather than translating them like this: "*Blessed* is the man who is poor in spirit...*blessed* are those who mourn, etc." William Barclay and other scholars suggest a more accurate translation: "O the *bliss*" of such persons! God gives *bliss* to the meek, *bliss* to the peacemakers, *bliss* to the merciful, and *bliss* to the pure in heart! And the beatitudes culminate with this:

> *Yours is the* bliss, *when men shall heap their insults on you and persecute you, and tell every wicked kind of lie about you for My sake* (Matthew 5:11 Barclay).

This type of pleasure is simply irrational. It is otherworldly. That persecution would bring you jubilation is an unreasonable assumption! But nevertheless, it is a very tangible and *felt* euphoria. No matter what your enemies do to you, you are blissed! We have found this to be true in our own ministry. Many people like prophetic or healing ministries, but some have criticized us for being *too happy*. We get persecuted just for having fun in church. In the religious mindset of many, prophetic maturity is marked by bland, somber stoicism. "You've got to take this stuff seriously, young man!" But we are wildly, obnoxiously happy. Joy is the serious business of Heaven.

Some find us controversial at times, going overboard on the drunken pleasure of Heaven. Nevertheless, we are not ashamed, and the more we are criticized, the more we get whacked with drunken glory! *For ours is the bliss, when men shall heap their insults on us and persecute us and tell every wicked kind of lie about us for His sake!*

We are actually commanded to enjoy God. *"Delight yourself in the Lord"* (Ps. 37:4 NIV). *"Rejoice in the Lord always. Again I will say, rejoice"* (Phil. 4:4). So why is it that so many Christians are depressed? Your quest for joy and your duty to glorify God are not in conflict. They are the same. We will either glorify God by enjoying Him, or we will face dire consequences. God demands that you have fun. Deuteronomy 28:47-48 says, "Because you did not serve the Lord your God with joy and gladness of heart...you shall serve your enemies." It has been said that God threatens terrible things if we will not be happy!

The play of God is more effective than the strife of man. If work was more important than play, Heaven would be a sweatshop. Instead, it is a place of eternal rejoicing.

> *...We rejoice and delight in you; we will praise your love more than wine. How right they are to adore you!* (Song of Solomon 1:4 NIV)

The friends of the bride are found "rejoicing" in this passage of Solomon's Song. It seems foolish to spend our time and efforts dancing, playing music, and building cathedrals to God, when there is work to be done in the fields. But the bride confirms what they are doing, "How *right* they are to adore you!" This rejoicing adoration is the most proper thing to do. The aesthetic, in its reconciled state, can ascend even the ethical. Remember that when Mary poured the costly oil over Jesus, He sharply rebuked Judas for suggesting it be given to the poor instead. What an extravagant waste this was on the feet of Jesus!

"We rejoice and delight in You."

This is what we are made for. Words such as "rejoice" and "delight" are not indicative of a religious suffering-centered theology. But they are the very essence of the Gospel. The *good news* of the Gospel is that God is happy, and He has stretched out His own arm to work salvation.

This term "rejoice" here is *samach*.[7] It is one of many forms of the word, but most have a common meaning: "To rejoice, to be glad. (The primary idea appears to be that of a joyful and cheerful countenance...). But its use is more widely extended, and it is even used for louder expressions of joy, *as of those who make merry with wine*…and who utter merry cries." It can literally mean "leaping for joy," and is "said of those who held sacred feasts in the courts of the sanctuary."[8]

Is it possible that true Christian worship should be as extravagant and wild as those who make merry with wine? How productive is this? How practical?

Yes, we have serious business to do. We are called to destroy the works of the devil—but that won't happen through our solemn assemblies. As we get infused in the wine room, it is the very revelry of God that inspires, equips and empowers us. God too rejoices over His people, *as of those who make merry with wine.* In fact, God wants to drink *you* like the finest wine.

Bartender Angels

Play is such a priority with God that Heaven is full of it. Let there be a supernatural element to your play. Angels are very playful creatures. Did you know there are actually angels assigned to help you drink?

We have a number of *bartender angels* that travel with us in our ministry. We see them regularly; they are little fat Friar Tuck sorts who roll the barrels right into our meetings and begin to mess people up. These are not the huge, towering warrior type of angels you may have seen or read about. They look more like rosy, drunken little cupids than anything else! But the Lord has shown me they are some of the highest level beings and not to underestimate their power. The joy of the Lord is their *strength*! And they drink up a lot of joy juice. These little fat friars are *very* intense if the situation demands. Although they are merry, robust little cherubs, the demons know not to mess with them.

Everywhere we travel these days, it seems that people are caught up into ecstasies. Angels begin to come and yank on their arms and legs. Bodies begin to shake and hit the floor en masse. Sometimes angels will come and begin to spin people around. Certain angelic portals will open up in areas of the room at times, and anyone who steps near cannot help but spin in circles! This is often a prophetic sign that angels are helping people to shift to a new season, career, anointing, or perspective in God. But when these angels appear, you are not trying to analyze what all the prophetic signs might mean. You are just overwhelmed as you get absolutely whacked.

One of our associates, Shawn Gabie, had an open-eye encounter with an angel playing peek-a-boo with him in Moravian Falls, North Carolina. Our friend Todd Bentley has walked up and "surprised" angels in the woods of Moravian Falls. Those particular angels were playfully wrestling with one another and appeared to snap to attention when they realized they were being watched. Roland Buck, the Boise, Idaho, pastor who received numerous angelic encounters in the late 1970s before his death, noted the relaxed demeanor of the angels as well. They assured him that Heaven was far more laid back than we make it out to be!

Jesus said that unless we *"become as little children, you will by no means enter the kingdom of heaven"* (Matt. 18:3). This has much to do with the playful nature of Heaven. We should never despise the childlike quality of play any more than we should despise children themselves. The Lord also warned us to *"take heed that you do not despise one of these little ones, for I say to you that in heaven their angels always see the face of My Father who is in heaven"* (Matt. 18:10).

Becoming a Drink Offering

God wants to thoroughly enjoy you. When He looks at you, He sees perfect beauty. You are so pleasing to Him that He wants to drink of you.

> *I have come into my garden, my sister, my bride; I have gathered my myrrh with my spice. I have eaten my honey-comb and my honey; I have drunk my wine and my milk* . . . (Song of Solomon 5:1 NIV).

Despite your feelings of inadequacy or spiritual immaturity, Jesus loves you. He sees you perfectly whole through His finished work, and He enjoys you. He has already come into you, His garden, and has feasted upon you. The wine of intimacy you provide to Him is the very thing that intoxicates Him, even as you are mesmerized by Him.

> . . . *Eat, O friends, and drink; drink your fill, O lovers* (Song of Solomon 5:1 NIV).

This verse is translated in a bit more straightforward fashion from the Septuagint: *be drunk, brothers and sisters.*[9] This is a prompting not just for you to drink, but for Him to drink as well. The honey, wine, and milk are all representative of His Spirit, which He freely receives from you. Did you know that you are called to refresh, encourage, and even counsel the Lord? This may sound far-fetched, but it is true. He is looking for a resting place in you. God doesn't need encouragement—He is not insecure. Yet your adoration of Him is a pleasant fragrance. He is not in need of counsel. But like Moses, He wants you to be so possessed by His own Spirit of Counsel that He can ask your advice and it will be trustworthy. Moses was so full of God that he changed God's mind (see Exod. 32:14)! God doesn't *need* relationship, but He desires it. And therefore He makes Himself vulnerable to you, risking the dangers that come with intimacy.

> *...and your mouth [is] like the best wine. May the wine go straight to my lover, flowing gently over lips and teeth* (Song of Solomon 7:9 NIV).

This is the wine that Jesus drinks. It is the wine of your deep fellowship. God loves you so much, He just wants to roll you up and smoke you!

Catherine of Siena in the 14th century points to the very drunkenness of God Himself. What is God drunk on? *Your love.*

> You, high eternal Trinity, acted as if You were drunk with love, infatuated with Your creature ...You, Sweetness itself, stooped to join Yourself with our bitterness. You, Splendour, joined Yourself with darkness; You, Wisdom, with foolishness; You, Life with death; You, the Infinite, with us who are finite. What drove You to this?[10]

The thought of God's drunken love caused Catherine to feel "inebriated," saying, "I sense my soul once again becoming drunk! Thanks be to God!" Catherine writes:

> O priceless Love! You showed Your inflamed desire when

You ran like a blind and drunk man to the opprobrium of the cross. A blind man can't see, and neither can a drunk man when he is fast drunk. And thus He [Christ] almost like someone dead, blind, and drunk, lost Himself for our salvation![11]

According to Catherine, the very reason God created us—knowing we would fail miserably—was to have communion with His creation, which He loved immensely:

O unutterable Love...even though You saw all the evils that all Your creatures would commit against Your infinite goodness, You acted as if You did not see and set Your eye only on the beauty of Your creature, with whom You fell in love, like one drunk and crazy with love. And in love You drew us out of Yourself giving us being.[12]

Catherine also encourages us to stay whacked, saying, "Let us behave like the drunkard who doesn't think of himself but only of the wine he has drunk and of the wine that remains to be drunk!"

Chapter 5

high on Jesus

The marketplace and every sector of society is about to be invaded by an ecstatic group of champions. They will be a paradoxical blend of joyous celebrants and fiery prophets. God is releasing a greater intensity of His glory like the church has never seen in these days.

Where are those who will go deeper still, to the level of full possession? To go into the Most Holy Place means that you may be dragged back out by the rope around your ankle. There are higher levels of glory and power that you do not control; the glory controls you. God is preparing His Church to operate in a greater anointing, but most are not capable of it right now. It is a level of glory like was common in Acts 5 when Ananias and Sapphira dropped dead for their sins. In comparison to what squeaks by in our church services today, their sin was very minor! In fact, their sin seems nobler than many of today's best Christian acts of service!

If the *greater glory* killed Ananias and Sapphira, what will it do to such a backslidden church when it comes again in our day? And come it will. In greater measure than before. The church of our day is playing a grand song and dance, but this will be a messy thing when the glory of God actually shows up!

The Wine of Boldness

The manifestations God is releasing today are sometimes both pleasant and volatile. Blissful, but intense. He is teaching us to operate in the glory, not by using and marketing His presence, but getting possessed by it. The sword of the Spirit is one that you do not bear—the sword itself wields you. And sometimes strikes you. Remember when Joshua asked the angel of the Lord before the battle of Jericho, "Are you for us or for our enemies?" How did the angel respond? He said, "Neither." He represented the interest of One who was altogether above the fray (Josh. 5:13-14 NIV).

This level of glory is not about twisting God's arm and pleading for Him to back your own cause. This is a level of glory wherein we get on board with *His* agenda. And since we are no longer in control, there is a certain holy wildness that comes over us. It is the unfettered wildness of love. The wildfire of His Spirit.

Playfulness and might are interconnected in the Spirit. The Bible says that the *joy of the Lord is our strength.* The Prophet Joel speaks of the wine of God flowing freely in the latter days. In addition to this, Joel also champions a dread army of supernatural magnitude that will emerge in the might of the Lord. Wine drinking and boldness are intrinsically connected. What do soldiers do on furlough? Do they get pedicures on their free time, or volunteer at the local floral shop? No. Stereotypically, they tend to hit the pubs. They drink!

Consider this, when someone has been drinking a bit too much, do they suddenly become prim and proper, carefully choosing their words in public? No way! They lose all inhibition and they boldly blurt out anything that comes to their lips! A drunken man says things a sober man never will. The term is called flexing your "beer muscles." The same is true with the wine of the Spirit. As you drink, you lose all apprehension about what others are thinking. The fear of others drops off you like an old shirt. You suddenly become clothed with might.

In Acts 4, the apostles were *seeking* signs and wonders that Jesus would be glorified (consequently, you should seek signs and wonders too for His glory, despite what you may have heard to the contrary!). The apostles also prayed for boldness. Signs and wonders are an outworking of the Spirit of Might. Might, boldness, signs and wonders. They are all linked. But none of this came about until the apostles were filled with the Spirit's wine! The apostles prayed:

> *"Now, Lord, consider their threats and enable Your servants to speak Your word with great boldness. Stretch out Your hand to heal and perform miraculous signs and wonders through the name of Your holy servant Jesus." After they prayed, the place where they were meeting was*

shaken. And they were all filled with the Holy Spirit and
spoke the word of God boldly (Acts 4:29-31 NIV).

This infusion of Holy Spirit wine ultimately releases courage and miracles. In Acts 2, they had to get loaded before the miracles exploded! All the
apostles were gathered in the upper room on Pentecost when, "a sound like
the blowing of a violent wind came from heaven" (Acts 2:2 NIV). Next,
cloven tongues of fire rested on their heads and they spoke in the native
languages of every nation of the earth, as thousands of people gathered. By
this point, they were completely sloshed.

Some, however, made fun of them and said, "They have
had too much wine" (Acts 2:13).

Peter let them know that, *"These men are not drunk, as you suppose. It's*
only nine in the morning!" (Acts 2:15 NIV). It was Peter who explained, not
because he was the only one sober enough to stand—though that may have
been the case as well—but because the wine released a powerful preaching
anointing upon him and he spoke boldly, leading 3,000 people to the faith.

Wine drinking releases great boldness—but this is not just a natural
courage, mustered up by the mind of man. It is utterly supernatural
strength. In fact, when this same Spirit of Might rested on men throughout
the ages, it caused some to become miraculously invincible. The Spirit of
Might is what clothed Samson when he was able to kill a thousand men
with a bone and pick up a huge city gate to wipe out his enemies. The Spirit
of Might clothed David's mighty men, the men of renown who slaughtered
thousands supernaturally. They were not empowered by working out at the
gym. They had a supernatural force field of power that caused their enemies
to bounce off them like a sci-fi film.

The Spirit of Might is what releases miracles in our meetings when we
see God supernaturally cause fat to disappear from bodies, dissolve tumors,
or create gold teeth in people's mouths. His might makes you bold, but it
also releases signs and wonders. The reason the apostles prayed for signs and
wonders in the name of God's holy "servant Jesus" instead of "son Jesus," is
because they were asking for might. I will explain.

The four faces of the living creatures in Heaven reveal aspects of Christ's nature. Jesus is the Lion, *the King of Kings*. But He is also the Ox, *the Servant of All*. He takes the highest position, as well as the lowest one. Jesus is the messy Ox in the stall who will bring the increase and pull the yoke in the end-time harvest (see Prov. 14:4). Psalm 92:10 says:

> *But my horn You have exalted like a wild ox; I have been anointed with fresh oil.*

My *horn* is my authority or power, which God lifts up like an ox. Not just a domesticated ox, but a wild one! This is the oil of the anointing of the Spirit of Might. The ox is being released for harvest.

Don't be proud when Jesus comes to wash your feet like Peter. Let Him *serve* through you in great demonstration of power. The bliss infusion will bring a mighty harvest on the streets.

Buzz Evangelism

We have found that ecstatic drinking is the most powerful God-given tool for evangelism. There are many great spiritual gifts for evangelism today. We have friends who do prophetic evangelism (giving people prophetic words on the streets), dream interpretation, healing booths, spiritual reading booths, etc. Some of our friends are brazen enough to put up a "palm reading" sign. They don't really read palms; they just hold people's hands, prophesy over them, and lead them to Jesus! We do prophetic outreaches as well. But sometimes, I am honestly just too drunk in the Spirit to be coherent for this kind of stuff.

For example, while visiting the nation of Wales some time ago, we thought about doing a prophetic evangelism outreach on the streets. At the time, we were overwhelmed with the heavy, weighty glory of God, and it just seemed like a lot of work to do an outreach in our state of drunken bliss. Instead, we simply went to the streets holding a sign that read "Free Buzz." Instead of preaching, prophesying, or doing the "work" of evangelism, we just waited for people to approach us. As people stopped, we merely told them that we would pray and God would touch them with His tangible, manifest presence. Then they would know He was real. We led many in a prayer of salvation in a very short amount of time because they "felt" the presence of God. We touched them, they literally experienced the intoxicating presence of Jesus, and they knew He was real.

I only operate in evangelism when I am buzzed in the Spirit. So many people are religious in the way that they approach evangelism, but I have determined only to have fun with it. The results are that I now *enjoy* evangelism; I don't care what people think about me; and I see much more fruit than many people.

I think that the only danger the church faces today regarding "prophetic outreaches," like dream interpretation booths and the like, is that we could make them the next *formula*. Prophecy, healing, and such are just spiritual gifts. They are tools. We cannot have more production-line mindsets and a guilt-driven emphasis on evangelism, while simply using the shiniest new spiritual tools. Evangelism is necessary, but we must be motivated by the desire and delight of God's presence in the midst of it. We always have to leave room for the glory to come and possess us on the streets. God must be able to spontaneously switch things up in the streets. It is the tangible glory we need, not just the tools. This is how we will truly see the Last Great Awakening break loose in the Americas.

I have come to grips with the fact that I have no boldness or strategy to talk to people without the glory. Unless I am drunk on God, I can't do much. However, I do a lot of evangelism because I am buzzed most of the time. When the Spirit fills you, you can easily move in and out of the prophetic, and gifts of healing flow freely in the marketplace. Sometimes I do not even have a prophetic word for someone, but if I stop trying to evangelize and just get tanked up in the Spirit, something is bound to happen.

Satanic Ritual Squashed

Once we were ministering at a church in Florida, where powerful miracles took place. We watched as God caused physical rain to fall in the building! After the service, we took an evening stroll through a city park. As we were walking along, suddenly we heard a group of teenagers loudly worshiping satan by name. Someone in our group was recognized by the teenagers, so they knew we were a church group. They began to openly mock us for being Christians. It was time for a power encounter.

There is a prevailing "sissy spirit" that most Christians operate in fluently today. Although we profess to be lions, most Christians are pussy cats when it comes to sharing their faith. Sure, they may spray paint "Jesus Loves You" on an overpass, or scribble a Bible verse on the bathroom stall occasionally. But few believers are bold enough to actively evangelize. This is because they don't know how to drink.

As we heard the satanists mocking us, I could feel the sissy spirit trying to creep in. My children were not going to put up with it though.

"Dad, did you hear what they said?" my 9-year-old daughter asked, with such an outrage. She matter-of-factly stretched out her hand toward them and began violently speaking in tongues. Hers was an attitude of, "Who are these uncircumcised Philistines that they should defy the armies of the living God?" Had I cut her loose on them, she probably would have come back with a bag of foreskins.

Next thing you know, my 1-year-old son is pointing directly at them across a huge open lawn. Though he could barely walk, he began running toward them as if he saw what was about to take place. He must have seen the angels preparing for battle. All the kids were ready to go—but not me.

I had nothing. No words of knowledge, no prophetic strategy. No faith to call fire from Heaven. The whole church group was looking at me since I was the guy talking about miracles all the time. And here goes my toddler, running into the den of satanists! No silly little Gospel tract is going to help you at a time like this. All I knew was to get blitzed and see what happened. I needed to get whacked by God. I had no choice but to get tanked up! I started to get high on the Most High.

Before I knew it, my feet started moving underneath me. Keep in mind that this was the most foolish, non-seeker-sensitive evangelism strategy known. I got so smashed so quickly in the wine room that I started singing out loud in tongues and dancing around in circles as I approached the satanists. Moments before this, they were mocking us. Now they just shut up, dumbfounded.

I approached one of them with a gleam in my eye.

"I've got more power in my pinkie than all the antichrists of hell!

Because *Almighty God* lives inside of me!" I bellowed while absolutely hammered. It was like a hurricane struck. Several of them started to scream and manifest demons. Others were getting saved as the church group descended on them. Before long, the former satanists were laid out on the grass as several received the Lord. Others vanished into the darkness, screaming. It was not very difficult work, and I did not need any big showy gifts in operation. I just dived into Papa's cabinet upstairs and got hold of the fire water. The séance had been obliterated.

God is most definitely releasing a new wineskin to handle the fresh thing He is doing in this hour. Adam was given a skin garment, which showed that something had to die to cover his nakedness. In the same way, something has to die in order for us to have a wineskin. Jesus is the veil of flesh that was torn for our open Heaven, and whenever we drink of Him at the table of communion, we are drinking an open Heaven over our lives.

The thing about new wine is that it is always *new*! Although God trains us in the ways of His Spirit, no two experiences should be exactly the same. He has fresh wine and manna for us daily. There is a fresh thing He is doing today which cannot be contained by an old package. Even an old, brittle wineskin can be renewed if it is softened with oil. I don't even know if there is a wineskin left that can contain what God is pouring out today! It is truly an uncontainable wildfire. We had best just throw our heads under the tap of Heaven and turn the nozzle!

This crazy love is more than you could ever hope for. The rampantly wild joy of the Lord is what overwhelms the *prisoners of hope* in the day of God's restoration. In Zechariah 9:15, He says, *"They shall be roaring drunk as with wine"* (The New English Bible).[1]

Centuries ago, Dominican mystic Catherine of Siena understood the courage afforded to the one who drinks the strong wine of the Spirit. She speaks of this drunken boldness in the life of Mary Magdalene, saying, "She didn't think or worry about anything but how she could follow Christ.... She was no more self-conscious than a drunken woman." Mary Magdalene, according to Catherine, "wasn't afraid of the Jews, nor did she fear for herself. No, like a passionate lover she ran and embraced the cross.... Surely you were drunk with love, O Magdalene! As a sign that she was drunk with love for her Master, she showed it in her actions toward His creatures, when after His holy resurrection she preached."[2]

Drink deep and you will preach with fire.

Want to Get High?

On yet another visit to the U.K., we had just come from a powerful meeting where the glory of the Lord showed up tremendously. As we were driving away from the church, well after midnight, we paused at a railroad crossing for a train to pass. Seeing two young people passing by the car on foot, I casually reached my hand out the window as if I were holding a marijuana joint.

"Do you want to get high?" I asked them from the window. They were all ears, and quickly approached the car. They seemed eager to partake. I explained to them that there is no high like the Most High. "Do you want to get high on God?" I asked.

At first they were a bit suspicious. But when they saw that I was serious, they allowed me to pray for them. Before long, I had led them both to the Lord, prayed for an infilling of His Spirit while prophesying tremendous destiny words into their lives. They were noticeably touched by God, and before I left, the girl said to me, "I believe God really did send you here to speak to us today."

Her boyfriend snapped at her, very matter-of-factly: "*Of course He did!* God always sends His disciples to do these sorts of things!"

There is new wine for harvest. If we open our eyes, the fields are white for the reaping. It all starts with a little sip!

Taking Drug Culture

Ever since I first became a believer, I have had a constant addiction to the presence of God. I do not know of any other way to live the Christian life, apart from a loving compulsion to continuously be near this God of gladness. One of the primary things the Lord showed us years ago was that intoxication on Him is the very essence of "first love." God is not interested in your dispassionate praise or disinterested service. He is going for the depths of your heart strings. The thing that intoxicates you to the core is the very thing you worship. There is a deep, inner craving that draws us outside ourselves and into the realms of divine ecstasy. This is our inheritance as children and lovers of God. The only kind of love that will lay down its life is a love that has transcended life itself.

Heaven should be the prevailing norm. Ecstatic trances may seem strange or unusual to the natural mind, but they are the ordinary effect of Heaven's joy poured out on the average believer. Wherever the church has failed to set the standard in this regard, the enemy is ready to offer a cheap counterfeit.

Everyone is created for love's delirium, and this is why drug addiction is such a major draw not only for our youth, but in every sector of society today. Mind-altering drugs, like many occultist religious practices, do induce trance-like states. But these are illegal means of channeling spiritual activity, and they open adherents up to demonic influence. Pharmaceutical means to altered states of consciousness are direct counterfeits to the ordinary state of bliss humankind should experience in Christ. Adam was created to walk in bliss with God in Eden. Humanity was not created for depression, toil, and the curse of a fallen world. People unknowingly pursue drugs and alcohol to recapture this lost sense of the presence of God that man remembers from the garden. As we know, these addictions only provide a fleeting, momentary sensation that is followed by devastation to health and homes, ending in broken families, poverty, suicide, and destruction for future generations.

Even the temporary pleasure offered by drugs is shallow and utterly incomparable to the surpassing ecstasies of the Living God! Only believers have access to the purest stash of open Heaven delights. Though they do not realize it, drug addicts are trying to find this pleasure for which they were created. But most believers are also clueless to the infinite kilos of ecstasy available in their own bellies!

We are tired of seeing the church forfeit inner trance experiences to drug culture, new age, and the occult, which can only offer imitations at best and demonic counterparts at worst. As believers, we should be the most intoxicated people on the planet—blissed out on the God of ecstasy who has rivers of pleasure flowing at His right hand! We were never created for a dry, boring, sober religious existence. True spiritual "sobriety," of which the apostle Paul speaks, is coming into a vivid awareness of the unseen realm of Heaven. In Acts 2 and elsewhere in the Scriptures, this "spiritual sobriety" looked like complete drunkenness to the natural eye. The new wine of God's Spirit is the daily fare of the believer. The church started in the heavy drunken glory on Pentecost, and we are moving from glory to glory. God would never give us a lesser experience for a greater one. What the apostles tasted in part, we will overdose on in full!

There is a supernatural bliss that the world longs to see demonstrated in the people of God. To live by the rules and regulations of naturalistic religion, without encountering the Spirit of God Himself, is to already be drunk on the ways of the world. The Scriptures have long commended us to be inebriated without limit on God, as we are told to *"Eat, mates, and drink, and be drunk, brothers and sisters!"* (Song of Sol. 5:1, Septuagint).

We want to be those who partner with Heaven to see a redemption and restoration of true supernatural, mystical experience by finding our intoxication in the Holy Ghost! God will never put a limit on your joy levels. It will take all of eternity to explore the depths of God's gladness.

God is truly *restoring all things* in this hour. For instance, He is bringing the arts and media back to the church. The church was always intended to be the most creative arts center of the community. Likewise, all the sciences originated in the church, and prophetic scientists are again going into Heaven to make new discoveries. All major genres of music started in the church. And many people want to *take these back*. Furthermore, there are many people focused on taking back the government, taking back the education system, and taking back the courts. It is time for restoration.

I love all of this. I love the restoration movement, as God sends the spirit of Elijah to restore all things. But my question is this: *why did we give all of this stuff away to begin with?* Quite honestly, we cannot continually play defense. I think it is time that the church goes on the offensive by going out and taking the devil's stuff. Instead of waiting for him to take something else, let's put him on the run for a change!

This is something our ministry has determined to take: *drug culture.*

Taking It to the Street

When I go out for evangelism these days, I rarely ever start with the "four spiritual laws" or try to convince people they are sinners. I say this not to criticize anyone else's evangelism method. If it bears fruit for you, go for it. But most people already know they are sinners.

More often than not, I ask young people on the street if they want to get high! And more often than not, they do.

"Presence evangelism" is the most effective mode of making true converts, because people are not simply making intellectual decisions based on points of doctrine. Instead, they are truly *encountering* the Lord of glory through a tangible experience, and the explanation follows. Yes—of course we must give a rational exposition of the Gospel. But without tangible demonstration, the Gospel will be all talk and no show. Everybody is looking for interior fulfillment at a heart level, and we are carriers of that to a broken world. We pray, and people get rocked. They feel. They taste. They see.

It is amazing how drug culture and all manner of sedation are so prevalent in our society today. At best, everyone is addicted to television, food, and materialism. But more common than you realize, even in the church today, people are addicted to mind-altering substances—from Prozac, Xanex, and alcohol to marijuana or hard street and party drugs. I cannot begin to count how many people we have seen set free when the liberating pleasures of the Holy Spirit are released. *The anointing breaks the yoke* (see Isa. 10:27). We have seen many thousands get rocked who once suffered from depression that also led to physical ailments such as chronic fatigue, chronic pain, and fibromyalgia—all because the joy of Jesus broke a spirit of heaviness from their lives!

Humankind is designed to live in an alternate state of reality. You were made to walk in the Spirit. If someone is not plugged into the ecstasies of Jesus, they are naturally going to look for their fix in a perverted form. Although the source of our intoxication is two worlds apart, secular people at least understand the principle of *intoxication*. There is an issue of *relevance* and *reality* here. Although religious spirits hate it, I have no problem drawing parallels between the ecstasies of God and a drug-induced state of consciousness. The latter is only a counterfeit of the former. My goal is to bring the spiritual principles to street-level language, where people need the revelation. Most nonbelievers think God wants to take away their fun. I encourage them to "Toke the Ghost" or take a psychedelic trip with Jesus—not by using drugs of course, but by imbibing the Spirit of God.

A Personal Testimony

Drug-induced trances are only shallow, deadly substitutes for Holy Spirit trances. We can convince people that they don't need drugs by getting them high on the Most High. Then and only then, freedom and deliverance are simple, if not instant. The best way to convince them is to give them a taste of what they are missing out on! This is the "one-step program" for deliverance. But this is not just for the street—the majority of Christians are missing out on the trance realm as well.

I am living proof of this principle. I received an instant deliverance from drugs as a teenager, and I was the worst substance abuser of all my friends. The thing that finally broke my addiction was getting whacked by the thrilling pleasure of the infilling of the Holy Spirit! How could I ever choose a lesser substance after tasting divine bliss? Most of the strongest drug addicts consequently have the strongest call to raptures and the seer realm. Consider how every class of drug specifically imitates something produced in rapture. *Sedatives* only counterfeit the deep, supernatural peace of God. Stimulants, or *uppers*, only imitate the power and stamina of the breaker anointing when the Spirit of Might comes upon you. *Hallucinogens* only simulate the visionary realm. It is completely normal that people would want to experience peace, power, and see things! These are God-given desires, but we should fulfill those desires in Him, rather than substances. Bono, from the rock band U2, makes a great point when he sings: *there's nothing better than the real thing!*

Our ministry has taken it as a sort of personal mandate to influence the church toward the ecstasies and living a lifestyle of spiritual drinking. This is because the new wine has everything to do with intimacy, and love is the highest way. God wants junkies, and I have resolved to be a Holy Ghost *pusher*. Pharisees often get offended when I talk about smoking

"Jehovah-wanna," popping a "taste and see pill," or drinking "Godka." Of course we never have nor ever would encourage the partaking of drugs. But we strongly encourage the partaking of God! Hearing these sorts of analogies is like sweet water to the thirsty soul who was born to live an intoxicated lifestyle. There are many desperate people out there who are ready and willing to embrace a God who is tangible, loving, joyful, and full of mystical surprises and intoxicating delight. This revelation of first-love intoxication drives young people through the roof. They know that this is what they were made for: to live more whacked than their friends who are on drugs.

The truth is that we are not really comparing God to drug use. The world has already done that! The very existence of a drug culture shows that the comparison has already been made. We are simply reversing the comparison by choosing the true experience of divine ecstasy. You do not need to inhale marijuana when you can inhale the *ruah*—the very life-breath of God's Spirit! We are simply reversing the idea that substances (or anything the world offers) can fill a void of pleasure and experience reserved for God alone.

We have seen numerous drug users set free, prostitutes converted, and countless people filled with the Spirit, simply by offering them valid impartation in a language that is accessible. Entire secular schools have been turned upside down as God has invaded the marketplace with His mystical presence.

Shock Language

Imbibing the pleasures of God is the most critical, key component for the preservation of society. Finding God as our holy "addiction" goes much further than a tactic for ministering to drug users. We must all learn to love God at the deepest, most compulsive levels of our existence.

All of mankind is called to find its identity as lovers of God. The essence of true love goes far beyond our works or service. True love must *find pleasure* in the object of its affection. While Christianity is full of cliché terminology to describe *love, joy, worship, adoration,* and the like, I have found that it is sometimes more effective to use shock language and wild demonstration to convey how extreme is the joyful possession He offers us!

We have had many pastors ask us to "tone down" the vernacular when paralleling God encounters with drugs. But by the grace of God I will not tone down an ounce of what He is doing until the day I die. Jesus never toned it down, and He never held anything back. One of the very reasons we use this type of language is to dismantle religious strongholds that keep people from "going too far" in the Spirit. Heaven is all about a great party.

Even the great evangelist Billy Graham has made the analogy between conversion to Jesus and drug use. Taking the stage at the request of rock concert promoters in the late 1960s, he encouraged young people coming to hear the Grateful Dead and Santana to "get high without hang-ups and hangovers"...on *Jesus*.[3] Graham used to quote the testimony of pop star Cliff Richards in interviews, saying, "When I accepted Christ as my Lord and Savior...this was 10,000 times more of a turned-on experience than any trip I took on LSD."[4]

It was very common for converts in the Jesus People Movement of the 1960s and '70s to make these analogies as a way of relaying the pleasurable ecstatic experiences of the Gospel. As former dopers flushed their drugs down the toilet in Arthur Blessitt's Sunset Strip headquarters, a typical convert would be heard to say, "I don't need this anymore. I'm high on the Lord."

"Blessitt became one of the first to adopt the argot of the street for his evangelistic pitch. If the jargon of the 'Jesus trip,' 'Jesus the everlasting high,' 'dropping Matthew, Mark, Luke and John,' 'dealing reds' (Blessitt stickers, not pills) had its origin in one man, it was Arthur Blessitt," notes the historical work, *The Jesus People.*[5]

Blessitt is the same man who led the later-to-be U.S. President, George W. Bush, to receive the Lord in a Texas restaurant in 1984.[6] Blessitt would often approach a junkie and strike up a conversation: "Hey, man, let me say a word about Jesus. Man, He's out of sight. He really is. You think you've got a high? Man, Christ can take you higher, all the way to Heaven. You ever think of getting spaced-out on Jesus?"

In his book, *Turned on to Jesus*, Blessitt addresses his audience:

> You're spaced out on acid, some of you are high on speed,
> or you've been smoking grass. Some of you are loaded on
> downers or maybe you've hit up and felt the rush of
> heroin. Let me tell you, brother, if you really want to get

turned on, I mean, man, where the trip's heavy, just pray to Jesus. He'll turn you on to the ultimate trip. He'll give you a high that will keep you for eternity.[7]

Jesus Is Better Than Hash

In the Jesus Movement, the commonly heard term "just drop Jesus" replaced "dropping" acid for many hippie converts. Thousands upon thousands of new believers were being added to the church, as some of the fastest growing denominations were birthed in this movement, including Calvary Chapel, Vineyard Churches, and Hope Church, along with parachurch organizations like Jews for Jesus and the massively influential contemporary Christian music industry (CCM).

Hundreds of thousands of copies of the *Hollywood Free Paper*—a Jesus People magazine that regularly touted Jesus as a better alternative to drugs—were distributed in California and beyond. A 1971 issue of the *Free Paper*, for instance, heralded the edgy front cover headline: "Jesus Is Better Than Hash." Another popular Washington-based magazine of the day, *Truth*, had a massive influence of the revival culture. Here is an excerpt from a 1971 issue of *Truth*, entitled "The Parable of the Parsley and the Acapulco Gold." It is emblematic of the language one would regularly find in the magazine and other Jesus Movement publications of the day:

To what can we compare the Kingdom of Heaven? ...Do you smoke dope? Have you ever smoked bad dope? You know, full of stems, maybe mixed with parsley and catnip. Yeh, you burn your throat, and the only way you can get high is hyperventilating.

Let's say you just bought a lid for fifteen bucks. Bad dope. You're sitting there, puffing away. Maybe you're getting a little high hyperventilating. Maybe you're getting a little bummed out because it's a burn.

I come tripping up to you, and I have a big sack of Acapulco gold. Say it's one of those plastic garbage sacks full. And I say, "Man, if you'll just throw down that lid, I'll give you this Acapulco gold, free. It's already paid for, but the only way you can get it is to throw down your lid."

What would you do?

Well, that's what Jesus is saying to you. He's just saying, "Man, if you're getting a little tired of your trip, of getting burned. If you just give up your trip and accept My life, I'll give it to you free with all the love and all the joy and all the peace that comes with it."

You know, only a fool would smoke parsley when you could have Acapulco gold.

Not only were thousands coming into the Kingdom through the church's invasion of popular culture, but secular journals were forced to take note of this unlikely revival among hippies and drug users. "The word 'trip,' as used by the counter-culture and now by the Jesus People, is a synonym for experience; a 'high' is an experience. To be high on drugs means to have a drug-induced experience. To be high on Jesus means to have a certain religious experience. When those in the counter-culture talk about being turned on to Jesus, they are referring to an emotional experience that, for them, has striking similarity to the emotional experience induced by drugs," explain *The Jesus People* authors.[8]

Secular social science magazine *Society* ran a 1972 article titled, "Mainlining Jesus: The New Trip," analyzing the Jesus People, their drug culture metaphors, and the spreading movement among the young. The magazine commented, "The Jesus trip is The Great Awakening of 1740 (Jonathan Edwards) revisited; it is American frontier religion revisited with Volkswagens and amplifiers supplanting the horses, wagons, and saddlebacks of Cane Ridge, Kentucky, 1801." The magazine estimated that of the many thousand new converts being baptized along the coasts of California and elsewhere across America during this revival, most had a high incidence of past drug use, "with 62 percent of those over 18 and 44 percent of those under 18 having used dope. Only a few individuals were extremely light users, usually of marijuana. . . . A common description of the conversion experienced is: 'It's a rush like speed.'"[9]

The music of the era likewise invaded drug culture by using common metaphors understood in popular culture and focusing listeners toward Jesus as a better, alternative experience than substances. Artist Marj Snyder produced a hippie ballad in 1972 titled "High on the Love of Jesus," while pre-CCM era Mike and Karen Johnson released a track the same year titled "I'm High." His slurred vocals did sound as if he was high, but the song was an anti-drug tune with references that encouraged people to get their fix on Jesus. As late as 1976, a Jesus People song from the U.S. Apple Corps was titled "Get High on Jesus." The Joyful Noise band also produced a "High on Jesus" song in 1971. Overall, there are literally dozens of albums, spanning nearly every genre of music—from country to rap to reggae—that have some derivation of a "get high on Jesus" track. Popular billboard-charting bands of today still get away with these edgy metaphors, such as Plumb's "Drugstore Jesus" or Grammy-nominated CCM band Skillet, whose song "Better Than Drugs" screams:

Your love is like wine
Feel you comin' on so fast
Feel you comin' to get me high
You're better than drugs
Addicted for life
Feel you when I'm restless
Feel you when I cannot cope
You're my addiction, my prescription, my antidote.

The Ambrosial Drug of the Jews

These types of analogies have a much deeper history in the church. Philo was an ancient Jewish Bible commentator whose works shaped the thought work of the early church in the first centuries. Consider his writing, as he said:

And when the happy soul stretches forth its own inner being as a most holy drinking vessel—who is it that pours forth the sacred measures of true joy but the Logos, the Cup-bearer of God and Master of the feast—he who

differs not from the draught he pours—his own self free
from all dilution, who is the delight, the sweetness, the
forthpouring, the good cheer, **the ambrosial drug** ...
whose medicine gives joy and happiness.[10]

Ultimately, there is even scriptural precedent for making such typological analogies between God's presence and mind-altering substances. Proverbs 9:1-5 reads:

> *Wisdom has built her house, she has hewn out her seven*
> *pillars; she has slaughtered her meat,* **she has mixed her**
> **wine***, she has also furnished her table. She has sent out*
> *her maidens, she cries out from the highest places of the*
> *city, "Whoever is simple, let him turn in here!" As for him*
> *who lacks understanding, she says to him, "Come, eat of*
> *my bread and* **drink of the wine I have mixed***.*

The Holy Spirit is, of course, the *Spirit of Wisdom*. But what is the *mixed wine* of the Spirit? For this, we must look into the customs of the times. According to Bible commentator Adam Clarke, "probably the *yayin masach*, mingled wine, was wine mingled, not with *water*, to make it *weaker*; but with *spices* and other ingredients to make it *stronger*. The ingredients were *honey, myrrh, mandragora* [an aphrodisiac], *opium*, and such like, which gave it not only an *intoxicating* but *stupifying* quality also. Perhaps the *mixed wine* here may mean *wine* of the *strongest* and *best quality*, that which was good to cheer and refresh the heart of man."[11]

Clarke is essentially saying that the Holy Spirit has mixed "opiated wine" for the believer. Of course, God is not endorsing the use of opium here. We must remember that this is symbolic of "tripping on Jesus."

Mystic writer John of the Cross further draws this analogy between the mixed, or spiced, wine and the interior graces of divine love:

> "The spiced wine" is that exceedingly great grace which
> God sometimes bestows upon advanced souls, when the
> Holy Spirit inebriates them with the sweet, luscious, and

strong wine of love. . . . Such wine is prepared by fermenta-
tion with many and diverse aromatic and strengthening
herbs; so this love, the gift of God to the perfect, is in the
soul prepared and seasoned with the virtues already
acquired. This love, seasoned with the precious spices,
communicates to the soul such a strong, abundant inebriation when God visits it that it pours forth with great
effect and force those acts of rapturous praise, love, and
worship . . . and that with a marvelous longing to labor and
to suffer for Him. . . . The spiced wine continues for a
considerable time, and its effects also; this is the sweet love
of the soul, and continues occasionally a day or two, sometimes even many days together, though not always in the
same degree of intensity, because it is not in the power of
the soul to control it. Sometimes the soul, without any
effort of its own, is conscious of a most sweet interior
inebriation, and of the divine love burning within, as
David says, "My heart waxed hot within me, and in my
meditation a fire shall burn."[12]

Chapter 6

dispensers of the glory

You have authority to bliss people. You are a wine barrel. Inside of us are rivers of living water—we are simply containers for Heaven. You are a temple—a house full of Him.

Under the Old Covenant, God's Spirit primarily rested *on* an individual, but now, He comes to dwell *within* us. Gain a deep revelation of this. Instead of seeking the anointing, we become a *source* of the anointing. As David said, *"I am like a green olive tree in the house of God..."* (Ps. 52:8). From us, the olive grows and the oil flows. We have become carriers of the glory, and the *golden oil of bliss* pours freely from within us. You've been grafted into the anointing of the *sons of golden oil,* the mantle of the two witnesses that rests on the Lord's end-time church:

> *"What are these two olive-branches, held by the two golden spouts that empty oil into the golden bowl?"* ...
> *Then he replied, "These are the sources of the oil of bliss, the two men who stand before the Lord of all the earth"*
> (Zechariah 4:12-14 Moffatt).

You are the branches flowing with sap; you are the golden bliss spout of God into the earth. Perhaps you have run to church services, chased anointed men of God, hopped conferences, or even spanned the globe chasing a drop of this oil. That is great! Many never get off their comfy recliner to pursue the anointing—blessed is the heart set on pilgrimage. But now, let your journey be from the *inside out!* You are an ecstasy tap! The glory that is *within* you yearns to pour out and touch that cloud of glory from *without.* Deep is calling out to deep.

Understand the dynamite that is inside of you. *Christ in you the hope of glory* will revolutionize your perspective about yourself. No longer will you perceive yourself as needy for an external blessing you must pursue. Instead of seeking a blessing, you will *become* a blessing. Instead of looking for a drink, you will become a watering hole for others.

One of the greatest tactics of the enemy to stifle the church from operating in her fullness is to attack her identity. In the desert fast of Jesus, satan repeatedly attacked His identity, asking, "If You are the Son of God...." If the enemy can sow doubt into your heart and mind concerning your spiritual identity, he can block or divert the eternal power that resides inside of you. You are a source, a headwaters of God's very anointing on the earth. The enemy cannot stop the all-powerful flow of God's power from blasting out of you.

You are already seated in the House of Wine. You are already in the ecstasy of God. As your eyes of faith allow you to believe this truth, a state of rapture begins to manifest. However, if the enemy can cause you to believe his empty lies, then you will turn off the valves of your heart through disbelief of God's word. Then the waters cease to flow. Believing is the key. Less thinking and more drinking!

It is imperative that we reverse the age old lie that we are merely saved sinners—worms in the dirt who are unworthy of anything. God has absolutely eradicated our sin nature, burying us with Christ and therefore resurrecting us with Him (see Rom. 6:4). You are not just a refurbished sinner. You are a *new creation* in Christ, and furthermore, He has placed the full worth of His Son on *you*! If we constantly focus on a false perception of unworthiness, we call God a liar and the work of the cross null and void.

Taking this principle further, did you know that you are no longer in need of a blessing from God or from man? You already have everything! We now have *"every spiritual blessing in the heavenly places in Christ"* (Eph. 1:3). We simply need to walk out what we already have inside of us:

> As you therefore have received Christ Jesus the Lord, **so walk in Him....Beware lest anyone cheat you** *through philosophy and empty deceit, according to the tradition of men, according to the basic principles of the world, and not according to Christ. For in Him dwells all*

*the **fullness of the Godhead** bodily; and **you are**
complete in Him, who is the head of all principality
and power* (Colossians 2:6, 8-10).

What could we possibly ask for that has not already been given us through the cross? All blessing and power has been released through the atonement because the heavens themselves were torn open through the veil of Christ's flesh. Christ in you, the hope of glory, allows *you* to do all things through Him who strengthens you (see Phil. 4:13). You can do anything because you are truly a container of never-ending supernatural power. Theoretically, you should never get tired, never get frustrated, and never face any obstacle that you cannot pulverize your way through without the slightest effort. You are a source bed of God's eternal strength and might. Don't lower this standard.

Someone will say to me, "You can't possibly believe that!" I say that you have more power in your pinkie than all the antichrists of hell.

The Power of Benediction

In the state of ecstasy, you cease to pursue God for things, and instead, allow Him to *be* through you by grace through faith. If you already have everything, then why ask God for anything else? Prayers of petition are really only necessary because we lack faith. The only prayer we should ever have to pray is one of adoration and worship for eternity. Nevertheless, the New Testament is clear that we should offer up requests and petitions to God. We will do this our entire lives because we are always growing into new levels of faith. We "have not because we ask not." But truthfully we already *have* everything positionally in Christ. Asking God for things simply reminds us where it all comes from, keeping us dependent and thankful. Yet it is not our requests to Him that bring about answered prayer—it is our faith to believe what He has *already given us.*

*Therefore I say to you, whatever things you ask when you
pray, believe that you receive them, and you will have
them* (Mark 11:24).

Faith is the key ingredient to answered prayer. Once faith comes, we know that we already have what we have asked for. It was there all along through the atonement. This is why proclamation and declaration are more effective forms of prayer than petitions. Through a proclamation, you are aware of the vested authority of Christ in you to do a thing, and so your words are simply framing up a reality. Your words speak not vertically, but horizontally to the environment and situations around you, as you command it to line up with Heaven. You are no longer asking God to heal your knee; you are commanding the knee itself to be healed because you have faith that God is already here and available to back the word.

There is a process of growth and maturity that enables us to jump from petition to effective proclamation. But the highest form of prayer is neither petition nor proclamation. It is worship. Worship is a prayer of intimacy. In the place of worship, the need for any other kind of prayer no longer exists, because *need* itself does not exist. He is the Answer. The Beginning and the End. You simply become lost in Him.

In the place of intimacy and the simple practice of His presence, other forms of prayer lose their necessity. Requests and petitions are the prayers of hope. Proclamations and declarations are the prayers of faith. Praise and worship are the prayers of love.

"Love prayer" is far more effective than "faith prayer." *"Delight yourself in the Lord and He will give you the desires of your heart"* (Ps. 37:4 NIV). In the place of *delighting in God*, you become a magnet for blessing because God's favor spills over you. If you have needs, you are unaware of them in this place of bliss.

Many spend hours in successful intercession, and this is noble. But it is never sustainable without a deep-seated enjoyment of God's tangible glory. The deeper we venture into His glory, the more words often fade away. The most effective prayer is to spend hours getting blasted in His presence. Brother Lawrence says the following:

> I have quitted all forms of devotion and set prayers but those to which my state obliges me. And I make it my business only to persevere in His holy presence, wherein I keep myself by a simple attention, and a general fond

regard to God...which often causes me joys and raptures inwardly, and sometimes also outwardly, so great, that I am forced to use means to moderate them, and prevent their appearance to others....

The King, full of mercy and goodness, very far from chastising me, embraces me with love, makes me eat at His table, serves me with His own hands, gives me the key of His treasures; He converses and delights Himself with me incessantly, in a thousand and a thousand ways, and treats me in all respects as His favourite. It is thus I consider myself from time to time in His holy presence.

My most useful method is this simple attention, and such a general passionate regard to GOD, to whom I find myself often attached with greater sweetness and delight than that of an infant at the mothers breast; so that, if I dare use the expression, I should choose to call this state the bosom of GOD, for the inexpressible sweetness which I taste and experience there....

At other times, when I apply myself to prayer, I feel all my spirit and all my soul lift itself up without any care or effort of mine, and it continues as it were suspended and firmly fixed in GOD, as in its centre and place of rest.[1]

Brother Lawrence explains that this state of encountering and abiding in God's presence is the very essence of prayer itself, for it is a state of *being in God*, versus a mere exercise of rhetoric with God. It is also the state in which God pours out through us. When we arrive at ecstasy in the Spirit, we simply stand under the fountainhead and God pours through us. Thomas Aquinas says that we have most fully come into true mysticism the more we lend ourselves to passivity in this state. We are merely a valve or a hose for His love to channel through to the world. You really don't do much, except love Him. We never read of Adam "working" in Eden. He simply walked with God and the garden was tended.

When we live in the place of intimate union with God, living the "love prayer," we find the "faith prayer" much easier to administer. Rather than vainly trying to *name and claim* a thing through our proclamation, we simply speak out of the cloud of glory and things happen. This realm of glory is far higher than approaching God through mental prayer. Many people are very religious in their prayer routines, but we must be moved by the cloud of His presence.

St. Ignatius, like Brother Lawrence, recommends not forcing ourselves into various acts of mental prayer. "If any particular point causes me to experience the grace which I am seeking, I must remain there calmly until my devotion is satisfied, without caring for anything more," he says.[2]

We as believers possess an authority to pronounce blessing upon others. This is the principle of *benediction*. It is especially true with prophets and apostles, but even in the Old Testament, priests were divinely authorized to bless the people. In Deuteronomy 10, the Levites were separated to minister to God, but also to *bless the people* in His name. We understand that life and death are in the power of the tongue (see Prov. 18:21), but rarely do people realize that powerful men of God have a mandate to release blessings and even creative miracles on behalf of God. In this, I am not talking about petitions (asking God to do it) but proclamations (telling it to be done). Let us look at how the Lord, through Moses, commissioned the Levites to bless people:

> *And the Lord spoke to Moses, saying: "Speak to Aaron and his sons, saying, 'This is the way you shall bless the children of Israel. Say to them: "The Lord bless you and keep you; the Lord make His face shine upon you, and be gracious to you; the Lord lift up His countenance upon you, and give you peace."' So they shall put My name on the children of Israel, and I will bless them"* (Numbers 6:22-27).

God told Moses to tell Aaron to tell his sons to tell the people: *the Lord bless you*. Talk about delegated authority! Throughout the New Testament in the Epistles, Paul, Peter, and others on numerous occasions release apostolic benedictions to believers. *Grace be with you. Peace be with you.* Here, they are not asking for grace and blessings. Rather, they are bestowing them, because of their authority to do so.

This is a mandate. You are a royal priesthood, and you are called to bless people! You have authority to speak and declare blessings and to carry an atmosphere of blessing everywhere you go. You are to be an agent for God's pleasure and goodness in the earth. On one side of the cross you were always looking for a blessing. Now you *are* a blessing.

But what does it mean to speak blessing? The word "blessed" is perhaps one of the most overused and despiritualized words in the Christian vocabulary. We have even reduced it to a trite greeting: "How are you?" "I'm blessed." In the same superficial way—when a person is asked "How are you?"—although they are depressed and on Prozac, they reply, "I'm fine." *Blessed* means nothing to us today.

What does it truly mean to be *blessed* by God? One of the Greek words for "blessed," as we mentioned earlier, is *makarios*. It means "to enlarge or prosper; *to make happy.*" To be truly blessed is to be truly happy—not the make-believe, put on your Sunday face kind of happiness. This is gut-busting, exhilarating, in-your-face elation. You are on cloud nine. You are caught up into another realm. You are *ecstatic*.

You are literally commissioned by God to *bliss* people. Sometimes, I even frame up my own glory experience through the spoken word. I say to myself, "John, you are going to be drunk in the Spirit for the next 36 hours straight." The funny thing is, it works! I am lining myself up with a pre-existing heavenly reality. I am not striving to enter the Holy of Holies from the outer court. My faith tells me that I am already there with Christ. When I believe it, I begin to manifest it. Living as a passive instrument of His grace means that you are a vessel, continually dispensing His presence and purposes.

But this authority is much broader than its application to ourselves. God wants you to exercise your authority to bliss-bless entire people groups and regions. The church is about to stop giving lip service to their royal priesthood, and actually start to operate in it! We will not just talk about being sons and daughters of the King—we will actually use our princely authority to command the earth into alignment with Heaven!

It is good that you believe you are a child of the King. Now what are you doing with this power? Are you giving divine mandates to your city? To your school system? Are you making royal proclamations and releasing royal blessings?

Isaiah 32 tells us that there will be princes (you and I) who actually use their God-given leadership to release justice into the world. To set things straight in this fallen society we live in:

> *Behold, a king will reign in righteousness, and **princes will rule with justice**. A man will be as a hiding place from the wind, and a cover from the tempest, as rivers of water in a dry place, as the shadow of a great rock in a weary land. The eyes of those who see will not be dim, and the ears of those who hear will listen. Also the heart of the rash will understand knowledge, and the tongue of the stammerers will be ready to speak plainly* (Isaiah 32:1-4).

When we begin to rule justly with our delegated authority from our Father the King, we become a place of blessing, a refuge from the storm and a shelter from the wind to those around us. You begin to frame up a new life, vision and voice for those in your sphere of influence, because you sit on a throne with God and have a mandate to do so.

I have seen the Lord do some tremendous things, simply because I learned to approach the heavenly courts and release the glory from that place. In our ministry, the more I began to believe in my divine authority to bless others, and the more I exercised it with the spoken word, the more I began to see some fantastic miracles. We have seen the Lord heal thousands of people from sickness and infirmities. I have watched people come out of wheelchairs and walk after years of disability. I have seen dozens if not hundreds of deaf ears open, seen cancerous tumors disappear from people's bodies, and watched as new teeth grew into people's heads. We have seen hundreds of phenomenal creative miracles, such as people losing weight instantaneously in meetings, and more, all because we became dispensers of God's blessings.

There are many people who are oppressed, sick, broken, and lost in the world, but few Christians who will actually exercise their God-given power to do something about it. We display faithlessness when we keep asking *God* to do something when He has clearly given the task to *us*. Who will be the ones who boldly approach the throne of grace and become a mouthpiece for restoration? Isaiah 42:22 says:

But this is a people robbed and plundered; all of them are snared in holes, and they are hidden in prison houses; they are for prey, and no one delivers; for plunder, and no one says, "Restore!"

Decide today that you will be a prince who releases justice and restoration in the earth. Stand in the gap and boldly say, "Restore!" This is more than the working of miracles. This is about becoming a source of blessing and fulfillment for entire nations. This is about carrying an open Heaven everywhere you go.

If Moses had benediction authority from God to split open the Red Sea, how much benediction authority is afforded to New Covenant believers, who are the very houses of the Spirit of God Himself? God is waiting for people to be just crazy enough to believe Him for bigger and bigger things.

Out of this place of intimate suspension between Heaven and earth, God has used countless forerunners as firebrands, heralding another realm of power and glory. Such ones who have lived a rapturous lifestyle have manifested radical reformations on the earth. Do not settle for a mediocre existence that ignores the unseen realm. By dwelling in unbroken union, you will do much more than prophesy with goose bumps. As you speak, nations will be established and overthrown. Poverty will be eradicated. The deaf will hear and the blind will see. You will become a source of life, happiness, and hope to your community, region, and world!

Part III

a history of trances

Chapter 7

from biblical prophets to the outer fringes

There is something solid in the surreal. The existence of a realm outside the known parameters. It is a place of divine mystery. The path of Life. The ecstatic prophets of old knew this place. These men were radicals. Unpredictable. Fiery. These were unbalanced men, their lifestyles marked by the strange and uncanny. They lived somewhere between Heaven and earth. These men were well outside the established circles of their day. They belonged to a company of fanatics and mystics—an eternal generation that is strewn timelessly throughout all the ages to be paraded at the end in a grand apostolic processional—these men who never danced for mainstream society nor fit within the tailored hem of manmade religion.

These men were a loud and grinding catalyst in a white-picket-fence world, a reminder of another place. They were a preservative of truth who endured social distaste, persecution, and misunderstanding for our sakes and for the hope of a better resurrection.

Most people are quite comfortable with a faith that fits within the boundaries of their own understanding. But these men lived outside themselves. Consider Isaiah, who wrote 66 chapters in our gold-gilded Bibles. He looked millennia into the future through multiple dimensions of reality. And he walked the earth naked for three years.

Ezekiel cooked with dung cakes (see Ezek. 4:12). John the Baptist lived in the desert, wearing animal hair and eating bugs (see Matt. 3:4). Their approaches were unorthodox. Their truths were inconvenient. Their ideas were forbidden by the world and the clergy of their day.

Contemplative author Thomas Merton said, "One of the first signs of a (great saint) may well be the fact that other people do not know what to make of him. In fact they are not sure whether he is crazy or only proud:

but it must at least be pride to be haunted by some individual ideal which nobody but God really comprehends.... He cannot seem to make his life fit in with the books."[1]

The Scriptures and the annals of history are chock full of these ecstatics, who somehow tasted the invisible and were too captured by the siren melodies of Heaven to turn back around. The Lord speaks most highly of these men whom we despised in life but honor in death. He also speaks of more to come—*many more to come.*

There is coming to the earth in these last days a generation that will walk in the *spirit of Elijah.* They are a coming wave of ecstatics like no age has seen and no successive generation will ever see again. Even as John the Baptist was the "Elijah to come" who ushered in the advent of Christ, so will there be an entire company in these last days who will be clothed corporately in this same mantle, ushering in Christ's second coming. They will be the final fulfillment of Malachi 4:5-6 (NIV):

> *See, I will send you the prophet Elijah before that great and dreadful day of the Lord comes. He will turn the hearts of the fathers to their children, and the hearts of the children to their fathers; or else I will come and strike the land with a curse.*

Through this move, God is restoring all things. Primarily, He is restoring intimacy between Heaven and earth. Beyond the visions, the prophecies and miracles—beyond all the supernatural accessories that accompany this Elijah spirit, there is one hallmark feature that stands out among the rest: brazen *unpredictability.* Elijah prophets are extreme. They always have a measure of eccentricity and wildness. John the Baptist, who walked in this spirit, was untamed and unfettered. These persons embody what composer Oscar Levant once quipped, "There is a fine line between genius and insanity."

Biblically, Elijah most typifies what we technically call the *ecstatic prophets.* They lived in a realm of trance and rapture, but out of that state, their movements were frenzied, irregular, and volatile. There was nothing about Elijah that was formatted, pre-calculated, or routine. He was fully possessed by the Divine Wind. The Scriptures say his movements defied all human anticipation (see 1 Kings 18:12). This was not a quiet monk, softly meditating on a cloud. Mocking the idol of baal, he called fire from Heaven at Carmel and bloodied the ground with the slaughter of 450 demonic priests.

God sends ecstatic prophets, not to pamper and massage us in our immaturity; He sends them to prod the lion until it wakes up. To shatter established parameters and rip through religious strongholds. God sends them to intentionally irritate the old order, like a grain of sand in an oyster that will one day form a pearl.

Because they draw so sharp a line in the sand—a bitter sharp line indeed—their penchant for truth is often construed as a lack of compassion. But they care little for man's opinion. No man-pleasing spirit has taken root in them. They are addicted to One and One only. They are driven by the glory like madmen. They are hurricanes blown by the Spirit.

Ecstatic Prophets of the Bible

God did not begin shaking and zapping His prophets at Toronto or Azusa Street. Not only is church history full of ecstatic prophets, but so are the Scriptures brimming with examples of visions, trances, and rapturous experience. Ecstasies were common among the early Israelite prophetic bands. Not only did individual prophets gain revelation in trances, but the glory of God would come in a corporate nature on entire groups of people who would prophesy at once. God has always longed to have a prophetic generation, a movement of people who know Him and live in His heart.

There are two scriptural accounts of Samuel the seer's relations with King Saul in which this corporate trance glory was present. Both in First Samuel 10:10-12 and First Samuel 19:23-24, Saul is pulled into the furious worship and atmosphere of the spirit of revelation that rested mutually upon the entire group of prophets.

In one of these instances, Saul approaches the prophets in a search for David. He first sends several regiments of soldiers ahead of himself, but they all get wrapped up into the corporate trance of the prophets. All of his soldiers end up joining the prophets. Finally Saul himself comes to the scene at Naioth at Ramah. He is so overwhelmed by the glory that he also begins to prophesy and continues the entire way there. Saul then has such an uncontrollable frenzy that he strips off his clothes and lays on the ground all day and all night! An individual has to be quite whacked in the Spirit to do this.

Saul perfectly exemplifies how God can give trances, regardless of a person's spiritual state. He will even give them to unbelievers as a sign. The pagan seer Balaam, who was not even an Israelite, began to give an elaborate Messianic prophesy after "falling into a trance" (Num. 24:16 KJV). God will speak through an unbeliever, just as He spoke through the unbeliever's donkey. God often moves, not *because* of our theology, but *in spite of it!*

Quite often, I have run into individuals who were drawn to Jesus, even in the midst of a pharmaceutical drug trip. God does not endorse drug use, but He will use any means available to reach the lost. God will invade even a demonic trance and reverse it for good, if He so chooses. My own testimony is similar. I was tripping on LSD when Jesus began to draw me and reveal Himself to me. On one hand, He caused me to instantly sober up from the drug, but on the other hand, He saved me and filled me so remarkably with His Holy Spirit that I was immediately switched over to a Holy Spirit trance!

One of our associates, Shawn Gabie, led one of the top drug dealers in his city to the Lord by interpreting one of the man's drug trips for him! The dealer was so radically converted that he flushed a massive quantity of cocaine down the toilet on the spot. Even in our sin, God is drawing us and trying to speak to us through many means. Daniel interpreted Nebuchadnezzar's dream, while the king was pagan, leading him to honor God. Sometimes when reaching out to unbelievers, the best thing to do is ask if they have ever had a "spiritual experience." The Lord will often help you to interpret it and show the person how He had been reaching out to them with His love the entire time. While we were still sinners, Christ died for us (see Rom. 5:8). Jesus does not hide from bars and strip clubs and block parties. He is there in the midst of them, trying to convict hearts and draw them to Himself.

Consider how the witch of Endor, in the midst of her pagan sorcery, was screaming when the spirit of the dead prophet Samuel appeared and rebuked Saul (see 1 Sam. 28:7-25). Rest assured that no one can hide from the Lord, even in a demonically inspired trance. No drug can hide you from His all-seeing eye. As David said: *"If I ascend into heaven, You are there; if I make my bed in hell, behold, You are there"* (Ps. 139:8).

We also see examples of demonic trances in the Scriptures, such as the prophets of baal who worked themselves into a fit and cut their own bodies on Mount Carmel, trying to get their idol to respond with fire. How sweet it is that our God makes the first move! Jesus, in His grace, is a God who came from Heaven and was cut for us! We never have to work ourselves into an ecstatic state: for us, *ecstasy is a free gift.*

Not all prophets throughout Scripture necessarily experienced *frenzied* ecstasies of physical manifestations. But all of the writing prophets were caught up into visionary experiences and inward raptures to some degree.

As for those radicals like Isaiah, Ezekiel, and John the Baptist—what realms of glory had these men tasted inwardly to drive them to such exterior madness? David played music under a cloud of revelation until he possessed God's very heart. When it was time to bring the Ark of Glory into his city, he danced his own royal robes off for nine miles in worship, stopping every six steps to butcher an ox or fatted sheep before the Lord (see 2 Sam. 6). Imagine the long, red trail of sacrifice, with David whirling about, barely clothed in the blood of bulls. His appearance would have fit more in line with a Gothic rave or horror film than a Sunday morning service. But his abandonment in passion and in sacrifice brought the glory into his city.

The Dance Trance

What David clearly understood in the Psalms was the obvious connection between music, dance, and ecstatic experience. David had a revelation of abandoned worship, and his writings are full of prophetic utterance and visionary experience.

In the prophetic bands of Samuel's day, their prophesying was accompanied by "lyres, tambourines, flutes and harps being played before them." This music and dance assisted their prophetic trances. When the Spirit came in power upon Saul as he met these minstrels, he began prophesying and was "changed into a different person" (1 Sam. 10:5-6 NIV). Music and

dance are important aspects of worship, and historically, have always facili-
tated ecstatic states. This is why satan used gnostic influence in the early
church to quickly stamp out the use of instrumentation in music.

Often, in large meetings and conferences we have seen the Lord release
a massive *trance dance* where people are veritably unaware of their surroundings and corporately caught into a heavenly consciousness. The assembly
enters a simultaneous spiritual experience in a massive collision with the
glory. Our good friend and South American missionary Jim Drown has told
us many accounts of trance dances in his evangelistic campaigns that could
last for hours, followed by multitudes of souls being saved.

Music is a neutral commodity that has the power of facilitating
raptures, either for God's glory or for demonic hypnotism. Instruments are
natural tools that provide accompaniment to the spiritual realities at hand,
whether good or evil. Before delving further into the spiritual nature of
trances themselves, I would like to briefly discuss this natural aid that God
has given us in music. First the natural, then the spiritual. On a practical
note, playing an instrument or listening to praise and worship albums is of
great benefit in contemplative prayer, especially at the start of your journey.

Sound and music have always accompanied heavenly experience. David
constructed a 4,000-piece orchestra that played openly before the glory of
God for 33 years. Jesus sang a hymn with the disciples before going to the
Garden of Gethsemane, and Paul and Silas, in Acts 16:26 (NASB), sang
and praised God in prison until "suddenly there came a great earthquake,
so that the foundations of the prison house were shaken; and immediately
all the doors were opened." Paul and James, in their epistles, both encourage
believers to sing and make songs to God. In Heaven, we see the living creatures and 24 elders each having a harp (see Rev. 5:8) as well as countless
verses depicting angels with trumpets, along with various heavenly sounds.
Consider Revelation 14:2 (NIV):

> *I heard a sound from heaven like the roar of rushing
> waters and like a loud peal of thunder. The sound I heard
> was like that of harpists playing their harps.*

Sound, song, and dance have always played a strategic part in facilitating divine communication and rapture. In the early church, there were literally thousands of new songs written around the early apostolic teachings. Many ancient Greek manuscripts have been found with Christian odes. Ignatius, in the first century, wrote a hymn just before he was martyred, and Pliny, in A.D. 79 wrote that Christians "have a custom of meeting before dawn and singing by turns hymns to Christ." Josephus also reports that Christians would sing out songs as they awaited their turns to be eaten by lions in the coliseums.

Physiologically, man is a being designed for sound. Sounds can assist in opening the soul to God. Satan was once a chief worship leader in Heaven, before his fall, and he knows the power of sound and dance implicitly. This is why church history is full of assaults against sacred music and dance. Today, with the modern worship movement, we are seeing a revival of song, dance, and worship arts in the church. But let us not quickly forget how the use of instrumentation and creativity has been suppressed during the past centuries. Because of the direct link between sound and trance, there has been massive warfare against the mere use of instruments.

Clement of Alexandria (A.D. 150–220) was considered a church father and was one of the earliest hymn writers. Although he wrote hundreds of hymns, he also condemned the use of instruments in public worship because of their association with pagan rituals and superstitious rites. For the first time in Judeo-Christian history, questions began to be raised in the post-apostolic era as to whether music should be instrumental or vocal only. Two major errors surfaced here. Because instruments are natural, external devices used for worship, they were not deemed as being spiritual in themselves and therefore evil. This subtle assumption that all natural things are evil is gnostic and antichrist in origin. Furthermore, since instruments were widely associated with pagan worship, this further solidified that they must be evil.

Clement tried to allegorize the hundreds of references in Scripture to instrumental worship. He said that each instrument in Psalm 150 represented the believer worshiping God with his whole body. Although Clement was a staunch defender of the faith against gnostics, a reading of his work still shows a powerful gnostic influence in his own life.

In A.D. 190 he wrote, "Leave the pipe to the shepherd, the flute to the men who are in fear of gods and intent on their idol worshipping. Such musical instruments must be excluded from our wingless feasts, for they are more suited for beasts and for the class of men that is least capable of reason than for men."[2] Following this exhortation, Clement gives us a legalistic diatribe on the tone of laughter that is permissible among Christians, as well as a rulebook on when blushing should be done instead of smiling. Sounds like a happy camper.

John Chrysostom, in the fourth century, warned against the licentious nature of the Christian chants and warned that there was no need for instruments. Around this time, the Synod of Laodicea (aptly named considering Jesus' warning to the church there in the Book of Revelation) ruled that no one should sing in the church except for appointed singers. Furthermore, women could not even sing in public worship, unless they were in a convent.

Augustine in A.D. 354 described the singing at Alexandria under Athanasius saying, "musical instruments were not used. The pipe, tabret, and harp here associate so intimately with the sensual heathen cults, as well as with the wild revelries and shameless performances of the degenerate theater and circus, it is easy to understand the prejudices against their use in the worship." Martin Luther pointed out Augustine's self-deprecation on the issue, saying he was "afflicted with scruples of conscience whenever he discovered that he had derived pleasure from music and had been happy thereby; he was of the opinion that such joy is unrighteous and sinful."[3]

By the sixth century, bad had gone to worse. Pope Gregory (A.D. 540–604) launched perhaps the most demonic assault ever against sacred music in the earth. Although we know his name from the Gregorian chants, most of us are unaware that Gregory shut down congregational singing altogether. He allowed only the paid priests to sing, essentially saying that the people were not allowed to worship God—*the priests will do it for you.*

Gregory also turned the singing to Latin, so no one in the congregations could understand it in their native languages. He limited the scale of music in his approved chants to an extremely narrow number of variations. These somber, monotone sounds offered no freedom for harmonies or creativity. This clinical strip down of allowable music brought generations of frustration to people who could not worship God in a free and individual expression.

Obviously this was entirely unbiblical; but moreover it prevented the church from receiving her bliss, accessing the realm of the Spirit and moving in great power. Praise always releases intimacy and power. Unlike Elisha of old, the prophets could no longer say, *"Now bring me a harpist"* for *"while the harpist was playing, the hand of the Lord came upon Elisha"* (2 Kings 3:14-16 NIV). It was a jezebellian tactic to castrate the wildness and spontaneity from a Spirit-driven people. Chants are great, but sometimes I like to hear some *Demon Hunter* on my iPod.

Nevertheless, there were a few shining voices who could be heard in the Middle Ages, such as Bernard of Clairvaux and Francis of Assisi who both emphasized the importance of singing and wrote upbeat tunes. But while the world was inventing new instruments: the psaltery, lutes, flutes, bagpipes, and organs—the church was officially rejecting it all.

Musicians who were born to praise God had no outlet in the church, and they fled to the world. And by the age of the Renaissance, music and creativity was flourishing at a height in the secular arena. It was at this time that the Reformation brought awakening to the worship arts as well. Although John Calvin was staunchly opposed to instruments—melting down pipe organs in churches throughout Europe—Martin Luther ran an opposite course. Luther was trained in music and was a breath of fresh air. He believed that music should be sung by everyone, not just the clergy, and that it should be in the common language of the people—not Latin. He was a skilled lute player and translated songs to German, modifying tunes. Luther rewrote secular pop songs of the day, making them Christian. His songs had a massive popular appeal, and he understood the ability of music to move the emotions. "Music is a beautiful and lovely gift of God which has often moved and inspired me to preach with joy," he said.[4]

Others throughout history would follow suit. William Booth, founder of the Salvation Army, once asked, "Why should the devil have all the best tunes?" Like Martin Luther, Booth also rewrote bar tunes of his day and changed their lyrics to honor Christ.[5]

We should not underestimate the great power of silent contemplation here. In the quiet hours of meditation, we can surely be still and know that He is God. But the Lord's presence is limited neither by the lack of music, nor the presence thereof. We should neither vilify music, nor use it as a crutch to experience His presence. On the subject of music, there is great freedom.

Music has a powerful way of elating the soul and bringing the heart and mind into harmony with the Spirit of God. In today's multimedia culture, there is another virtual renaissance at hand for the church, in terms of sound, technology, visualization, and creation of altogether new genres of worship mediums. New forms of trance music are coming to the church that drip with encounter in every beat and every note. The problem today is not so much the legitimacy of musicianship in the church, but the exploitation of it. In today's Christian contemporary music industry of pop stars and glam, the dangerous temptation is to package and sell God's glory, while missing it altogether.

The glory being released in our day is going to be uncontainable and widespread; it will strike like wildfire in the streets as entire populations of people will come under a corporate cloud of His presence. There is little precedent to describe what is coming, only to say that it will be alive with color and motion, sound and wonder, dancing and celebration in the streets. There will be little that can be done to contain the divine outbreaks of revival and the corporate trances God will release en masse in these last days.

Dancing Mania

An archaic shadow of what is coming could perhaps be seen in the *dancing mania* that swept through whole towns and regions in the Middle Ages in the days of the Black Plague.

Known also as St. Vitus' dance or St. John's dance, dancing manias swept across Europe through the 11th and 17th centuries as tens of thousands of people participated in these frenzied spectacles that lasted for days and sometimes weeks. One of the first outbreaks began in Aix-la-Chapelle in 1374 with a group of people dancing uncontrollably in the streets, screaming of wild visions. They kept dancing until they collapsed with exhaustion, even foaming at the mouth, and still they flailed on the ground. The dancing caught on, sweeping through a whole town then jumping over to a neighboring community. This irresistible urge to dance spread rapidly throughout France and the Low Countries. Some people would dance until they fell over dead.

Though scholars have tried to attribute this dancing to sickness, disease, psychological mass hysteria, spider bites, or even dietary conditions of the day, it was clearly a spiritual issue. One BBC news commentator reports, "My explanation rests on the fact that the dancers were in a trance state.... The epidemic, I argue, was a result of both desperation and pious fear."[6] There was a contagious impartation that tangibly spread from person to person, block to block, city to city. It was supernatural in origin.

The clergy of the day held religious ceremonies in an attempt to exorcise the demons they thought were the cause of the mania. Music would be played to soothe the dancers. But some sociologists like Robert Bartholomew believe the dancing was actually initiated by ecstatic sects of pilgrims who were traveling through Europe at the time. Bartholomew says the following:

> Based on an examination of a representative sample of medieval chronicles, it is evident that these episodes are best explained as deviant religious sects who gained adherents as they made pilgrimages through Europe during years of turmoil in order to receive divine favor. Their symptoms (visions, fainting, tremor) are predictable for any large population engaging in prolonged dancing, emotional worship, and fasting. Their actions have been "mistranslated" by contemporary scholars evaluating the participants' behaviors per se, removed from their regional context and meaning.[7]

The source of these wild outbreaks now becomes clear: *religious fanatics.* A morbid tune from the Straussburgh Chronicle of Kleinkawel in 1625 describes another outbreak of dancing mania:

> *Amidst our people here is come*
> *The madness of the dance.*
> *In every town there now are some*

Who fall upon a trance.
It drives them ever night and day,
They scarcely stop for breath,
Till some have dropped along the way
And some are met by death.

We should not believe that these flare-ups were without extreme mixture. I would venture that it was the grandest combination of hedonism and true worship that ever occurred side-by-side in the streets, at a time when the populace was faced with a major pandemic. Since these outbreaks allowed people to exhibit social behavior that was prohibited at any other time by the church and social order of the day, many took the opportunity to tear off their clothes, prancing naked through the streets, or took the occasion for sexual immorality. But other accounts clearly recorded visions and divine encounters among the dancers.

"Some screamed and beckoned to be tossed into the air; others danced furiously in what observers described as strange, colorful attire. A few reportedly laughed or weeped to the point of death. Women howled and made obscene gestures while others squealed like animals. Some rolled themselves in the dirt or relished being struck on the soles of their feet," writes Bartholomew.[8]

Like everything else in the Dark Ages, the church itself was full of gross mixture. On the one hand, the church was wide open for the supernatural in the pre-Enlightenment era. Phenomenal miracles occurred in those days. But on the other hand, the church was in a theological quagmire. Besides that, remember that there was very little free expression of worship, dance, and celebration in the church. Women were prohibited from singing. Few men were allowed to sing, and only in a few notes allowed in the chants. Most services were in a language that people didn't understand. So, as many of these dancers hit the streets, they reported experiencing heavenly visions and encounters when this liberty was afforded them.

Very often the light and darkness are juxtaposed in times of intensity. I would not doubt that divine and demonic trances were taking place side-by-side. In these last days, we can expect the same. *"For behold, the darkness shall cover the earth, and deep darkness the people; but the Lord will arise over you, and His glory will be seen upon you"* (Isa. 60:2). As open satanic worship, orgies, and cults go mainstream in these days, expect also that the latter rains of God's glory will fall like no generation has ever seen before. The greatest clash between light and darkness is coming. Both camps will go unrestrained. We will not be somber little church mice tucked away in our caves, waiting for the end to pass us by. Ready yourself for widespread Holy Ghost dance trance explosions that will even sweep up the Sauls, the Balaams, and the unbelievers into the fray. Some who have no context for what's going on may even strip off their clothes as the glory expels their demons! It could get messy.

We simply do not have enough recorded evidence to determine how much of God was in these manias. We often bark up the wrong tree trying to determine if something was God or the devil. The wheat and the tares were probably growing together. So, instead of wondering about the past, we can use it to gain insight into the future. Even if the devil could pull off something this big—with thousands of people dancing in a wild trance in the open squares—then how much more of a party can God throw in the streets?

Whatever the origin of these mysterious events in the quagmire of the Dark Ages—even here we see a foreshadowing of the glory outbreaks that will occur in these endtimes. The principle of wild, abandoned worship in the streets is something we should recover from these cases. The striking nature of the dance mania—like the mass trances of other great revivals—is that these were *contagious* and transferable moves that swept through the populace in an instant. As we see the dancing hand of God land on one person and then another, His glory will begin to catch and infect entire crowds, neighborhoods, cities, and regions in mere moments.

Chapter 8

trances, fits, and enthusiasm in revival

There has always been a remnant lineage of ecstatic, Spirit-driven prophets—shakers, seers, and fanatics who accessed Heaven and brought a firestorm of revival to the earth. Physical manifestations have always signaled the ecstasies of God as people in every great revival have been corporately pulled outside of themselves in trances. These ecstasies have been termed *fits, enthusiasms, the jerks, convulsions,* and many other names in various revivals. But the similar thread of losing control to the Spirit of God has always been present.

It is humorous to consider the writings of great 18th and 19th century revivalists and missionaries of the past, when they spoke of gathering together to be "refreshed" in the Holy Spirit. Ever wonder what that looked like? We've stereotyped so many of our forerunners as stiff-necked, starch-collared holy rollers. But many of them were complete Holy Ghost drunks. Ecstatic trances and manifestations of spiritual intoxication did not end with the days of Samuel, David, and Elijah.

The First Great Awakening is a classic example. In Jonathan Edwards' meetings, people swooned and fell over and entered trances under the weighty hand of God. Describing the revival of 1740–1742, Edwards notes, "It was a very frequent thing to see a house full of outcries, faintings, convulsions, and such like, both with distress, and also with admiration and joy."[1]

Edwards' wife was an absolute lush. Sarah Edwards would often show signs of "enthusiasm," to say the least. Once in a meeting in 1742 she stayed after for three hours, while her "'bodily strength was overcome' and she was so full of joy and thankfulness that she conversed with those who were with her 'in a very earnest manner.'" She was still so excited the next day she couldn't do her daily tasks. During the sermon, she sank to the floor and people had to pull her back into the chair while "earnestly she shared with them her sense of God's wonderful grace towards her in redeeming her from hell." During the next hymn, she "leaped spontaneously from her chair, feeling as if she were ascending to Heaven." Two hymns later, she was back on the floor and they took her to bed! There, she continued to "contemplate the glories of the heavenly world."[2]

During this one instance, Sarah Edwards felt "wholly indifferent" to the affairs of the world and to earthly glory and ambition. "Her heart was filled with love and she felt so exhausted by emotions of joy that she could not rise or sit up for about four hours. That Thursday night she described as 'the sweetest night I ever had in my life,'" notes Dr. Barry Chant. "Furthermore, her 'sense of the glory of the Holy Spirit' was such as to overwhelm her in both soul and body."

Edwards himself spoke of his wife's behavior saying, "Now if such things are enthusiasm, and the fruits of a distempered brain, let my brain be evermore possessed of that happy distemper! If this be distraction, I pray God that the world of mankind may be all seized with this benign, meek, beneficent, beatifical, glorious distraction!"

Jonathan Edwards on Enthusiasm

Jonathan Edwards consistently challenged the people to experience God in a deep and emotive fashion:

> How can they sit and hear of the infinite height, and depth, and length, and breadth of the love of God in Christ Jesus, of His giving His infinitely dear Son, to be offered up a sacrifice for the sins of men, and of the unparalleled love of the innocent, and holy, and tender Lamb of God, manifested in His dying agonies, His bloody sweat, His loud and bitter cries, and bleeding heart, and all this for enemies, to redeem them from deserved, eternal burnings, and to bring to unspeakable and everlasting joy and glory—and yet be cold and heavy, insensible and regardless![3]

Realize that Edwards was a Great Awakening revivalist of mainstream rapport, both of Congregational and Presbyterian influence—as well as founder of an ivy league college, Princeton University! This begs the question: "Would Edwards' ministry be welcome in the very churches he founded today?"

Edwards was by no means the only great mainstream revivalist who experienced the manifest glory in his meetings. John Wesley, George Whitefield and countless other popular forerunners held meetings that were full of wild and crazy ecstatics.

Even Edwards was stretched at times by the preaching of his own young protégé, Samuel Buell. During Buell's sermons, people would begin to encounter prolonged ecstasies and such freedom from religious bondage that the revivalists attributed much of the "wildness" to the enemy:

> There were some instances of persons lying in a sort of trance, remaining for perhaps a whole twenty-four hours motionless... but in the meantime under strong imaginations, as though they went to Heaven, and had there a vision of glorious and delightful objects. But when the people were raised to this height, Satan took the advantage ...a great deal of caution and pains were found necessary to keep the people, many of them, from running wild.[4]

In Edwards' day, these manifestations of God's Spirit (which included trances, visions, falling and the whole gamut), were termed *enthusiasms*. This word "enthusiasm," which emerged in the 17th century, comes from the Greek *en theos*, which means *to be filled with or inspired by God.*

Edwards said that many who were converted in the revival experienced supernatural waves of joy: "Their joyful surprise has caused their hearts as it were to leap, so that they have been ready to break forth into laughter, tearing often at the same time issuing like a flood, and intermingling a loud weeping."[5]

I would contend that this was just a foretaste of the latter-day wildfire God is releasing on His church. Had there been a greater historical context of ecstatic trances, visions and a biblical paradigm for understanding heavenly encounters, perhaps Buell could have notched the fires to another level at Edwards' church at Northampton. But instead, much of Edwards' work would succumb to attacks by cessationist critics like Charles Chauncy who opposed the revival (*cessationism* is the demonic belief that spiritual gifts, miracles and the supernatural operations of God through the church ceased with the first century apostles). Because of persecution from the church, Edwards edged away from his strong support of bodily manifestations and enthusiasm in his later years, though he never fully disavowed them. Had he chosen to run with the young bucks like Buell, instead of hedging, I believe the revival could have continued. Many of the revival's most vocal antagonists, like Chauncy, who opposed enthusiasm, went on to fully apostatize their faith. Chauncy helped form the Unitarian Universalist group— one of the most relativistic, syncretistic, bogus religions that allege to be part of the Christian church.

The enemy will distract revivalists by sending Pharisees to get them defensive and apologetic. Don't defend a move of God, just run headlong into it even faster. John Arnott, pastor of Toronto Airport Christian Fellowship, said that his number one regret during the Toronto Blessing outpouring of the 1990s was that he tried to defend the move of God. Never let the enemy pull you down into the legal realm of debate, bickering and defensiveness.

A man's ignorance will be made clear when he attacks a true move of God. As soon as we *defend* that move of God, we cease to be on the offense. My wife and I learned long ago how to ignore criticism and click the "delete" button when people send us nasty emails. I don't waste time apologizing and defending ourselves to religious devils when there's Kingdom work to be done. The age of apologetics is over. There is always further to go in the Spirit, and we can no longer afford to slow down over trifles. The great miracle revivalist A.A. Allen once said, "If you are walking with Jesus, in the Spirit, you need not fear going too far. No believer has gone as far as God wants him to go."[6]

If you are on the cutting edge, keep truckin', and don't let the fires die down. Stoke the fire. Feel the burn. The enemy of desire is not hatred. It is *moderate* desire. Like an addict's cravings that never decrease or level off, our appetite for Jesus should ever increase, ever pushing us further into the intoxicated lifestyle of abandonment to Him. *You need not fear going too far.*

The Flemish mystic John of Ruysbroeck (1294–1381) writes, "Those who flow by desire into the boundless sea, feel the hunger, feel the thirst, and taste unity. But a *moderate* desire insufficient to *suspend the soul to the Divine Essence* is a sad hindrance. The men of moderate desire do not receive the ray; they are not touched by the sublime ignorance which knows no human measure. They exist in themselves, and are not swallowed up here below by the gulf of beatitude."[7]

Elsewhere, Ruysbroeck comments on this holy intoxication:

> The spiritual inebriation leads to many and unaccustomed actions. Some, in the abundance of happiness, break out into canticles and sing God's praises. Others shed tears of joy. Some feel an eager longing for movement in their limbs, they cannot remain still; they must run, leap, stamp their feet, clap their hands vigorously. Others show their delight by loud cries. Others, again, find all their faculties taken possession of to such an extent that they stand silent, and as it were, melting with love.[8]

Even Chauncy, Edwards' chief critic, gives us some fun accounts of what those wild Great Awakening meetings must have been like. He described "swooning away and falling to the Ground, where Persons have lain, for a Time, speechless and motionless; bitter Shriekings and Screamings; Convulsion-like Tremblings and Agitations, Strugglings and Tumblings," adding that those who received assurance of salvation were almost always given to "Raptures and Transports." Many, he said, "shew this Joy by clapping of Hands, by jumping up and down, by Congratulations in the Way of Kissing, by breaking out into hearty loud Laughter." Others, noted Chauncy, gave manifestation to "Swoonings, and Out-cries, and Screamings, so like to these same Effects under Terror, that it han't been known, whether persons were in Joy or Sorrow [*sic*]."

In one home meeting, Chauncy recorded two women who fell into a trance together, "depriv'd of their bodily Strength; but yet, were by Turns able to speak, which they did...." By the next evening, the women "fell down unable to walk...(and) continued in a Sort of Extasie, either lying as though in a Sleep, or uttering extatic Expressions of Joy, of the Love of Christ, and of Love to Him; of Concern for the Souls of Sinners, and the like."[9] At other times, when preachers began to lay into their sermons, Chauncy wrote, "Young Women were presently thrown into violent histeric Fits" [*sic*].[10]

We should get accustomed to physical manifestations in the church—every revival has been marked by them. For one, the state of bliss and a routine of exciting encounters should be the norm of both Heaven and earth. But God also sends manifestation because He's ready to shake up our pretty services and remind us of His ever-present reality. If we can't handle someone falling over in a church service, how will we cope with blood and fire and billows of smoke when the Lord releases Mosaic signs and wonders back into the earth? Do we want revival, or a funeral dirge?

Quakers and Shakers were so aptly named because they physically shook and trembled under the mighty presence of God. In fact, early Quaker literature records visions, healings and prophecies as well. And though their founder, George Fox, discouraged them from speaking in tongues, many Quakers have continued to do so.[11]

The joy and the wildness of God is our inheritance. The wine room of Heaven is a place of spiritual fertility where movements were birthed. The most unsuspecting heroes of our faith learned to drink deep of this strong wine. Second Great Awakening revivalist Charles Finney wrote about his baptism in the Spirit that it was "like a wave of electricity, going through and through me," and that immediately afterward, an ordinarily serious elder in the church "fell into a most spasmodic laughter. It seemed as if it was impossible for him to keep from laughing from the very bottom of his heart."[12]

Finney was a staid Presbyterian, not bothered with excessive emotion or shallow conversions. But the first time that people began to be overcome by the Spirit in his meetings, he was preaching in Utica, New York. Four hundred people fell off their chairs and hit the floor after he spoke for only 15 minutes.

Finney said, "In every age of the Church, cases have occurred in which persons have had such clear manifestations of Divine truth as to prostrate their physical strength entirely....The veil seems to be removed from the mind, and the truth is seen much as we suppose it to be when the spirit is disembodied. No wonder this should overpower the body."[13]

Oswald Chambers, the Scottish Baptist revered among believers for his devotional writings, entered in his diary on April 19, 1907 that "we had a blessed time. I was called down by the teachers to pray and anoint a lady who wanted healing, and as we were doing it God came so near that upon my word we were laughing as well as praying! How utterly stilted we are in our approach to God. Oh that we lived more up to the light of all our glorious privileges." Chambers acknowledged that laughter was a sign of Holy Spirit baptism.[14]

Trance in the Early Church

Clean cut, predictable worship services may seem nice, but God is about to make a royal mess, within and without the four walls of the church. We must learn to embrace the glory realm, so that we do not get hung up on manifestation, laughing and flopping. This is tame activity compared to what is coming. Many are so focused on the natural effects of manifestation, they miss what God is doing and saying in the midst of it all. Often, He is simply moving on hearts and playing with His children. Usually, He is filling us with power.

True mysticism is losing yourself in the delicious sweetness of God. The anonymous author of the *Cloud of Unknowing* says it is "a blind feeling of one's own being, stretching unto God." Teresa of Avila says it is "awareness, absorbed and amazed," and Walter Hilton says it is "the enlightening of the understanding, joined to the joys of God's love."

In the early days of the Christian church, many fathers of the faith documented the prevalence of their ecstatic experiences. In the first century, Clement of Rome and Ignatius both wrote of the continued operation of spiritual gifts in the lives of ordinary believers. Irenaeus of Lyon in the second century wrote of Charismatic gifts flowing in modern France, especially the gift of prophecy.

Tertullian (c. 160–225) gives us a great account of the Montanists, the "new prophets," who operated in healing, tongues and the prophetic.

Though the Montanists were condemned as heretics by the Catholic church, modern scholarship puts to doubt any serious error in their theology. Tertullian himself even joined their group, which flourished around A.D. 170. The facts show that the Montanists were persecuted, merely because of the ecstatic nature in which they worshiped and were filled with the Spirit. The Montanists were never criticized for what they said, but for how they said it. When prophesying, they were reportedly "filled with spiritual excitement and fell into a kind of trance and unnatural ecstasy."[15]

Montanism, like many movements after it, "was soon outlawed by the mainstream church of the day. At a time when the church was settling down and developing stable patterns of leadership and order, the popularity of the prophets and their teachings were seen as threatening the growing authority of the bishops," notes an article in *Christian History & Biography*. "Moreover, the movement was marked by extremism and fanaticism, and its intense religious excitement aroused suspicion."[16]

In later centuries, both the French prophets of the Cevennes as well as the Methodists would be critically compared to the Montanists by cessationist heresy hunters. John Wesley read *The General Delusion of Christians* (later retitled *The Spirit of Prophecy Defended*) by critic John Lacy (1713), a book aimed at discrediting revival. But the book did just the opposite for the founder of Methodism. Wesley was convinced from the book "of what (he) had long suspected," that the Montanists "were real, scriptural Christians." Wesley also concluded that "the grand reason why the miraculous gifts were so soon withdrawn [from the church], was not only that faith and holiness were well nigh lost; but that dry, formal, orthodox men began even then to ridicule whatever gifts they had not themselves, and to decry them all as either madness or imposture."[17]

Many of the early Desert Fathers, in the third and fourth centuries, experienced tremendous supernatural encounters, trances, visions and prophetic utterances, while also working signs and wonders. An eastern mystic, Simeon the New Theologian (949–1022), reported a "baptism in the Holy Spirit" that was distinct from the graces given to him through the sacraments, and which was "accompanied by compunction [awareness of one's guilt before God], penitence, copious tears, and an intensified awareness of the Trinity as light dwelling within."[18] The Christian mystics of the Middle Ages provide countless stories of ecstatic trances, providing us reams of theological understanding on such supernatural experience. Theresa of Avila, for instance, was a virtual cartographer of the soul. But there were many others. Hildegard of Bingen (1098–1179) experienced ecstatic visions along with all manner of revelatory and healing giftings. Gregory Palamas (1296–1359) stressed the need for laying on of hands to impart gifts of healing, miracles, prophecy, divine wisdom, tongues and interpretation.

The life of Thomas Aquinas was marked by frequent miracles, in addition to regular ecstasies, especially toward the end of his life.[19] Around this same time period, Bonaventure gives reports of Francis of Assisi, an untrained minister full of the Holy Spirit and power who works miracles, heals the sick, prophesies, communicates with animals and is regularly lifted from the ground in ecstasy. Running parallel to the frenzied Great Awakening revivals—a mostly Protestant revival—we have powerful stories of Orthodox Charismatic leaders, such as Seraphim of Sarov (1759–1833). This Russian mystic said the entire aim of the Christian life is to be filled with the Holy Spirit. Seraphim is largely known for his transfiguration experiences—being changed, while still in the body, into divine light. Seraphim was also known for his gifts of prophesy and healing.

Methodists Struck Down

Beyond the ministry of Jonathan Edwards, one does not have to look far into the Great Awakening revivals of the 18th and 19th centuries to find swoonings, trances, prophetic utterance, holy laughter and violent "moshpits" of glory. John Wesley writes of prayer meetings with George Whitefield and others where they all fell to the ground in awe and amazement as God's power overwhelmed them. An early Methodist convert wrote in 1807, "I thought they were distracted, such fools I'd never seen. They'd stamp and clap and tremble, and wail and cry and scream." An even earlier such gathering in 1776 was described as follows: "the assembly appeared to be all in confusion, and must seem to one at a little distance more like a drunken rabble than the worshippers of God."[20]

The acceptance of raptures within the heart of Methodism lasted well beyond the Great Awakening. Many a Methodist preacher was known for his wildness, such as Benjamin Abbott. Seven years before he was saved, Abbott had two dreams, one of Heaven and one of hell. His conversion was no academic exercise in theological principles. He was saved in a supernatural experience when Christ appeared to him in yet a third dream. He was later baptized in the Spirit, falling to the floor as he "felt the power of God running through...(his) soul and body, like fire consuming the inward corruptions of fallen depraved nature." Abbott would later be described by his contemporary Robert Southey as "a sincere and well-meaning enthusiast, upon the very edge of madness himself."

Southey claimed that Abbott, "not only threw his hearers into fits, but often fainted himself through the vehemence of his own prayers and preachments." Abbott spoke of his meetings, saying that "many fell under the mighty power of God, like dead men."[21]

One of Wesley's friends, John Berridge—who consequently was deemed to be a very level-headed person—preached with such power that "great numbers, feeling the arrows of conviction, fell to the ground, some of whom seemed dead, and others in the agony of death, the violence of their bodily convulsions, exceeding all description."[22]

Consider Wesley's own journal entries from the following meetings:

> At Limerick in 1762—"Many more were brought to the birth. All were in floods of tears, cried, prayed, roared aloud, all of them lying on the ground."

> At Newcastle in 1772—"An eminent backslider came into my mind, and I broke off abruptly... 'Is James Watson here? If he be, shew thy power.' Down dropped James Watson like a stone."

> And at Coleford in 1784—"When I began to pray, the flame broke out. Many cried aloud, many sank to the ground, many trembled exceedingly."[23]

The Methodist circuit riders spread like a holy plague in the land. In the early 1800s, people would crumple under the weightiness of God in the revivals of famous Methodist circuit rider Peter Cartwright, including countless numbers of Baptists.[24] Ecstatic experience was not limited to Presbyterians, Congregationalists, or Methodists. As the flames of revival burned in the first and Second Great Awakenings among people of every denominational background, God began to pour out a foretaste of corporate trance upon His people. Experiencing Heaven on earth. All of the manifestations now associated with the "Toronto Renewal" were present, including raptures, visions, violent shaking, and holy laughter.

Extasis Explodes Through Pentecostalism

The trance experiences of Methodism made a natural progression to the deeper embrace of raptures at Azusa Street and the birth of the Pentecostal movement. Pentecostalism is widely known for its adherents falling over, going into trances, speaking in tongues and receiving prophetic utterances. There is little need to discuss early Pentecostalism, as this activity has virtually been the movement's trademark throughout the last century.

But there is a greater glory now pouring from the throne room that is exponentially more explosive than Azusa Street. The urgency of the times demands that we keep flowing with the River, not looking back at Azusa Street or any given revival as if those were the "golden years." God wanted those revivals to be signposts of something greater, not just monuments of times gone by. He wants us to be pioneers of something new, not curators of dusty mausoleums.

The only reason we study old movements is to get prophetic blueprints for the new thing God is doing today. I can honestly say without apology, from my reading and research, that the glory in our own meetings today—as well as many of our friends—is far greater than the glory that hit Azusa Street. Although it was big and new for its time, now those days have passed. It is time for us to make the leap forward into what God is doing today. Build on the past; don't try to repeat it. The Last Great Awakening is at hand.

As a greater glory was being released at the turn of the 20th century, it took a great leap for many Methodists to move into the new thing God was doing at Azusa Street. While Methodists had a long history of trances and ecstasy, the Pentecostal experience provided a far more intense, full-body possession experience than most Methodists had ever seen.

William Durham, a Wesleyan Holiness evangelist, describes this fiery baptism experience at Azusa Street. Durham had already been saved for years. He had also experienced the "sanctifying" work of the Holy Spirit in his life, as the Methodists referred to it. But now he was presented with something remarkable: *Azusa Street presented a whole new level of glory.* As the power of God came upon him one Friday night, he "jerked and quaked under it for about three hours," adding that God "worked my whole body, then my head, then my face, then my chin, and finally at 1 A.M. Saturday, Mar. 2, after being under the power three hours, He finished the work on my vocal organs, and spoke through me in unknown tongues."

Durham said that "I was conscious that a living Person had come into me, and that He possessed even my physical being, in a literal sense."[25]

The Pentecostal experience spread like wildfire. Bodies hit the floor like clockwork. One early meeting in Zion City, Illinois, was reported like this: "The Holy Ghost fell, as they were praying for Him to come and manifest Himself. First one began to drop and then another until the floor was covered. The first to speak in unknown languages was a young man who spoke in Chinese, Italian and Zulu, which were identified. Then it was not long till the flood of joy began. . . ."[26]

Trance Evangelist Brings Slaying Power

As Pentecostalism began to flourish, America saw perhaps her greatest introduction to the glory realm yet, through the ministry of Maria Wood-worth-Etter. Etter was years ahead of her time. She was known far and wide as the "trance evangelist." Consider this newspaper report from her meeting in Hartford, Indiana in 1885:

> Thursday night five more were in a trance, and a man operating a restaurant was in a like condition for several hours at his place of business. Many went to see him. He had one hand uplifted and eyes wide open, and seemed to

be muttering a prayer. When he came from under its influence he praised the Lord for an hour or more.... Saloons closed doors early in the evening to attend the meetings, and the different 'poker dens' shut up shops, and the inmates wended their way to church. Not only so, but many persons who never go to church are regular in attendance. These meetings are the theme on every hand, and each one has his opinion, and is free to express it.[27]

There was a strong, canopy-like atmosphere of the glory that would envelop entire regions when she came into town. Beginning in the latter part of the 19th century, Etter's meetings were marked by entire crowds of people being carried into corporate trances under this cloud of glory. Well before Azusa Street, people traveling to Etter's meetings would be catapulted into trances from 50 miles away. Entire congregations would be pinned to the floor, carried away in the Spirit. Even skeptics would find themselves completely whacked. Often, Etter herself would fall into a trance in the middle of her preach, struck mute. She would stand there frozen, hand in mid-air for entire days! These mass trances would last for multiple hours—often catching up tens of thousands of people simultaneously, as well as individuals throughout the region who were not even aware that her meetings were being held. Consider the following newspaper report from 1885:

The announcement yesterday afternoon that Mrs. Woodworth, the evangelist, was in a trance caused hundreds of people to make a break for the place of meeting. She lay on the platform from 2:30 in the afternoon until 8:30 at night before recovering her senses. The daughter of John Malone soon after was similarly affected, and so death-like was her appearance that some of the members thought that she was dying, and her father was summoned. As he was known to be a man of violent temper, trouble was looked for. He was aroused from sleep, and at once commenced vowing all kinds of vengeance on Mrs. Woodworth and her assistants, keeping it up until he was inside the church. He soon weakened, however, and in ten minutes he was the noisiest convert in town, praising the Lord and shouting that he was glad he had found Christ.[28]

Stories of visions, transformed lives and saved souls abound from these revivals. Before launching her into ministry, the Lord showed Etter a vision of the harvest fields, telling her that she would see people fall as "grain fell from wheat."

Through Etter's ministry, the concept of trances, raptures and being slain in the Spirit would go to mainstream in America. She called this experience "the power," but her critics were quick to dub her as the "voodoo priestess." She was frequently charged with hypnotizing people, and once in St. Louis, two doctors attempted to have her committed as insane during the meetings she conducted there in 1890.[29]

Etter's crowds ranged up to 25,000. It was not uncommon to see such a vast swarm of humanity mowed down together, "when the Holy has fallen on them, and swept over, wave after wave, till the multitude would sway back and forth like the trees in a forest or grain in a storm. Many of the tall oaks would be laid prostrate over the ground, and many were converted standing, or sitting on their seats."[30]

Etter was front page news. Dozens of reporters would follow her, and crime would often be eradicated from entire towns after she visited, leaving saloons out of business and communities impacted by the glory. Finally, consider this *New York Times* report on one of Etter's Indiana meetings:

Mrs. Woodworth, a lady evangelist, still continues with the most unusual manifestations. . . . Scores have been stricken down at these meetings, and whatever form the limbs or body chance to assume in that position, immovable as a stature, they remained—sometimes the hands were uplifted far above the head, the eyes open wide, and not a muscle of the entire body moved; they were as immovable as in death. Many have gone to these meetings in a spirit of jest, and were the first to be under the influence pervading the assembly. The people are wonderfully excited, and neighbor asks neighbor, 'What is it?' It is what is known as catalepsy, or is it a form of ecstasy where the mind absorbs an idea until every faculty of the soul is under its control, and the body becomes stilled as though dead—naught by circulation and the act of respiration remain to signify life. The features are as pale as marble, the pulse weak and feeble. This morning a young lady was found in a trance or ecstasy in bed and could not be aroused for hours. The eyes were lifted to the ceiling and the hand pointed to heaven. When she was restored to consciousness she shouted, clapped her hands, and sang 'hallelujah' for an hour, and said she was perfectly oblivious and totally unconscious to all about her. Is it contagious or infectious, epidemic or endemic, good or evil?[31]

It is worth noting that Carrie Judd Montgomery, an early leader in the Christian and Missionary Alliance (C&MA) movement, got blasted by God in Etter's meetings before the turn of the century. In fact, the C&MA movement also has a rich history with trances, manifestations and prophetic utterance.[32]

Raptured Roots of C&MA

The Christian and Missionary Alliance churches were steeped in trances and ecstasies in their formative years. In an 1897 camp meeting in Pennsylvania, General Field Superintendent Dean Peck preached over three days, saying: "At service after service...I saw people fall as dead under the power of God." He added that it was a *legitimate* revival, like those experienced by the Methodists decades before, which were now less commonplace because of the tendency of human manufacture.[33] Famous C&MA leader A.W. Tozer even spoke favorably toward holy laughter:

Now I say that worship is subject to degrees of perfection and intensity. There have been those who worshiped God to the place where they were in ecstasies of worship. I once saw a man kneel at an altar, taking Communion. Suddenly he broke into holy laughter. This man laughed until he wrapped his arms around himself as if he was afraid he would bust just out of sheer delight in the presence of Almighty God.... So worship is capable of running from the very simple to the most intense and sublime.[34]

Consider the following accounts from early C&MA pastor Dr. E.D. Whiteside. When being healed by God in 1888, he reported being over-whelmed by the Spirit: "Like a flash of electricity, I was instantly thrilled. Every point of my body and nerves was controlled by a strange sensation that increased in volume, until I bowed lower and lower to the floor. I was filled with the ecstatic thrill. My physical frame was unable to stand the strain." This was so powerful, he reports nearly "dying from overjoy."[35]

For a most accurate account of the origin of the C&MA movement, let us look at its founder, A.B. Simpson. He wrote in 1897 that one of the effects of the Spirit's infilling is "fullness of joy so that the heart is constantly radiant. This does not depend on circumstances, but fills the spirit with holy laughter in the midst of the most trying surroundings."[36] Later, on September 12, 1907, Simpson writes in his journal of experiencing holy laughter for *more than an hour straight.*[37] C&MA was strongly based on a mystical foundation; Simpson established the church's entire mission emphasis based on a lucid dream from the Lord, from which he awoke shaking.[38]

Prophetic Origins of Adventism

Earlier in the 19th century, before C&MA ever took root, another well-known denomination was being born in the womb of ecstatic experience: the Seventh Day Adventists. Though sometimes criticized for doctrinal eccentricities, the manifestations of prophetic trance are undeniable in the movement's origins.

A newspaper reporting an Adventist camp meeting in 1844 wrote that "the mourners or converts, of whom there were a very large number, threw themselves in the dust and dirt around the pulpit, and for nearly an hour, men and women were praying, singing, shouting, groaning and weeping bitterly."

Furthermore, people were hammered throughout the prayer tent, "men and women down in the straw lying and sitting in every conceivable posture; praying, shouting, and singing indiscriminately with all their might." It was common for Adventists to be "slain by the power of God" both in public and private meetings.[39] Historian Milton Perry gives abundant evidence of "emotional and ecstatic experiences" among the early group.

The Adventists had their start in the *Millerite* movement. Sparked by the teachings of William Miller, these were largely believers who came out of Methodism. Despite whatever valuable teachings he may have left behind, Miller will always be remembered for the "Great Disappointment." Miller wrongly predicted the return of Christ on a date in 1843, and later revised that date to 1844 when He didn't show up on time. Miller finally had to confess his error when Jesus was a no-show for two consecutive homecoming parties. The Millerites relied heavily on prophecy and experiential enthusiasm. But after Miller missed the mark on his Second Coming prophecy, many of his followers became disillusioned and regrouped. The Seventh-Day Adventist church was actually birthed because of a botched prophecy!

It is common for prophetic movements and individuals to sharply recoil after making an error. Rather than find a center point, we tend to make knee-jerk decisions and revert to opposite extremes after *great disappointments*. After the Great Disappointment, some of the moderate Millerites wanted to distance themselves from prophecy altogether. They also wanted to avoid the practices of the radicals, saying "we have no confidence in any new messages, visions, dreams, tongues, miracles, extraordinary revelations, impressions, discerning of spirits or teachings not in accord with the unadulterated word of God."[40]

Nevertheless, the "radical" element of the movement forged on, pursuing prophetic downloads, and forming the Seventh-Day Adventist church. In the mid-1840s, the main prophetess of the movement was Ellen G. Harmon, and a number of prophetic persons would lie on the floor during meetings, going into trances and prophesying. There is no doubt that the Adventist church was steeped in visions and trances. Although their interpretations of these experiences were not always the best, and at times, their application was worse—it must be credited to the Adventists that they were a pioneering movement pressing into terra nova. Perhaps the greatest error of the Adventists, like the Millerites before them, was the emergence of a *single prophet* as an authoritative visionary. A cult can be defined by any group of people who listen to only one prophet. They lack checks and balances and the wisdom that comes through the counsel of many. This accounted for the way early Adventists placed too much focus on minor doctrines and petty legalisms at times. However, it must be credited to them that they stayed orthodox on the essentials of the faith. Regardless of Adventist doctrinal turbulence, a rich traditional platform for trances and visions exists solidly in the movement's origins.

More Movements Spawned in the Wine Room

It bears repeating that no major revival or denominational birth came without the presence of trances and ecstatic experience. In the meetings of the great revivalist Charles Finney, people would often hit the deck with manifestations of swooning or ecstasies, which he called "falling under the power of God."[41] As 100,000 were converted through the preaching of David Morgan and others in the Welsh revival of 1859, the move was accompanied by swooning as "waves of power often overwhelmed" people.[42] At the famous preacher Andrew Murray's church, in the 1860s, he spoke out against those who shouted, cried and swooned in a revival there—but only until a visitor from America shared with him about similar manifestations happening in the U.S.[43]

Revivalist D.L. Moody spoke fondly of his own infilling of the Holy Spirit while in New York, after which many more came to salvation during his sermons. His associate, R.A. Torrey, also testified of people falling to the ground during meetings. There are recorded instances of pedestrians in Chicago passing the door of the hall where Moody was preaching, and crumpling to the sidewalk under the power.[44] Torrey himself fell into a trance when he was baptized in the Spirit.[45]

Baptists in the Bliss

Baptists are another denomination whose founders cut against the grain of religious orthodoxy in their respective era. When considering modern-day cessationist denominations, who cannot help but think of the Southern Baptist church? And yet Baptist origins were some of the craziest of all.

It was the Anabaptists, a 16th-century movement in Europe, which spawned a number of modern-day denominations, including the Baptists, Mennonites, Church of the Brethren, Brethren in Christ, Amish, and Hutterites. The Anabaptists were on the radical, utopian side of the Protestant reformation. They were ruthlessly oppressed by Catholic, Lutheran, and secular authorities. Ecstatic experience was common, and at times extreme. Speaking in tongues and prophetic utterance was widespread, and many were influenced by the German mystics. The following are just a few stories of their shenanigans.

In the early 1530s, an ecstatic circle of Anabaptists gathered around a miracle worker and prophet in the southwest corner of Thuringia, under the jurisdiction of the abbot of Fulda. Facing persecution, about 40 men and women barricaded themselves into a house, resisting capture. Then finally captured and sent to prison, "they astounded their jailors with their singing, dancing, visions, and spiritual raptures. They confronted their judges joyously and serenely went to their deaths as if in a trance."[46]

But there were by and far wilder stock of Anabaptists than these. Consider this pre-Southern Baptist meeting held in 16th-century Holland:

> About the beginning of the year 1535, twelve Anabaptists, of whom five were women, assembled at midnight in a private home at Amsterdam. One of them, who was a tailor by profession, fell into a trance, and after having preached and prayed for the space of four hours, stripped himself naked, threw his clothes into the fire, and commanded all the assembly to do the same, in which he was obeyed without the least reluctance. He then ordered them to follow him through the streets in this state of nature, which they accordingly did, howling and bawling out, Wo! wo! the wrath of God! the wrath of God! wo to Babylon! When, after being seized and brought before the magistrates, clothes were offered them to cover their indecency, they refused them

obstinately, and cried aloud, We are the naked truth! When they were brought to the scaffold, they sung and danced, and discovered all the marks of enthusiastic phrensy [*sic*].[47]

Like the Camisards of France, the inspiration of the Anabaptists was often used to incite war against their persecutors, but it is difficult to be critical of this considering the mindset of the times, when politics and religion went hand in hand. The Anabaptists suffered horrendous abuse and torture. King Ferdinand advocated drowning them all—which he called the *third baptism*, saying it was "the best antidote to Anabaptism." Even Martin Luther advocated their death. Nevertheless, their lives shone with true Christian virtue. It is said that "a 16th century man who did not drink to excess, curse, or abuse his workmen or family *could be suspected of being an Anabaptist* and thus persecuted."[48]

The Anabaptists are often lumped together with their most violent fringe elements, like Thomas Müntzer (1490–1525), a radical German reformer and leader of the *Peasant's Revolt*, a war aimed at establishing a communistic theocracy. Despite the extreme nature of Müntzer, he staunchly believed in continued divine revelation in the post-apostolic era. Though his inspiration was clearly filtered through personal anger and carnal means to an end, he is an indicator of the prophetically inspired origins of modern movements like the Baptist church. Müntzer criticized those priests who rejected personal divine revelation: "These villainous and treacherous parsons are of no use to the church in even the slightest manner, for they deny the voice of the bridegroom, which is a truly certain sign that they are a pack of devils. How could they then be God's servants, bearers of His word, which they shamelessly deny with their whore's brazenness? For all true parsons must have revelations, so that they are certain of their cause [*sic*]."[49] Müntzer emphasized direct revelation through dreams and visions, the need for baptism of the Holy Spirit and the need to rely on the "inner word" of the Lord.

Obviously, these are very fanatical and arguably immature examples among the early Baptists, but my point is to make clear how extremely open they were toward ecstatic activity and spiritual gifts. The wild, uninhibited abandonment with which they pursued God was a major catalyst for their growth and spread throughout Europe and beyond.

Chapter 9

recovering the experience of trance

It is nearly impossible to explore historical ecstatic movements without discussing the French prophets of the Cevennes.

In 1688 in the Cevennes, 16-year-old Isabeau Vincent began to have ecstatic experiences, shaking and fainting, and displaying keen prophetic abilities. She could quote Scriptures she had never read, preach in her sleep, and soon, a prophetic movement was launched that spread rapidly through the French countryside. Visitors flocked to the area, and many were saved, as their meetings were marked by extreme spontaneity, demonstrative worship, and physical manifestations of God's presence on believers.[1]

The Cevennes prophets were Huguenots (French Protestants), and the revelatory wave swept through from about 1685 to 1707. It is important to realize that this movement ended in carnal warfare, as they organized an armed insurrection in opposition to Louis XIV's persecution of Protestantism. At that time they were known as the Camisards. France is soaked in martyr's blood on both sides of the Catholic/Protestant divide.

Looking at the roots of the movement, there were significant lessons to be learned. Vincent was a young shepherdess who began to draw debate between theologians, bishops, and royal authorities. She sparked the ministry of many others, including Gabriel Astier, a prophet who would "preach in a trance, and other prophets and prophetesses would fall to the ground, shake violently, then begin to speak in a calm and ethereal voice as frightened listeners gathered around to hear their words. The miraculous nature of the experience was heightened by the fact that illiterate women and children as young as five or six spoke French rather than Occitan."[2]

For peasants to begin speaking in other languages, whilst experiencing such exotic manifestations, this caused an extreme stir. But like many early prophetic movements without solid teaching foundations, the gifts of prophecy found their abuses. This was accelerated in a time of religious hatred and war.

Prophets felt the Spirit was instructing them to strike war with the hierarchies that persecuted them. Following the French war, many of the original prophets fled to England for refuge. There, they caused no small splash, as pamphlets and books debating their experiences flooded the English market.

At first, prophets like Vincent called for simple repentance. But later on, other prophets used their office to issue directives for resistance and defiance of the royal orders that forced them to take Catholic mass.

The French prophets were not without miracles. Near the village of Sérignan in 1703, the prophet Pierre Claris was consumed by fire, but walked miraculously out of the flames unharmed. There were numerous miracles reported both before and during the Camisard war.[3]

It is good to put the French prophets in context with the Great Awakening of the Wesley brothers and George Whitefield, if we are to truly gauge society's popular opinion on prophetism, trances, and the supernatural in general.

There was no lack of public opposition to the French prophets who came to London in 1707–1708. Their influence filtered over to the Great Awakening revivalists, causing many to take a hesitant stance toward their embrace of *enthusiasm*—the common term in that day for ecstatic manifestations. Although the revivalists (Whitefield, Wesley, and others) all allowed physical manifestations to occur in their meetings to differing degrees, many would have seen the French prophets as an example of extremism. To be compared to the Cevennes prophets would not have been complimentary to someone like Wesley, though personally, he fully embraced the similarities between the two moves of God.

The Cevennes revival occurred in a very unique and transitory time, when the public was undergoing drastic social change. The bloody religious wars of that post-Reformation period (France itself had eight civil wars) put distaste in the hearts of many for anything that smacked of religious extremism. When the French prophets hit England, lines were being drawn in the sand regarding spiritual experience.

Nevertheless, the French prophets ignited a fire in England, despite their controversy. And like all ecstatics, they served as perhaps unpopular reminders that there is more to Christianity than religious formalism. They often fell, fainted, or swooned. One English critic gave the following description of French Prophets who had arrived in London:

> ...their Countenance changes, and is no longer Natural; their Eyes roll after a ghastly manner in their Heads, or they stand altogether fixed; all the Members of their Body seem displaced, their Hearts beat with extraordinary Efforts and Agitations; they become Swelled and Bloated, and look bigger than ordinary; they Beat themselves with their Hands with a vast Force, like the miserable Creature in the Gospel, cutting himself with Stones; the Tone of their Voice is stronger than what it could be Naturally; their Words are sometimes broken and interrupted; they speak without knowing what they speak, and without remembering what they have Prophesied.[4]

The Growing Fear of Enthusiasm

The enthusiasms of Jonathan Edwards' meetings in America and the fresh memory of the French Prophets in Europe provided a backdrop for the groundbreaking ministry of John Wesley and George Whitefield. The Cevennes revival dovetailed together with the start of the First Great Awakening.

Enthusiasm was strongly identified with puritanical strains at that time. In fact, Puritans had always emphasized revelatory experiences such as dreams, visions, and audible voices. But secular society was growing weary of ecstatic experience. Because of the immaturity of some and misconceptions of others, any type of "religious extremism" was linked with political dissent. In an age of bloody revolutions that had been married to religious disputes, people in the Enlightenment era began valuing reason over enthusiasm. They were tired of so-called "God-inspired" wars. And so here were the birth of Methodism and the revivals of Jonathan Edwards, both coming at the heels of bloody revolutions in Europe.

It was during this time that personal spiritual inspiration became the enemy of reason in much of the popular thought. It did not take long for opponents of revival (both religious and governmental) to attribute all enthusiasm to *mental insanity*, rather than attacking it on doctrinal grounds. Religious leaders who opposed the revivals rarely turned to biblical argument, as is so common today. Rather, they opposed the glory with *medical arguments*. The Pharisees of the day turned to science, not Scripture, to attack revival.

It was right then, in the heart of awakening, that we begin see the emergence of a new form of science called *psychology*, whose initial aim had a very specific purpose in mind: it was pioneered by anti-enthusiast religionists such as Frank Manuel, whose chief task was to *explain and discredit enthusiasm*.[5] Psychology was born as a science aimed at equating personal inspiration from God with *insanity*. Psychology was birthed from the antichrist seedbed of the cessationist "church."

Before long, secular society was thronged with psychobabble language. Mesmerism, somnambulism, animal magnetism, pathetism, somnium, and somnipathy were all terms that attempted to explain away trances in naturalistic means with pop-psychological lingo. All of this psychological nonsense was a direct result of detractors of revival who sought to condemn spiritual experience by attributing it to the imagination or outright insanity. Consequently, the mind sciences followed. New age was born, not as the seed of pagan witchdoctors, but as the direct prodigy of unbelieving cessationists who turned to pseudoscience instead of God. *It was the religious spirit that gave birth to new age.* Just as Presbyterian anti-revivalists like Charles Chauncy turned to universalism in Jonathan Edwards' day, so did the religious clergy open the door for the mind sciences and spiritualism in their quest to quench the Spirit in the 1800s.

Obviously, psychology holds a number of valid truths. Please understand that there are many effective, Spirit-filled Christian psychologists in practice today. Prophetic counselor John Sandford is a great example of one who has redeemed true psychological principles through cross-centered, biblically based methods. For years, Sandford would go daily into Heaven in trances, and his pioneering work has brought mental, emotional, and physical healing to thousands. But apart from a supernatural perspective and an understanding of spiritual dynamics, psychology can only offer counterfeit solutions and deceiving diagnoses. Its quackery can muddy the waters.

Over the past two centuries there have been countless prophetic persons locked away in mental institutions for their claims of divine inspiration. Whether misunderstood, lacking proper "prophetic etiquette," or merely unable to explain the spiritual dynamics they were perceiving, very many authentic believers have suffered under the label of "insanity." And on the other hand, there are countless people diagnosed with mental disorders who simply need a good old-fashioned exorcism.

The first time I ever personally tried to prophesy, my own family thought I was crazy, had me arrested, and I was locked up for three days! Get ready for the sanity of prophetic believers to be questioned in these last days like never before! Forerunners are always misunderstood. Don't be afraid that people will think you are crazy. Just drink your bliss! If you are pursuing God at all, there are plenty of people who already think you are nuts. Just accept the fact. The wisdom of God is foolishness to the world, so in their eyes you are verifiably *insane*.

During this time period in the 19th century, it seems the enemy was scrambling to counteract what God had been doing. With powerful preachers like Maria Woodworth-Etter going coast to coast with trance evangelism, the world was curious and hungry for true spirituality. The mind-science religions began to flourish, along with spiritualism, mediums, clairvoyance, and all manner of new age thought and practice, including the popular Christian Science cult. Prophetic teacher Rick Joyner rightly points out that Christians need to reclaim the term "new age." We have the most optimistic, utopian hope for the coming age of any other religion on the planet!

The enemy loves to steal meaningful terminology. This is the reason our society has a popular street drug today called *ecstasy*. During this same era of history, around the late 1840s, an apostate Methodist preacher turned spiritualist, La Roy Sunderland, began to use the word "trance" in his terminology, to describe ulterior states of consciousness *outside the Christian context*. We can trace theft of the word "trance" by the new age movement back to this time period. The experience of trance belongs solely to the church. Any other foreign spiritual experience is an illegal one. We trance out through the one true Door that is Christ.

The enemy used spiritualism and the mind sciences to fill a gap of true mysticism in areas where much of the church was bereft of supernatural experience. The spiritualist William Howitt, in his book *History of the Supernatural* in 1863, seemed to hit the nail on the head regarding the modern church's lack of supernatural power. He said that the problem of doubt did not lie in the skepticism of the age of Enlightenment. He traced it all the way back to the Protestant Reformation. Howitt said that Protestantism had built itself by attacking the miracles of Catholicism.

"In endeavoring to pull up the tares of false Roman miracle, they have …pulled up the root of faith in miracle, and in the great spiritual heritage of the Church with it," wrote Howitt.[6] What wisdom from a syncretistic new ager! In attacking the perception of false miracles, Howitt says that the reformers threw the baby out with the bath water. The early new agers clearly saw that the church was forfeiting spiritual ground, which is why they looked elsewhere for experience. To this day, cults like Christian Science still understand that naturalistic explanations of life offered through secular psychology are a sham.

The exciting thing to see in our day is a remnant of believers recovering mystical Christianity. It is such a radical notion to consider what God is doing in the church in our generation. There is truly a glory revolution at hand. I do not say it is another reformation, because God is not re-forming an old wineskin. He is attacking the religious idolatry and priestcraft of our day, and giving us a whole new God-centered perspective on the Christian walk that is utterly supernatural. It is revolutionary. I believe that in many ways, we are returning to supernatural roots that were severed in the Protestant Reformation. I do not even consider myself a Protestant anymore. Why? Because I'm not protesting anything—I am pursuing Someone. We are in a post-Protestant era. Of course I am not Catholic either. I am just a drinker.

Unbelieving Believers

In the midst of today's supernatural revolution, the most scientific persons are having their framework of reality stretched far beyond what their education or religious backgrounds have taught them. When gemstones appear out of thin air and missing limbs regrow instantly with a word, we are forced to confront the existence of the supernatural realm.

Signs and wonders are proofs for the unbeliever. But in our ministry, the Lord generally sends me to work miracles within the church. Why is this? There are lots of "unbelieving believers" out there today—Christians who still live the vast majority of their life by the natural laws and parameters of the seen universe. If science is the study of the "observable universe," rest assured that Jesus was never a scientist. He does not "judge by the sight of His eyes, nor decide by the hearing of His ears" (Isa. 11:3).

True science has never been an enemy of the cross, but much of what we have today is not science. It is the religion of *scientism*. Writer Lambert Dolphin sums it up: "Most all of modern secular science today is actually scientism, a branch of secular humanism. Instead of giving nominal assent to, or at least tolerating a biblical world view, the climate in our land is now antichristian."[7]

You may think the skepticism of modern science is the selfsame *spirit of doubt* that has infiltrated the very church of God regarding the miraculous. But the opposite is true. Sadly, this antichristian worldview is the very *fault* of the church. Countless multitudes of "Christians" deny the supernatural realm, or at the very least, the free accessibility of the supernatural realm. To them, Heaven may be floating out in the clouds somewhere, but surely the Kingdom of Heaven is not *at hand!*

We could just call it *cessationism* and pretend that this is a trifling doctrinal issue—something debatable on theological grounds. Religious spirits love debate. But the very real and available power of the Kingdom is not something relegated to deliberation or consensus opinion, as if truth can be hawked off at the pawn shop to the highest bidder. The spoils do not go to the man with the best argument. To pretend that cessationism holds even a sliver of a valid point is to compromise Truth and to tolerate golden calves on the high places.

Nevertheless, for the sake of "unity," Charismatics often tolerate the unbelief of mainline denominationalists who reject the present-day miraculous workings of God. We can still love these brothers, but let us not pretend they bring something valid to the table. The man who rejects the

Spirit of God Himself brings nothing to the table. In fact, he is in danger of the fires of hell.

That may sound harsh, but think about this: *none of us* brings anything to the table. It is God alone who contributes anything of value. What a miserable, wretched failure all of us are, apart from the hope of present-day resurrection power! To reject God's Spirit is to reject God Himself, the very Paraclete who drew you to Jesus. Unless the power of God is for today, we fight a lost cause.

Discerning Enthusiasm

Your faith bolsters you in the bliss, not the opinion of society or the consensus of the religious order. I have gone to great lengths to show historical examples of ecstatic prayer in the church. But whether or not any given revivalist or favorite church leader approved of these trances is irrelevant. It was still a major part of church history and the experience is biblical reality. Jonathan Edwards looked for "signs" to determine the validity of experience, primarily the fruit of the Spirit in Galatians 5:22-23 (love, joy, peace, long-suffering, gentleness, etc.). These he called "religious affections." Revivalists like Edwards and Wesley said manifestations are not a necessary indicator of revival, but both recognized God's hand in the midst of them.

People often become anxious as to whether manifestations are legitimate or artificial. If this is a concern, then ambivalence can be the best course of action. Do people feign enthusiasms? Yes. Do people try to "recreate" previous experiences? Yes. This may involve a need for attention, a striving for acceptance, or any other less than perfect motive. But at the end of the day, all of these points are irrelevant. We have to trust God to sort these things out in the hearts of individuals, without micromanaging everyone else's day-to-day experiences. Whether Subject A's shaking was "in the flesh" or Subject B's shaking was "in the Spirit," should be my least of concerns. Chances are, you got "in the flesh" in traffic this morning. We need to learn extreme tolerance in this regard with one another. I would rather have God show up, while some people simultaneously manifest "in the flesh," than for God to never show up and everyone remains quiet. Chances are a lot of those quiet people are "in the flesh" already.

If someone begins in the flesh and ends in the Spirit, that is OK. But we do not want to begin in the Spirit and end in the flesh. This happens when we judge and criticize. We must learn to let the wheat and the tares grow up together, and let God sort it out.

I understand that many believers are afraid of deception. Fear-based "discernment" models won't cut it anymore. I would rather give freedom in these matters than formulizing a list of parameters and subsequently risk missing God.

In today's climate, the fear of "distraction" is not enough for me to quiet someone down who is manifesting in my meetings. Besides, I want God to come and show off His reality more than I want to entertain the ten-thousandth teaching we've all heard before. In fact, I find more often than not that God is trying to distract us from our bland religious exercises.

It is reasonable that leaders would want to safeguard their flock from an unholy "free for all." There is a lot of craziness that passes off as prophetic manifestation, but is actually witchcraft. It did not take much discernment to know she was a witch. Once a wiccan came into a service, blowing a shofar, and I immediately discerned by the Spirit that something was not right. He then came to me, demanding that he be allowed to anoint my head with oil along with the pastor in front of the congregation. When I rejected his request, he put his finger to my forehead and began reading curses over me, openly manifesting his devils.

Discernment is needed more than ever today. The problem is this: perceived craziness is not a valid indicator for anything. God and the devil both do crazy things. Again, Jesus did not judge by the eyes or by the ears. On the surface, both holy and diabolical possession can share some of the same traits.

One of the tools we have for discernment is the Word of God, but this is only part of the equation. We must also judge by the *Spirit*. Perhaps the number one key for judging manifestations is simply to determine whether or not there is *glory* on them. And you will only know the glory by staying in the glory. This is impossible for the leader who is not full of the Holy Spirit. A manifestation may be inconceivably crazy, but if there is glory on it, don't touch it. The Scriptures say that David "frolicked" before the Ark of the Covenant, ushering the glory of God back into Jerusalem from Obed

Edom's house. He literally danced the clothes off his own back. But when his wife Michal saw the king rejoicing in such an "undignified" manner, she criticized him. And for this, she became barren (see 2 Sam. 6). One of the number one ways we encounter spiritual barrenness is by criticizing another's spiritual experience.

John the Beloved tells us to "prove the spirits whether they be of God" (1 John 4:1). He never tells us to test the outward manifestations, but the spirits themselves. For this we need the *gift* of discerning of spirits. Notice also that John did not tell us to *disprove* the spirits. Discernment is not a paranoid hunt for devils in the middle of every manifestation. There are many people just itching to disprove something. Instead, John's admonition was positive and optimistic: he wanted us to constantly be looking for God in every situation, testing spirits to see if they are bringing something of value from Him.

This type of positive discernment is expectant, joyful—never anxious, worried, or fearful—with a penchant for mystery and open to the unusual. There are a lot of deliverance ministries today that see a demon behind every bush, and they are marked by fearful suspicions of everything that is not clearly understood by the discerner. They try to disprove and cast out everything. If you go looking for devils, you will find them. They really are behind every bush. But if you are always focused on devils, you will miss God in the process.

The problem is that paranoia has long masqueraded as the gift of discernment of spirits. Here is another way of explaining it: Instead of trying the spirits "whether they be of God," we have tried the spirits *whether they be of the devil.* Often in meetings, people will be shaking and writhing because they are being delivered in the glory. Someone may perceive the demonic coming out so they step in and stop the manifestation, putting their own hand in the mix and cutting off what God was doing. Even if a manifestation has a demonic root, the truly discerning person would be able to tell if it was coming or going, and whether or not to even get involved. The Lord is pretty good at casting out devils on His own in the glory, without our help.

Countless people are delivered in our revival meetings, but we are rarely aware of it. We don't go on a devil hunt. We just look for Jesus and allow the shaking and baking. Then the testimonies pour in afterward. We need an extreme tolerance for manifestations. Think of how patient the apostle Paul was with this stuff! When Paul visited Macedonia in Acts 16, a slave girl possessed by a spirit of divination followed him for "many days" saying, "These men are the servants of the Most High God, who proclaim to us the way of salvation" (Acts 16:17-18). Paul allowed this girl to rattle off for *many days* before getting "greatly annoyed" and casting out her devils. Why didn't Paul just shut her up to begin with? Paul afforded great leniency with manifestations. Give God room to work, and don't stress out about devils around every corner. Like Paul, I can often tell when someone is manifesting a devil because it is *annoying* and the disturbance lasts a long time. But even then, you need patience. It may just be your own religious spirit that is getting annoyed.

Overall, the simple rule of thumb is not to over-analyze manifestations. Rest in your faith. Follow the bliss, and roll with the river.

Diabolical Trances

A thorough study on the nature of trances would not be complete without addressing demonic or *diabolical* trances. But I do not feel it is necessary to focus too much attention on the ways of darkness.

Employees of the U.S. Treasury Department study real money for years before they ever look at a counterfeit note. For them, there is no need to study the false, in order to know the true. By thoroughly getting to know the *real bill*, they can spot a fake dollar any day of the week. Like a treasury official, we should always be studying the true ways of the Lord, and not overly focusing on the counterfeit ways of the demonic.

When looking at trances and manifestations, you will always know a tree by its fruit. Ask some easy questions when discerning an experience. Is there fear, oppression, anxiety, tension, ungodly confusion, or depression produced? If there are maniacal tendencies that produce harm to self and others, then the manifestation is not of God. Do these experiences draw the participant closer to God? The more time we spend in the glory, the more our lives should grow holier. Wrecked lives should change for the better. We can also ask ourselves, are actions produced by these experiences in alignment with the Scriptures?

The fact that someone trances out or manifests in the glory does not mean their lives are bearing the fruits of holiness. Mystical theologian Albert Farges writes, "First of all...it is not the ecstasy which proves the sanctity, but rather the sanctity which shows the ecstasy to be divine."[8]

Demonic occupancy varies dramatically from Holy Spirit possession, in that the individual feels enslaved against their free will. Farges notes that "The human will, in the ecstatic state, in no way loses its freedom, for it does not lose the concurrence of the understanding. The contemplative act, although passive, is therefore voluntary and meritorious, but indirectly, by compliance with an ineffable love."

A common criticism I hear regarding trances is that the subject *loses control,* which appears to be in violation of the free will.

There are momentary losses of reason and the most intense levels of passivity in divine ecstasy—at the peak of rapture, resistance is virtually futile—but this is all a welcome delight in the fires of holy love. In these instances, the Bridegroom may sweep you completely off of your own feet—but you would not consider *that* a loss of freedom, as He carries you over the threshold of His heavenly chambers. Possession by joy and possession by hatred are two different types of possession.

In the highest points of rapture, God's hand becomes utterly irresistible. Yet this is still a domineering hand of bliss. It is unlike the *involuntary* passiveness that marks the demonic trance. Demonic manifestations often come with all forms of hystero-epilepsy mannerisms: writhing, horrid convulsions, unseemly distortions of the facial muscles and limbs, foaming at the mouth, etc.

Do not discern the origin of a trance by its degree of intensity—instead, it must be discerned by its fruit. Depression can be extreme, but so can joy.

Manifestations can be quite "extreme" if not outright fanatical, yet still be divine in origin. The radical nature of the manifestation is *not in itself* a determining factor of its source. I have considered myself nearly on the brink of insanity at times when God swept over me for hours of uncontrollable drunken behavior, yet I was at peace, and the corresponding fruit was altogether tremendous, miraculous, and life-changing. I am always filled with joy and expectancy in these encounters.

Diabolical trances almost always produce a sense of paranoia or ungodly fear, and they lead to corrupt character, sensuality, and delusion. Conversely, humility and love will continue to grow in a true mystic. False trances can be suspected when a person regularly frequents spots where they can be observed by others. But even then, a person's need for attention does not invalidate their ecstatic states, as much as it simply highlights their immaturity or sense of rejection.

A number of states have been deemed "human ecstasy" or "natural ecstasy" in that they arise from intense mental concentration, mental ascension, or unlawful mental passivity. There are also states of catalepsy, hysteria, or epileptic-type seizures that are at best clinical cases of affliction and a worst, full-blown demonic possession. I do not intend to provide a comprehensive study of deviant trances, only to acknowledge their existence.

Spiritualism, hypnotism, yoga, spirit channeling, transcendental meditation, mediumship, spirit guides, and all manner of new age practice are altogether forbidden by Scripture. Mystical theologian Montague Summers notes, "There is an ecstasy of sorcerers, as well as an ecstasy of saints."[9] We should be aware of this, but not overly focused on it. Stay focused on Jesus, and you will be safe.

If your trances continually leave you nervous, fatigued, and agitated— if they leave you with no new revelation, no stronger convictions, or no fruits of sanctity—then you may reasonably suspect something askew. I believe one of the greatest dangers here is *pride*. But the other danger is *fear*.

For Western believers—and I speak to the "healthy," not the sick—I believe our propensity to fear the counterfeit often outweighs our willingness to pursue the genuine. From the rabid apologetics being taught in the church today, one would think that *all trances* are demonic in origin, a clear contradiction to the Scriptures. Discerning our experiences comes down to looking at fruit and knowing the source of your experience, which should always be Jesus. If you are afraid of deception, plead the blood of Jesus over your mind and body, soul and spirit before you enter in. Trust in the blood. Commit yourself to the guidance of the Holy Spirit. Stay in the word of God. Surround yourself with strong, prophetic, Spirit-filled believers. Do these things and you will not be led astray. Intimacy with Christ and the earnest pursuit of Him will not get you sidetracked into counterfeit experience. There is a trust issue at stake.

Teresa of Avila says that whoever loves and fears God is a safe traveler.

The way of mysticism will endeavor you to risk, experiment, and at times, make uncalculated mistakes. Grace gives you boldness on these paths, but the fear of failure will leave you fruitless. The fear of the Lord, on the other hand, is a fear you can *delight in* (see Isa. 11). Do not fear the enemy's ploys to delude and dupe you through a false ecstatic state if you are a blood-bought child of God. Risk is the common currency of true faith. You will not take risks if you are always afraid of the devil. Loving and fearing God is the answer.

In *The Way of Perfection*, Teresa of Avila writes, "love will make us quicken our steps, while (holy) fear will make us look where we are setting our feet so that we shall not fall on a road where there are so many obstacles."[10]

Many fear the devil's ability to deceive them, more than they believe in God's love to keep and sustain them. This is especially the case with mystical prayer, manifestation, and miracles. Teresa expounds on this:

> In order to disturb the soul and keep it from enjoying these great blessings, the devil will suggest to it a thousand false fears and will persuade other people to do the same; for if he cannot win souls he will at least try to make them lose something, and among the losers will be those who might have gained greatly had they believed that such great favors, bestowed upon so miserable a creature, come from God, and that it is possible for them to be thus bestowed, for sometimes we seem to forget His past mercies.[11]

In today's tamed-down, castrated form of religion, many people want to "play it safe." They want safe theology, safe services, safe worship, safe preaching, and safe, ordinary, contented little lifestyles. Even in our secular society today—especially in America—*safety* is touted as a virtue. We fear lawsuits, terrorists, non-organic foods, and cholesterol. We have safety bottles, safety lighters, safety belts, and safety meds. The church has wrongly embraced safety and *moderation* as marks of morality. God is neither safe nor moderate.

Fear of the devil will cause you to have a *moderate* pursuit of God. But God's middle name is *Danger*. Teresa says:

> Do you suppose that it is of little use to the devil to suggest these fears? No, it is most useful to him, for there are two well-known ways in which he can make use of this means to harm us, to say nothing of others. First, he can make those who listen to him fearful of engaging in prayer, because they think that they will be deceived. Secondly, he can dissuade many from approaching God who, as I have said, see that He is so good that He will hold intimate converse with sinners.

Activating Trances

Just as some criticize mysticism for being too *passive* for the free will, still others criticize it for being too *self-initiated.*

Many critics attack true mysticism claiming that it is an interior system of works for accessing the spirit realm. This, of course, is not true. It is an embrace of the finished work of the cross. However, we must dispense with the common superstition that trances, encounters, or any other divine activity in your life comes about with *no participation* of your own. God is looking for a lover to dance with, not a drone without a free will. Another generation cannot pass by, apathetically waiting on a lightning bolt from Heaven to solve our problems. He has already given us the lightning bolt on Calvary. It is now time we believe it and take our delegated authority to storm the gates of Paradise. I cannot stress enough that we should avoid striving in this area. However, there has always existed both the *ascetic* and *passive* (or mystical) way of encountering God.

In the ascetic mode, the soul *moves itself* toward God, but with the help of grace. In the passive way, the soul is moved altogether supernaturally by God. In these matters, I am referring to interior prayer.

If you are not whisked away into ecstasies like the great saints of old, do not think there is something wrong with you, or that you are somehow not qualified. It is very possible for you to *position yourself* for encounter with the Lord in this way. There are a number of interior disciplines you can learn, although I would not recommend you attempt a "suicide of the soul" in which some embrace a sort of internal religious masochism. We embrace the infinite pleasures of the glory realm.

Ultimately, it is grace through faith which causes us to access the realms of the Spirit. But it is OK to hunger and pursue these experiences.

We pursue ecstasies only in that they are a state of divine love to be eagerly desired. True contemplation is much deeper than verbal forms of prayer or worship. It is about intimacy, which is the foundation of revelation.

When we speak of activating a state of trance, or pursuing rapture, we cannot consider it a work or a formula in the Western, Greek rationalism sense. This is a deeper way. The mind alone cannot traverse these paths, nor is it sufficient to tread where the heart has not first ascended. The Lord says:

> *These people come near to Me with their mouth and honor Me with their lips, but their hearts are far from me. Their worship of Me is made up only of rules taught by men* (Isaiah 29:13).

What systematic approaches are powerless to accomplish, yet the blazing lamp of divine love achieves effortlessly, for *"the eyes of the Lord range throughout the earth to strengthen those whose hearts are fully committed to Him"* (2 Chron. 16:9).

There is no theological explanation. No form. No methodology to the practice of His presence. Its reliance is on the blind fury of faith—it hinges on abiding. It is a relationship.

> *This is what the sovereign Lord, the Holy One of Israel, says: "In returning and rest is your salvation, in quietness and trust is your strength..."* (Isaiah 30:15).

As my inner man learns to *be still and know that He is God* (see Ps. 46:10), I learn His still small voice. I begin to ascend.

It is OK to frame up mental pictures, meditate on scriptural imagery, or picture heavenly things on the backdrop of your sanctified imagination. This is how you begin to exercise your spiritual vision. This is how all true prophets, from ages past, have learned to access the heavens on a regular basis. To engage a trance does not mean you are trying to *create* supernatural experience. But the Lord does instruct us to *be still* and know that He is God. It is in the knowing that we get whacked. And the more accustomed we become to that state of being, we can easily move back into the glory when we find ourselves slipping out.

You do not need to strive for experience. *Faith* is what allows you to connect to all the mystical graces of the glory realm, through simply believing. This faith is a free gift, but true faith always produces within you a desire to do things that further your intimate experiences with God. Through faith, the heights of contemplation are available to all.

Though you may start in a mode of *participation with God*, the deeper states of ecstasy involve such surrender that the human will becomes completely passive to Him. This, says Teresa of Avila, is where "God does all." No longer does the will simply cooperate with grace, but grace becomes operative alone.

The apostle Paul tells us of an ecstatic encounter he had to the Third Heaven in which he was completely passive to the Spirit of God:

> *Fourteen years ago I was the subject of an **incomprehensible ecstasy**, in which truths too great for human language were imparted to me. I will base my boast on such experiences, in which I was but the **dependent, passive instrument** of the Lord* (2 Corinthians 2:5, George Barker Stevens).[12]

The paradox of our labors is this: we work to enter rest. We strive to cease from strife. Therefore the highest states of rapture—when God takes over and resistance is futile—should never be viewed as a loss of free will. They are a progression into grace.

Part IV

the way of
ecstatic prayer

Chapter 10

four stages of interior prayer

Until now, we have made a claim for living in the bliss of Jesus and given a brief history of those who tangibly experienced His ecstasies in various eras. But we shall now turn our focus to activating a lifestyle of mystical prayer for ourselves. We will explain the internal and external dynamics of the prayer of ecstasy, and give some practical, hands-on examples of supernatural phenomena you may experience in deep prayer.

In the rich tradition of "soaking" or inner prayer, many mystics and theologians throughout history mapped out certain *stages* of contemplation. Many writers have their own descriptions of these interior levels of prayer. Teresa of Avila, perhaps the premier mystical theologian of them all, talks about the seven stages or seven mansions of the soul. But when we step back and look at the mystics overall, there are four primary stages of prayer that can be found in most of their writings and experience. Here I will consolidate and discuss these four levels, or *stages of inner prayer*.

These levels are not formulas, nor is there a single biblical narrative to describe these levels, so I have tried to encapsulate them in as simple terms as possible. I have summarized the four stages of interior prayer as the following:

Recollection
Meditation (Prayer of Quiet)
Union
Ecstasy

Ecstasy is supernatural prayer. It is deemed the highest of these stages. Remember that contemplation is not "mental" prayer, per se, but the practice of the presence of God.

Throughout the course of the ancient church, ecstasy was always deemed the uppermost form of prayer. To again clarify terminology, *ecstasy, trance,* and *rapture* are generally one in the same. The word *rapture* is neither in the Bible, nor was it ever used traditionally to refer to an end-time event. It is only a modern pop-theology that the end-time church will *disappear* prior to the tribulation period described in the Book of Revelation.

The language in this section of the book will be slightly more technical. But for our purposes, we will be using the word *rapture* synonymously with the state of ecstasy. Later we will address some minor theological distinctions between the two words, delineating "rapture" as the *most intense segment of an ecstasy.*

All of the four states of prayer listed are inward. That is, they are internal experiences between you and the Lord in the hiddenness of the Secret Place. They are not external, in that dancing, shouting, singing, sitting, or standing are external positions of prayer. However, when one reaches the state of ecstasy or rapture, the experience becomes *both inward and outward.* That means there are visible, tangible manifestations that begin to occur, ranging from heavy drunkenness and fits to more extreme miracles such as one's body lifting off the ground. It was in this fourth stage of deep rapture that Teresa of Avila would begin to float about a foot and a half from the floor. Consider this eyewitness testimony from her fellow nun, Anne of the Incarnation:

> I was in the choir waiting for the bell to ring when our holy mother (Teresa) entered and knelt down....As I was looking on, she was raised about half a yard from the ground without her feet touching it. At this I was terrified and she, for her part, was trembling all over. So I moved to where she was and I put my hands under her feet, over which I remained weeping for something like half an hour while the ecstasy lasted. Then suddenly she sank down and rested on her feet and turning her head round to me she asked me who I was and whether I had been there all the while. I said yes, and then she ordered me under obedience to say nothing of what I had seen,

and I have in fact said nothing until the present moment.[1]

Each level of inner prayer we explore could be considered a stepping stone toward the ultimate state of ecstasy. Along the way, we grow so hungry for the Lord we eventually step outside of ourselves to reach Him. In fact, each of these first three states of prayer—*recollection, meditation,* and *union*—could be considered lesser degrees of ecstasy itself, until the culmination of full blown rapture.

The Prayer of Recollection

Let us begin with stage one of contemplative prayer: *recollection.* This is where we first settle in and get centered on the Lord. In this first stage, we are more geared on getting past distractions than anything else. We are expunging old things, before receiving something fresh from the Lord. Before we can hear from the Lord and get filled, we tend to spend considerable time just casting our existing cares upon Him. We are really just washing our hands on the outside, getting prepared for encounter at a deeper level.

You may spend the first 15 minutes of prayer just getting past the guilt of not having prayed for the past two weeks! In the place of recollection, all kinds of thoughts start popping into your head. Don't just try to shove these away, thinking they are distractions. This is often the biggest mistake we make in recollection. In this stage of prayer, you will *recall* things that need to be handed over to Jesus: the bills, the kids, the dog, the anxieties of the day, the cares and worries about all sorts of things that are going on in your life. As these things come to mind, don't ignore them. Just gently release them into the arms of Jesus, and allow yourself to fall deeper into His heart. We carry so many burdens needlessly, and this is why we become depressed and even physically sick. Take time to give your cares to the Lord. In this stage of prayer, we give our heavy burdens to Him and take up His yoke, *for His yoke is easy and His burden is light* (see Matt. 11:30).

In this state of recollection, there may be some intercession that takes place. You may be led to pray for a sick relative or the president or whatever.

Don't feel that you have to pray *silently* about these things. Get loud if you need to. Remember that there is no formula, so if you feel like pounding out some intercession, petitions, or even warfare prayer that is fine. You go for it. But the main purpose of *contemplative prayer* is not to intercede for others, as much as it is to focus explicitly on Jesus. It is a place of Holy Spirit infusion. The Lord may allow you to feel a burden for something; but after you have released it to Him, you should naturally be able to enter back to that place of perfect stillness, peace, and rest.

Remember, you are not trying to kill your interior thoughts, you are only holding them with open hands. Don't try to force yourself into any particular state. Give yourself grace and do not be frustrated with yourself. You are only allowing yourself to rest in a position where God meets with you.

On a practical level, it may help you to find a comfortable position in which to pray, but one where you will not fall asleep. If you are meditating, then sitting in a chair works great. There is nothing wrong with lying down, but if you have trouble staying awake, you may want to try something different. Remember: no external formulas here, just find what works best for you to tune in. After you begin learning to practice God's presence, none of these things make a difference to you anymore. In this place, you learn that "those who wait on the Lord shall renew their strength; they shall mount up with wings like eagles, they shall run and not be weary, they shall walk and not faint" (Isa. 40:31). Again, the Lord says in Isaiah 30:15, "In returning and rest you shall be saved; in quietness and confidence shall be your strength."

It is in the place of recollection that you reacquaint yourself with God's presence. You learn to taste and touch and feel Him. You are infused with His peace that surpasses understanding. Allow yourself to simply receive His rays.

Don't camp on a thought. Don't try to shove thoughts away. Find His presence. Follow His peace. Release yourself to Him.

It should be said that most people never penetrate past this level of prayer. Most Christians cap their prayer life right here, either for lack of patience or lack of hunger. At this level of prayer, after we have given our laundry list of needs, fears, or requests over to God, we begin to get some relief from the heavy yoke of our burdens. And naturally, many people feel they've had a *breakthrough* at this point, so they end their prayer. But this is just stage one! You have just begun.

Everyone feels relief from getting rid of those burdens which they never should have carried to begin with. Dropping off your cares is one thing. It is an altogether different thing to get a heavenly download and to be filled with the bliss that we are *designed to carry*! As we linger further in this place of inner prayer, we realize more than ever we are not alone. God begins to speak to us and show us things. We truly begin to enter in and go on a remarkable journey.

Meditation or the Prayer of Quiet

Stage two of contemplative prayer is often called meditation, or the *prayer of quiet*. Many writers break this stage into many levels, but there is no need to overcomplicate it. At this stage of prayer, you may meditate or chew over a verse of Scripture, an inner or outer vision—anything that helps to connect you to the Lord or draw your heart and mind to Him. This is also the place where you begin to experience the presence of God, though not necessarily in such an overwhelming way that you cannot easily pull out.

In this place, you have already become free from the distractions of the recollection stage, and now you can truly focus on what the Lord wants you to see. In this state, your inner eye, or divine imagination, may begin to see pictures, visions, or images on the backdrop of your Spirit's eye. Thoughts and impressions from the Lord begin to come.

It may start small. A little goose bump. A bit of Morse code through the canopy of unbelief. Just develop the small inclinations and keep waiting on the Lord.

It may be helpful, for instance, to read passages of the throne room in Heaven from the Book of Revelation and imagine yourself there. Allow your mind to become ablaze with the thoughts and images of God. Even if you don't "see" anything yet, you may feel waves of joy and presence on certain inspirations of thought, knowing immediately that these impressions are from the heart of God.

In this place, you become acutely aware of heavenly things. You are not just focused on natural cares and anxieties anymore. This is the place Jesus has longed to take you. He said in John 3:12, "If I have told you earthly things and you do not believe, how will you believe if I tell you heavenly things?" In this place, the realm of *heavenly things* begins to open to you. You have finally become curious enough to get past yourself and explore the place where He lives. Jesus always longed for His first disciples to ask Him about this place. He said again in John 16:5, "But now I go away to Him who sent Me, and none of you asks Me, 'Where are You going?"

Ask Jesus where He is going in this place. Ask Him what He is feeling. In this realm of meditation, you begin to see through His eyes and hear through His ears. *Meditation is where the prophetic opens up.*

In Isaiah 6:10, we see that a curse was leveled, so that people could not see or hear in the realm of the Spirit: "Make the heart of this people dull, and their ears heavy, and shut their eyes; lest they see with their eyes, and hear with their ears, and understand with their heart, and return and be healed."

This veil over the eyes and ears limits us to see and hear only the things of the natural world around us, unable to perceive spiritual realities. Paul calls this a "spirit of stupor" (Rom. 11:8). But in this place of meditation, as God's glory comes upon you, the blood of Jesus frees you from all spiritual rebellion. You become re-sensitized to His voice, so that you can see the images lying within and hear the still small whisper of His voice.

The curse is reversed, as Jesus said, "but blessed are your eyes for they see, and your ears for they hear; for assuredly, I say to you that many prophets and righteous men desired to see what you see, and did not see it, and to hear what you hear, and did not hear it" (Matt. 13:16-17).

Meditation is the stage where you begin to see angels. You may see Jesus Himself in vision form. All manner of prophetic visions and utterances begin to come to you. This is a stage of listening. A place of rhema revelation pouring from the Scriptures. There are reams of books and teachings on the market from prophetic instructors today that can give you insight on developing your eyes and ears at this stage of prayer. It must be said that this stage is wonderful, and honestly, most of today's well-known prophets visit this stage of prayer regularly to receive their revelation. However, this is *not the highest state of prayer*. Although it is the deepest level that many of our prophetic leaders have experienced, remember that this is only the *second level* of interior prayer.

The Prayer of Union

There is a deeper place on the journey that the mystics of old simply called the *prayer of union*.

In this third stage, I become so absorbed in His glorious presence that I can no longer tell where I end and He begins. There is a level where, although dreams, visions, prophecies, and angels abound, it all pales in comparison to this *greater glory* of just being with Him. You learn not to cling to a vision or experience. You are no longer distracted with interpreting a vision or trying to understand a Scripture.

He shows up, and you are undone. It is deeper into simplicity.

Bernard of Clairvaux writes in the 12th century: "I have no desire for visions and dreams. Clever stories and twists of language, even angelic visitors, bore me. Jesus Himself absolutely outshines them all."[2]

Although we should always have our eyes and ears tuned to see and hear from God, there is a place where visions can hamper us, if we cling to them too closely. Revelation can become an idol apart from Him. Often, we get befuddled in our prayer time, because we get stuck trying to decipher a vision and forget about the presence of God. It is OK to ponder the meaning of a vision, but only insofar as there is glory on the pondering!

A number of mystics claim that visions should be rejected altogether, as the soul is prone to cling to them idolatrously. This view is not only extreme, but ridiculous and unbiblical. Visions are beneficial to the soul. They are necessary for communication with God and carrying out the work of the Kingdom. The apostle Paul clearly directs us to *seek after* spiritual gifts, especially prophecy, of which visioning is an essential ingredient (see 1 Cor. 14:1).

Nevertheless, the darker mystics (i.e. the ultra-penitent ones) were onto something when they suggested that visions can hinder us from going deeper. The balance lies not in rejecting revelation, but holding it with open hands. Besides that, since we only see in part, we need to let the heart of

Jesus be our compass and guide as we navigate the deep waters, not just a shadowy vision that may still be underdeveloped.

Bartholomew of the Martyrs gives a good balanced understanding of this issue:

> Many persons have thought that this exceedingly pure union may be disturbed by all kinds of images, even by those that, in themselves, are most useful and had formerly produced excellent dispositions in the soul.... But we must accept this with discretion, for fear of falling into error. If they mean to say that the soul, resting in and tasting this pure union, should not persist in seeking them or in retaining them for any length of time, but should rather close the eyes of the spirit to such objects, well, yes, I allow that this doctrine is generally correct. But if they go to the length of claiming that these images always hamper or impede the vigour and perfection of the union, I think that it is false. In fact, experience shows that often, when the soul goes out to God with fervour, a thought suddenly presents itself to the mind. For example: "This God became man for me, and was crucified." Not only does such a thought not hinder the union, but it contributes to strengthen the love and the admiration which enter into the union.[3]

Visions are essential in that they would propel us deeper into the heart and bliss of Jesus. They are frivolous when they become a riddle of ends in themselves and distract us from the main thing. Because of the nature of our ministry at Sons of Thunder and our desire to pursue the enigmas and wonders of Heaven, it is not unusual for us to receive five-page e-mails detailing someone's random dream or vision. It is amazing how we can obsess over details and *lesser* revelation, and miss the intimate depths of His glory.

In the place of union, you are not focused on anything else other than His thick, rich honey presence. Visions and inspired ideas may come, and this is great. We do not reject them, but we no longer have strength to pursue them. We are lost in love.

Union is a *lesser ecstasy.* There is continuity between union and rapture.

"I wish that I could explain, with God's help, the difference between union and rapture, or elevation, of flight of the spirit or transport for they are all one. I mean that these are all different names for the same thing, which is also called ecstasy," says Teresa of Avila. "[Ecstasy] is much more beneficial than union, its results are much greater, and it has very many other effects as well. Union seems to be the same at the beginning, the middle, and the end, and is altogether inward. But the ends of rapture are of a much higher nature, and their effects are both inward and outward."[4]

In mystic *union*, feelings of love are always produced as well as sentiments of pleasure—Teresa speaks frequently of the "great delights," though these are not always present in the prayer of *quiet*. "There is always a pleasure inherent to the prayer of quiet. But at times, and even when it is of considerable strength, we are hardly aware of it. In such case we should feel more enjoyment, although of another kind, when reading an interesting book or engaging in conversation," she says.[5] Nevertheless, the prayer of quiet brings sudden bursts of "ardent spiritual delights," especially for those more exercised in it. There are often intermediate stages between union and ecstasy.

The Prayer of Ecstasy

Ecstasy, stage four, is the highest state of prayer. It occurred to me one day that there is no need of going back and forth from recollection to meditation to union to ecstasy to union to meditation and back and forth and so on all over again. Why not get stuck in stage four? How would you like to live a stage-four lifestyle, a continual happy collision with the glory cloud of His presence? I think it is more than possible—it is probable if you set your heart to it. It is easier to get into the glory than it is to get out of it. Once you get lost in stage four, it is like being smothered in honey and stuck to the wall of the Most Holy Place! You don't have to come out of the glory zone unless you want to. You actually have to *make efforts* to climb out of His presence. It is hard to get out of the Garden of Eden—there is only one tree that you don't eat from. Only one, clearly marked exit door. When God brings you into a place of glory and blessing, He surrounds, sustains, and keeps you there, just as the mountains surround Jerusalem. Don't be afraid His blessings won't last. He is a consistent Father.

There are many people who have lived in a consistent state of tangible, ecstatic communion with God. Many have possessed the *gift of contemplation*—this is largely a Catholic term used for one who regularly experiences a constant awareness of the presence of God. Continual bliss. Such a one could also be termed a "mystic." Don't think this is relegated to a select few. Remember, it is a "gift"—the very same gift we were all given on the cross—you have this grace already, just choose to believe it!

We will discuss the intricacies of stage four in the coming chapters on ecstasy. But let me reemphasize that there is no formula for contemplative prayer. We do see similar phases of recollection, meditation, union, and ecstasy in the lives of many great saints who often discovered these paths separately from one another. Let us pause to discuss one of the most profound mystics of the 20th century, whose life was marked by deep, inner prayer and an outflow of signs and wonders.

Lessons From the Sadhu

Sadhu Sundar Singh (1889–?) is a great example of one whose lifestyle was saturated with ecstatic prayer. Singh was a living mystic who spent hours a day in unadulterated communion with Jesus. Born in India to an upper-class sikh family, Sundar's mother taught him to pray for hours a day from the age of five. He prayed so often that his father worried something was wrong with him. Miraculously converted at age 14 in an open visitation of Jesus Himself, Sundar was immediately shunned by his family for turning to his newfound faith. They poisoned his last meal, booted him from the home and the family inheritance, and launched him on his own to fulfill his dream of being an Indian holy man, or *sadhu*. Like the Hindu sadhus, he kept no possessions, but wandered the streets until people would take him into their homes for a blessing. Then he would begin to teach them about Jesus, seeing tremendous success in winning souls.

Besides meditating on the Scriptures for hours, and sometimes all day and night, Sundar would spend much time in silent prayer and recollection. He also entered deep contemplation and fasted regularly.

This was Sundar's regular model of prayer: He would begin by reading a chapter of the Bible, quickly at first, then returning to reread passages that caught his attention. He would then begin to linger and meditate for any given length of time that seemed fruitful for him. Then Sundar went into a state of silence and listening for about 20 minutes, when his own heart and mind were stilled before the Lord. Sometimes he would just enjoy the Lord's companionship at this level, or go into deeper contemplation, which is suggestive of *union*.

Often during contemplation, Sundar would be plunged into ecstasies. He considered them to be no different from the apostle Paul's Third Heaven visitations. Toward his latter years, Sundar would have as many as ten ecstasies a month. He said, "I never try to go into ecstasy; nor do I advise others to try. It is a gift to be accepted, but it should not be sought; if given, it is a pearl of great price."

Do not try to get into Heaven. Just believe you are already seated there, and you will begin to manifest an ecstatic lifestyle. For true ecstatics, supernatural happenings begin to occur more frequently in their lives the more they encounter the bliss. Such was the case with Sundar. Stories of miraculous rescue abound, as he was severely persecuted for his faith. In one village where he preached, he was dropped into a well full of decaying bodies and left for dead. An unknown figure freed him from the pit at night, and the next day he returned to preach on the streets again. The grand lama of the village, terrified at his miraculous escape from the well (which was still locked), had the only key to the well still hanging under the fold of his robe.

Sundar was also beaten, bound to trees to be eaten by wild animals, and was once tied up in a wet yak skin to be crushed to death as it dried up in the sun's heat. Often he was rescued by a mysterious, hidden regiment of Indian Christians. Once Sundar visibly encountered satan, who offered him millions of followers if he would only bow down and worship him. When Sundar realized what was happening, he rebuked the devil. Just as soon as he did this, he turned his head to find Jesus on his opposite side, face to face. The Lord told Sundar that he was well pleasing in His sight—to ask what he wanted and he would receive it. Sundar only wanted to walk with

Jesus like Enoch, sitting at the Master's feet and asking Him questions. From then on, Sundar was able to ask the Lord questions face to face, and he went on to extensively document these detailed visions and encounters.

One of his most profound experiences occurred in the remote Himalayan Mountains on an excursion to Tibet in 1912. Sundar was walking along when he fell into a hole. Surprisingly, there sat a hairy old man surrounded by numerous leather manuscripts. The man who lived in this cave claimed to be nearly 400 years old, and said he was baptized by the nephew of Francis Xavier, the famous Indian missionary, in the 1500s.

"I pray for Tibet night and day," said the old intercessor, whom Sundar called the Maharishi of Kailas. No one knows the whereabouts of Sundar Singh today. He mysteriously disappeared in 1929, and his body was never found. No one knew the details of his final whereabouts. Many speculated that he went to live with the Maharishi, or that he took the hermit's place. Others feel that Sundar was simply taken into Heaven like Elijah or Enoch.[6]

A present-day minister friend of mine has been taken to see this Maharishi, asserting that he is still alive, but that you can only find him if the Lord takes you there supernaturally. Other modern prophets, like Bobby Conner, have reported meeting hermits 200 years old. Bobby says that this man knew of yet another person who was 700 years old. In the glory, even the human body is preserved. Think of the millions of children of Israel who never even wore out their sandals for 40 years in the desert, because of the preserving glory of God that was with them (see Deut. 29:5). There is so much glory in Heaven that nothing can die or rot away. Moth and rust do not destroy. There was still so much glory residue leftover from the Garden of Eden that in the early days of the earth, men could live for hundreds of years. Because the glory preserves, God had to keep Adam from the Garden, so that he would not live forever in a sinful state.

There are hidden remnants of persons still scattered throughout the earth that have been alive for centuries. I once asked modern-day prophet Bob Jones about these mysterious old hermits, sometimes called *those who remain* (see 1 Thess. 4:15). Bob said, "They go back and forth." These are men who are so lost in the realm of God's glorious ecstasy that they are continually between Heaven and earth outside the boundaries of time and space.

Ulterior Paths to Ecstasy

Although we are discussing contemplative prayer, remember that silence and stillness are not the only outward means of engaging a trance. There is only one Way to the spirit realm, which is Jesus. The exterior motions are negligible. Sometimes high praises and radical movement work better than silence. As we mentioned in previous chapters, you can literally dance yourself into an ecstatic state before the Lord. This is called a *dance trance*. If you are having trouble "soaking" before God, try getting up and doing something different. It is high praise that gives us entrance into His courts (see Ps. 100:4). Sometimes you need to dance until you can no longer move, and then the trance comes on!

Lots of people who learned how to soak during the Toronto renewal years ago are no longer soaking—they are snoring! If you are stuck in your prayer life, try doing something different. Many times, an ecstasy can come on a person suddenly if he or she is listening to a sermon, or just has a random thought about God while walking in the park.

All of the disciplines of interior prayer are good and beneficial, but quietness and solitude is only one part of the picture. Soaking is especially good for the beginner, because we tend to live our entire lives striving in an exterior mode of operation. We've never learned to go deep and search out the Kingdom of God within. And so finding that place of rest and internal refreshing is important. Find a comfortable place to sit. Put on some soft music. Tuck away. Drink His presence.

But God does not expect us all just to sit quietly and enter into a vegetative state. All the external helps (music, quietness, whatever) cease to matter when our faith grows strong. There comes a place of maturity, wherein we are aware of God both within and without. The more our spiritual muscles are exercised in ecstatic prayer, we can go in and out of trances with ease. It no longer takes you an hour to get hammered. You are no longer bothered by noise or commotion around you. In fact, things that first seemed to distract you from God's presence now become the trigger for an ecstasy! I can go into trances now listening to heavy metal just as easily as a Kumbaya soaking CD (in fact, probably more so)! But that was not always the case.

Wherein I once spent long hours in silence to engage the ecstatic realm, there is now a *greater glory* that has been cultivated. I can now enter in much more easily—often at the drop of a hat. When I speak of spending hours in ecstatic prayer, people get a picture of sitting cross-legged in a closet all day. But instead, it may look like standing in line at Burger King, glazed over in a haze of bliss. Anytime you are whacked in the Spirit, you are in prayer. Whether you are actively working or sitting still, as long as you are plugged in and aware of His glory, then you are harmonized with Heaven.

Chapter 11

the distinguishing marks of ecstasy

Ecstasy is not just the highest state of prayer; it is also the highest state of life. God's plan is not just to revolutionize your prayer life, but to make your life a prayer. In pursuing the ecstatic realms of God's glory, we are really just pursuing a higher state of living. Ecstasies are experiences of stepping outside oneself. We become so hungry for Him that, like the bride in Song of Solomon 5, we are willing to leave our darkened house to find Him. We have to *leave ourselves* to find Him.

More clearly, we are really just going *inside ourselves*, exploring the Kingdom of God that now lies within us as believers in Christ (see Luke 17:21). We are cultivating a God-consciousness—complete and unadulterated awareness of Him at all times.

Ecstasy is about union with God. Jesus, the God-man, was the supreme archetype and embodiment of this union. Jesus said, *"I and My Father are one"* (John 10:30). But He did not desire this union between Himself and the Father only. In every way, He hoped to dispense this truth and experience to all men, *"that they may be one just as We are one"* (John 17:22).

Understand that true raptures are nearly always accompanied by manifestations. These include the basics—visionary encounters, drunkenness, falling, fainting, shaking, convulsing—to the far more bizarre level of mystical signs and wonders such as floating, glowing, emanating fragrances, etc. Don't confuse the exercises of an ecstasy with the ecstasy itself. *Ecstasy is simply the experiential position of divine bliss in which we are open to the glory realm.*

Later, we will discuss a number of miracles that accompany ecstasy, but for now, let us look at raptures themselves. There are levels of the supernatural you will never reach until you are overtaken by joy. In the realm of ecstasy, there is a merger of divine pleasure, revelation, miracles, love, and all virtue. The ecstasy of God is about everything that flows from open heavens. We don't pursue this state just for prophecy or miracles, but for the intoxication of His holy love.

To separate signs and wonders from the joy of His presence is one of the most horrendous things we can do. I know ministers who love to work miracles, but they limit their "joy intake" so as to look presentable before the crowds. There are lots of prophets today who are full of revelation, but they are not *happy!* I think this is a foolish dilemma. Why do we take one part of God (let's say His miracles), but not another part (let's say His drunken joy!)? I think we need to take everything God gives us in extreme proportions. But when ministers tone down their "joy level" to appear serious or to avoid offense, they have missed the very essence of the Gospel and their ministry becomes counterproductive in the long run.

Absorption and Concentration Ecstasies

There are a number of ways that theologians classify trances. Traditionally there are two types: *absorption* and *concentration* ecstasies. Absorption is a type of holy possession wherein the person loses herself entirely into God. In absorption, you can no longer determine heads from tails. You are intoxicated to the point of immobility. Totally gone.

But in a concentration ecstasy, the person's senses are supernaturally heightened beyond their normal range for a period of time. In *absorption*, you may just be vibrating on the floor somewhere lost in transit. In a *concentration* ecstasy, however, you are somehow able to do things with superhuman ability. You may begin to bang out prophetic words with lightning accuracy or be clothed with the Spirit of Might to perform wonders. Both of these states—absorption and concentration—occur along with intermediary stages between the two.

From personal experience, I have found that concentration raptures actually heighten my ability to annunciate and preach sermons with power and prophetic accuracy. The etymological meaning of the word *ecstasy* can also mean "extra stare"; you supernaturally *see beyond*. In concentration, you are still intoxicated, but able to perform with divine ability or insight. I rarely preach sober, but when I am in a concentration ecstasy, revelation flows faster than I can keep track of it. If I ever try to preach in an absorption ecstasy, it is nearly impossible and I am soon struck mute on the floor with someone else reading my notes for me.

Often I preach in concentration ecstasy; but in the same services, others may be flattened to the floor by the same Spirit of glory, in a state of absorption.

At times when the ecstatic Carmelite Mary Magdalen of Pazzi spoke in this state of concentration ecstasy, her speech was so rapid that it took six secretaries at once to write down her utterances.[1]

Absorption ecstasy is perhaps the most common form of trance. Joseph of Cupertino, the 17th century was often called The Gaper, because his mouth hung open in a glorious daze. Joseph's life was a long string of absorbed ecstasies. He would often spend a whole day zoned out trying to pull off a preach, struck mute at the lectern having only turned pages all day without a word spoken. Society of Jesus founder Ignatius, in the 16th century, was dismissed from his office for the same reason. Catherine of Siena's raptures came to such a point that she could not even finish saying the Lord's Prayer without going into an ecstasy. Understand that this is not unusual behavior for an ecstatic, though extremely puzzling for the uninitiated.

Often I will be zapped with an absorption ecstasy while trying to speak—not only am I suddenly left mute in the middle of a sermon, but unable to read or find easy verses in my Bible. At times, I have had to give away the microphone after only a few short minutes of attempted speech, forced to lie on the ground in pure absorption. At times, I have given up trying to speak at all, and instead made paper airplanes of my notes!

Complete and Incomplete Ecstasies

There is another way that theologians specifically classify absorption trances. One such way is whether an ecstasy is *complete* or *incomplete*. The determining factor is simple: it all depends on how useless you become when you get whacked!

A complete ecstasy is when you are totally plastered and incapable of doing anything. If you are still sober and your legs work, then your ecstasy is still incomplete! Drink deeper. In a completed ecstasy, you have been fully possessed by joy. Stand on that promise of Isaiah 35:10 that gladness and joy will *overtake* you!

Ligature and Immobility

One of the first things that begin to happen in ecstasy is that one's natural senses are rendered useless. "The senses cease to act, or they convey a confused knowledge only," says R.P. Poulan in *Graces of Interior Prayer*.[2] The eyes are often fogged over. Many close their eyes instinctively during inner prayer, which assists them in recollection and staying focused. But in ecstasy, the sight tends to go whether your eyes are open or not. Hearing goes slower than sight. Hands lose their grasp. As the ecstasy intensifies, the imagination and the sensitive appetites remain "drowsy."

People would sometimes walk in on Sundar Singh in mid ecstasy, giving an account of what they saw. Though his eyes would be open and he was smiling from ear to ear, they could not shake him out of his trance. One of the things that begins to happen in this state, is that *ligature* begins to set in. Ligature is the inability to do normal, ordinary inward acts, such as *think, read, or speak.*

Consider Teresa of Avila's problems when the heavy ligature set in:

> While seeking God in this way, the soul is conscious that
> it is fainting almost completely away in a kind of swoon,
> with a very great calm and joy. Its breath and all its bodily
> powers progressively fail it, so that it can hardly stir its
> hands without great effort. Its eyes close involuntarily, and
> if they remain open, they see almost nothing. If a person
> reads in this state he can scarcely make out a single letter;
> it is as much as he can do to recognise one. He sees that
> there are letters, but as the understanding offers no help,
> he cannot read them, even if he wants to. He hears but
> does not understand what he hears. In the same way, his
> senses serve no purpose except to prevent the soul from
> taking its pleasure; and so they tend to do him harm. It is

the same with the tongue, for he cannot form a word, nor would he have the strength to pronounce one. The whole physical strength vanishes and the strength of the soul increases for the better enjoyment of its bliss. The outward joy that is now felt is great and most perceptible.

However long this prayer lasts, it does no harm. At least it has never done me any; however ill I might have been when the Lord granted me this grace, I never remember an occasion when I experienced any effects from it.[3]

Notice Teresa makes no guarantees for your safety here! "At least it has never done me any [harm]," she tells us. But you get to swim at your own risk! You never know what's going to happen when you encounter the living God.

Ligature comes in degrees. During the prayer of quiet, ligature does not lead to absolute loss of inward activities. But the more we lend our will toward the glory, the greater we forfeit control of our faculties. We may begin to say a prayer, "but after two or three words, some unknown and secret force often stops us. We hesitate and stammer. A new effort then enables us to resume, and so it goes on. We should soon be weary if we attempted to continue the struggle. The proper course is to resign ourselves," adds Poulan.[4]

When ligature sets in, don't fight it! Don't try to collect yourself. Just roll with it. Ride the wave!

When we walk, speak, try to read, or look around at our surroundings, we may feel a diminishing of the glory. After a while, you learn not to engage in activities or conversations that would kill your buzz. At first, people may have difficulty entering back into the glory after they get distracted. But the more accustomed we become to a *habitual state* of this union, we can break off momentarily, then pick back up again instantly without effort.

As a rule of thumb, your mobility usually diminishes in ecstasy. This is why, throughout the ages, people have fallen over in the presence of God, just as His ministers were unable to stand under the heavy weighty cloud of glory that filled Solomon's temple (see 1 Kings 8:11; 2 Chron. 5:14).

The great doctor of the church, Thomas Aquinas, says it this way—while in simple union, the external senses are generally asleep, but they can awake if disturbed. But in ecstasy, they are totally suspended, in a state of anesthesia. He writes, "It is impossible for a man, in the present state, to contemplate the essence of God, if he be not estranged from the senses."[5]

Mystical theologian Albert Farges says this anesthetic state is "to such an extent that even violent disturbance will not arouse them. The hand of an ecstatic engaged in prayer may be approached with the flame of a candle, without his feeling the least pain.... There is alienation of all sensitive life, or life in relation, as though the soul were no longer in the body...." Farges reminds us that these ligatures are only byproducts of something greater: "Occasionally total alienation of the senses is only a secondary phenomenon, an outward effect, and echo, as it were, of the more wondrous inward marvels."[6]

Sometimes when God allows a dry season in our lives, it works to bring us into deeper ligature in the long run. Deserts have a way of diminishing the strife of our souls. And in ligature, the soul ceases from its works in the bliss. Mystical writer John of the Cross correlates the purgation of the senses in the dark night of the soul (an intense season of aridity that some people experience in their Christian walk) to the degree of imbibed ligature that is experienced. In other words, if you are going through a dark night, don't be too distressed. God is just preparing you for extreme intoxication! God can redeem years spent in dryness and depression, and turn you into the happiest, craziest drunk on the block.

Often, 16th-century mystic Philip Neri could not say his liturgy without someone else alternating the sentences with him, because he was seized with ecstasy. There was such an intensity that, "in order to repress these transports he was in the habit of turning from right to left and rubbing his head violently with his hand."[7] And "at other times he made such violent efforts to repress his fervour that his whole body fluttered and made the predellae of the altar tremble.... The server was obliged to pull him by the chasuble and remind him of the epistle or gospel."[8]

Alvarez de Paz was a 16th-century theologian, who at times would fall into ecstasy while preaching, having to be carried away from the pulpit for his ligature. He defines divine *ecstasy* as "the complete and entire uplift of the mind and spirit to God, which is necessarily accompanied by a total abstraction from consciousness and the bodily senses, an inevitable and essential concomitant circumstance of the overwhelming force and power of this very uplifting."[9]

In ligature, adds Poulan, "as a general rule, limbs become immovable, and one can neither speak nor walk nor make any gestures unless God restores this power miraculously. This last state is called *mobile ecstasy*."

Active Contemplation and Mobile Ecstasy

There is an ecstatic state wherein the body and the senses are still able to function to some degree. Much like a concentration ecstasy, you are still able to perform certain functions, if not better than usual in this state. This is called a *mobile ecstasy*. I believe that all people, regardless of career, calling, or occupation, can learn to function in their daily, nine-to-five lifestyle in a continual state of being whacked. Historically, this lifestyle is called *active contemplation*. For centuries, monks and hermits have desired to live a lifestyle of being completely tranced all the time. But the problem is, they still had to milk cows and do the natural business of life. In *active contemplation*, you are still able to perform your daily tasks, but all the while, you are staying blitzed in the glory while you work.

Many people wonder how they could possibly live a daily ecstatic lifestyle by shaking and baking in their office cubicle. Not all degrees of contemplation involve or require bodily manifestation. You can enjoy God's presence without going into fits. There is an inebriating peace of God that enables this active contemplation, allowing the subject to still perform their needed routines. You can get plastered in your cubicle! Even though such a person is still very much experiencing the tangible presence of God, he or she can function. There is a *practical mysticism* for all. Remember the practical life Jesus must have led as a carpenter.

Brother Lawrence, subject of *The Practice of the Presence of God*, is a prime example. Lawrence made it his sole occupation to live in the cloud of God's presence, even though he still carried out his daily, physical routines of manual labor as a monk. It was such a powerful thing to witness that people would travel for miles, just to watch him wash dishes whilst whacked! We may go in and out of various modes of absorption and ligature (unable to move or function), but don't think the goal of inner prayer is just to arrive at a vegetative state 24 hours a day. The goal is His glory. Sometimes the glory infuses and empowers us to do things.

There is nothing wrong with stopping everything (career and all) to lay down in God's presence. Many people have done this throughout history. As long as God calls you to this (for a season or a lifetime), and it is not just your own romantic idea, go for it. Not everyone is called to be a hermit. But do not think that something of this extreme nature should be frowned upon. It may not jive with our Western work-ethic mentality, but God calls many people to the contemplative life. Somehow God will even get food into your mouth during the process. Elijah pulled aside, and God fed him by the ravens. Ezekiel lay on his side for more than a year in his house, but God instructed him beforehand to store up food for himself. Everyone is called to some season of contemplation in their life—an extended period of soaking and interior prayer—whether for a few weeks or many years. For Jesus, it was 40 days in the desert. He never returned to carpentry.

Most people will never cut out months or years of their lives like this to enter an extended trance. Whether hammered on the floor or running the company, just learn to enjoy the glory where you are at and expect the unusual! Even Brother Lawrence, amid his daily work, would have outbursts of joyful manifestation. There were times when he had trouble containing his childlike explosions of ecstatic frenzy.

There is one more technical point we should make here. While *active contemplation* means you are practicing God's presence while still doing your daily work or chores, *mobile ecstasy* is a bit different. Mobile ecstasy more closely resembles a concentration ecstasy, in that it causes you to perform *accelerated* activity. It is more of a supernatural thing, because the senses are heightened, enabling you to speak and perform tasks in a super-human way. A more biblical terminology for this would be the influence of the *Spirit of Might* mentioned earlier. Although you are in a trance, you are still doing things, but you are operating in power. This is often what I experience when conducting a healing service. In mobile ecstasy, the mystic Catherine Emmerich (author of the book that inspired actor Mel Gibson's movie, *The Passion of the Christ*) would ascend to heights inhumanly possible, climbing columns in the church building like Spiderman.

"It is during divine ecstasy that the highest phenomena of the mystical life occur, for the most part. It is during divine ecstasy that the choicest gifts are bestowed, that the Bridegroom adorns the Bride with the most radiant argentry of light," writes theologian Montague Summers in his work *The Physical Phenomena of Mysticism*.[10]

Vital Signs Begin to Slow

As ligature and immobility begin to set into the body and soul, ecstatics often slow down to an impossible vital sign rate. Often their breathing seems to stop altogether, or it reawakens with great gasps. Heartbeats and pulses slow. In fact, heartbeats have been known to stop altogether, as well as the pulse. Bodily heat vanishes at times, and the extremities turn cold. This has happened to many great men and women of God, such as German mystic Therese Neumann only a few decades ago. Like many other ecstatics before her, she *died* over and over again, without dying.

"In some cases the soul seems to have gone out of the body, leaving it— whether or not in an ecstatic state—seemingly dead. In fact, experienced spiritual directors of certain mystics often must decide whether to call for medical assistance or to wait (medical treatment at the hands of doctors who do not understand 'mystical states' is often a torture for a mystic), despite the cries around him that 'She is dead!' or 'She is dying!'" writes Albert Hebert in his book *Saints Who Raised the Dead*.[11]

Teresa of Avila reports from her own experience that "sometimes my pulse ceases, as it were, to beat at all—so the sisters say." She has this to say about the diminishing of vital signs during ecstasy:

> In these raptures, the soul no longer seems to animate the body; its natural heat therefore is felt to diminish and it gradually gets cold, though with a feeling of very great joy and sweetness.[12]

Furthermore, Teresa writes in *Interior Castle*: "When He intends ravishing the soul He takes away the power of speech, and although occasionally the other faculties are retained rather longer, no word can be uttered.

Sometimes the person is at once deprived of all the senses, the hands and body becoming as cold as if the soul had fled; occasionally no breathing can be detected.... This supreme state of ecstasy never lasts long."[13]

In no way does this type of manifestation imply true medical paralysis of any sort. Absorbed in God's presence, the phenomena could be deemed "more apparent than real."

Another common condition of raptures is called the *spiritual sleep*. Here, a person remains in an ecstatic state, even though their natural body is asleep. Sometimes we are so overwhelmed by glory that our physical bodies cannot stand under the pressure and we naturally doze off. In this state, the soul remains conscious of God, even though we bed down for the night. This usually amplifies the dream realm. At times I experience this in such a way that I wake up completely drunk in the morning, as soon as my eyelids open, as if I were still in a powerful prayer meeting from the night before.

Overall, if ligature and immobility set in with enough intensity, the body does appear comatose in the deepest throes of a trance. I believe that in the coming years, we will see more and more prophetic people being pulled out of their bodies for such extended periods of time (and to such a great distance) that their friends and families will assume them to be in physical comas. Sometimes, they will go out of their bodies for weeks at a time, perhaps to fight great battles in the Spirit or to take on supernatural adventures with the Lord. They will often bring back revelation and power to the earth realm. For those who have read Rick Joyner's *Final Quest*, imagine going into the spirit realm on a real, cosmic battle such as this, and leaving your body for weeks at a time to do it! Sometimes the bodies of these ecstatics will go with them, and they will seemingly disappear for long periods of time.

The child prodigy painter Akiane, who began painting masterpieces in pre-school, usually goes into Heaven to receive the subject matter for her work. Once her parents could not find her, and after scouring the block and calling a swarm of policemen, Akiane casually reappeared. Despite all the commotion and her parents' fears, Akiane had just been in Heaven—including her physical body.[14]

There are great heavenly excursions on the horizon for those who value God's presence above all else. Although you may appear comatose to the outside world, ecstatics usually do not lose consciousness on these journeys.

I have found that sometimes I remember everything that was going on around me during a trance, and at other times I do not remember a thing that was happening in the outside world. Our good mystical doctor Teresa of Avila further describes the loss of senses and mobility during rapture:

> During the rapture itself, the body is very often like a corpse, unable to do anything of itself. It remains all the time in whatever attitude it was in when the rapture came on it; seated, for example, and with the hands open or closed. The subject rarely loses consciousness; I have occasionally lost it entirely, but not very often and only for a short time. Generally the senses are disturbed; and though absolutely powerless to perform any outward action the subject still sees and hears things, though only dimly, as if from far away. I do not say that he can see and hear when the rapture is at its height; and by 'its height' I mean those times when the faculties are lost, because closely united with God. Then, in my opinion, it neither sees nor hears nor feels. But, as I said in describing the previous prayer of union, this complete transformation of the soul in God is of short duration. While it lasts, however, none of the senses perceives or knows what is taking place. We can have no way of understanding this, while we are on earth at least—or rather God cannot wish us to, since we have not the capacity for such understanding. This I have learnt for myself.[15]

Length of Ecstasies: Lost Forever in the Glory

The length of raptures varies from case to case. In general, ecstasies have tended to last for short durations at time. Teresa of Avila speaks of them lasting for about half an hour, but in this she was speaking of the length of their most *intense* duration. At other times, she speaks of longer periods:

> You will ask me, Father, how it is that a rapture sometimes lasts for many hours. Very often my experience is as I have

described it in relation to the previous stage of prayer, the rapture is discontinuous. And very often the soul is absorbed, or—to put it better—the Lord absorbs it into Himself. But after He has held it for a moment, the will alone remains in union.[16]

Generally, people tend to experience an intense wave of rapture that it is interspersed among the steady backdrop stage of *union*. Union, as we earlier mentioned, is a type of *lesser* ecstasy. But there is no reason for dismay! If God only blasts you for half an hour at a time, it is just to pace you, so that you don't get killed by His pleasure.

Keep your standard high. I believe we can get whacked, stay whacked, and never go back. I am a firm believer in getting stuck in the ecstatic realm. If I have a dry day anymore, I count it a write-off! I have determined to drink my fill of His wine every day.

Many have experienced ecstasies for several days at a time. Three consecutive days of trance were experienced by Catherine of Siena and other great men and women of God. Colomba of Rieti was whacked for five days straight. Ignatius was in rapture for eight days; St. Colette for 15 days; and Mary Magdalen of Pazzi was toasted on the Ghost for 40 days straight! For many of the saints, this was a very frequent occurrence. Catherine of Siena was seen in ecstasy thousands of times. Hermann Joseph, in the 13th century, was whacked almost every day in his later years, and Maria von Moerl was in *continuous ecstasy* all the time for the last 35 years of her life.

Imagine 35 years of straight bliss! But that's not all. The state of ecstatic contemplation is just a foretaste of the beatitude of our souls to be experienced forever in Heaven.

> *You will show me the path of life; in Your presence is fullness of joy; at Your right hand are pleasures forevermore* (Psalm 16:11).

The way of Jesus is the way of ecstasy. It is the path of life. And when we abide in His presence, we abide in *fullness* of joy. How much joy is available in this place? How much pleasure? Eternal *pleasures forevermore*.

Lengthening the Silver Cord

The more concentrated the joy becomes in rapture, the more our spirit thirsts to be propelled toward Heaven. Assisted by the Lord in this matter, the ecstatic can often leave his or her body without dying. This principle of *spirit travel* is very biblical. Your spirit man is actually at home in Heaven, which is where your true citizenship is located (see Phil. 3:20). You are a spirit walking out a natural existence. Furthermore, your spirit is already *positionally seated* in heavenly places (see Eph. 2:6). The blood of Jesus has already put you right in Daddy's lap, and trances merely enable you to bypass the soulish restrictions of mind, will, and emotions so that you can enjoy that heavenly estate that is already yours.

Some time ago, I was in a meeting in Cleveland, Ohio, when I saw a large angel in the room swinging a silver cord around himself. Suddenly, the angel snapped the cord at me, and it connected right into my chest. Then the Lord spoke: *"I am lengthening the silver cord in this hour."*

Immediately, my mind was brought to Ecclesiastes 12:5-7 (NIV):

> ...*man goes to his eternal home.... Remember Him—* **before the silver cord is severed,** *or the golden bowl is broken; before the pitcher is shattered at the spring, or the wheel broken at the well, and the dust returns to the ground it came from,* **and the spirit returns to God** *who gave it.*

In the spirit realm, there is a silver cord that connects your body to your human spirit. Even new agers are well aware of this. When your silver cord is severed, then you die. Your spirit is disconnected then from your flesh. Our friend Todd Bentley, a well-known evangelist, has had witch doctors astroproject into his room a number of times while on the mission field. Astroprojection is an illegal form of spirit travel, wherein one's spirit is able to leave their body through deviant means. Once when Todd could not get the person's spirit to leave his room, he threatened, "Leave, or I will cut your silver cord." At this point, the witchdoctor understood that he would die if his spirit was disconnected from his body, so he left the room.

In another instance, one of our associate ministers, Shawn Gabie, had just finished a series of meetings with me in Canada, in which there was intense warfare. We were seeing male and female prostitutes get radically saved and delivered. Yet immediately afterward, their pimps began tracking them down. Several people were stabbed and beaten, simply because of all these prostitutes coming to Jesus. After Shawn had finished some of the meetings in this town, one of the witches behind this persecution effort astroprojected into his room. Because of the harvest involved, there was intense warfare. Even in the demonic realm, spiritualists and mediums have learned to separate from their bodies, and there is a silver cord that keeps the flesh and spirit connected, so that people do not die.

Whenever you are praying for the dead to be raised, you should pray that the person's spirit returns to the body. The silver cord may need to be supernaturally reattached. This is so difficult a miracle, it is nearly impossible (if ever) for the enemy to effect a demonically inspired dead raising. It is a fact that witchcraft can manipulate a "zombie" type of resurrection, but it is not a true resurrection miracle where the person's spirit is reattached. God can easily reattach flesh to spirit. There are hundreds of resurrection stories throughout church history. Many were so dramatic that decayed flesh was reconstituted and revived. In some cases, bodies had rotted all the way to a skeletal state, but like Ezekiel's valley of dry bones, God miraculously recreated flesh and revived them.[17]

The Lord was telling me something powerful through this angelic visitation in Ohio. He is about to release us to travel farther in the Spirit than ever before. He is lengthening the silver cord so we can go deeper into Heaven. Even the occult world has learned to illegally spirit travel. But God is about to plunge His Body into a far deeper experience than any diviner or sorcerer could possibly obtain or imagine. His church is about to be exploring heavenly places to such a degree, it will be like nothing the earth has ever known before. Surely this is what the prophet saw in Joel 2:28, and what the forerunners at Pentecost proclaimed in Acts 2:17:

And it shall come to pass in the last days, says God, that I will pour out of My Spirit on all flesh; your sons and your daughters shall prophesy, your young men shall see visions, your old men shall dream dreams.

This outpouring of the Holy Ghost is far more than mere tongue-talking and *nabi* prophetic utterance that bubbles up by blind faith. As His Spirit is poured out, we will traverse the realms of the supernatural and step farther outside ourselves in trance like no previous company has ever done throughout history. This is the people of Joel 2:2, *"a people great and strong, the like of whom has never been; nor will there ever be any such after them, even for many successive generations."*

Imagine a people who can travel forward and backward in the Spirit. Time is no limitation. I have personally traveled into revival meetings from 50 years ago. Many people have traveled hundreds and thousands of years across time and space, as the Old Testament prophets did. We can also travel geographically and strategically, even as Elisha was able to travel by spirit into the enemy king's war chambers.

In the realm of trance, your silver cord is lengthened, and you are afforded the ability to *translate* or *transport*. This means your spirit could go to Heaven or to some other geographical place on earth. Even your physical body could jump with it, from one place on the map to another like Philip the evangelist in the Book of Acts. These translations allow you to traverse time (both forward and backward) and see all manner of insights that are humanly impossible to fathom. These are not strange concepts. Even the demonic world has understood this better than the church. Astroprojection is just an ungodly counterfeit for your God-given ability to move in the Spirit.

Brace yourself for spirit travel. The moment you begin to be sucked out of your body can be a fearful thing. It is quite common to resist at first. The realm of rapture opens vast doors of possibility, but it takes courage to jump into a million volts of bliss. The key is simply to ride the light, and press in only to those doors where the Lord Himself chooses to lead you in the experience. Teresa says:

For this, some courage is certainly necessary, since the joy
is so great, that at times the soul seems on the very point
of completely leaving the body.[18]

Revelation in Ecstasy

All manner of revelatory experiences accompany ecstasy and mystical
prayer. These include discernment of spirits, dreams, prophecy, visions,
infused knowledge, gifts of understanding, and all manner of divine insight.
Many books have been written about these gifts and experiences, especially
during the past few decades of the prophetic movement. Revelation *always*
accompanies true ecstasy.

In Peter's encounter on the rooftop in Acts 10, the apostle was in a
trance when he saw a vision. A large net full of non-kosher animals came
descending from heaven, and the Lord instructed Peter to eat. You will
never have a trance without God giving you something to eat! It is usually
a mysterious meal. It seemed quite strange for Peter to eat these creeping
critters. Likewise for the apostle Paul, he was shown such mysterious revelations in his Third Heaven rapture that he "heard inexpressible words,
which it is not lawful for a man to utter" (2 Cor. 12:4).

You will always come out of ecstasy with a deeper revelation of Jesus
Christ. An ecstasy that does not result in some type of encounter, visionary
experience, or deeper understanding of the Lord's nature is probably not an
ecstasy at all. Teresa writes:

In ecstasy come true revelations, great favours, and visions,
all of which help to humble and strengthen the soul, to
make it despise the things of this life and more clearly
realize the greatness of the reward that the Lord reserves
for those who serve Him.[19]

Earlier I said that the stage of *meditation* (the prayer of quiet) is the
backdrop for most visions. This is true in *quantity* but not *intensity*. At that
level, still much of your visionary material was being filtered through your
own mind and imagination. Of course much of it was *valid*, just not as

potent. Those visions were more intellectual. In rapture, however, there is a culmination of all the revelatory activities of recollection, meditation, and union—the best of every stage is somehow reconciled and thrown back to you at a much higher level. The revelation is purer and almost always comes unexpectedly, without looking for it.

Encounters in the prayer of quiet differ from ecstasy so much as to seem clumsy in comparison. Spiritual realities are much more vivid in deep trance—the things you see are instantly burned onto your soul like a tattoo. You never have to guess about this level of revelation. It is pure Third Heaven stash. It becomes part of you instantly. Teresa of Avila says the following:

> While the soul is in this suspension, our Lord favours it by discovering to it secrets such as heavenly mysteries...they remain so imprinted on the memory that it never forgets them. But when the visions are intellectual they are not thus easily related.... I think that if the soul learns no mysteries at any time during raptures, they are no true raptures.[20]

The visions and encounters in ecstasy come from a place so *beyond yourself*, there is absolutely no question to their origin. In the lower stage of meditation, you are still exercising your spiritual senses and sorting through your own ideas. This is perfectly fine and natural! Don't be afraid to experiment. But, in ecstasy, it is like God reaches down and taps you on the shoulder. You are suddenly shocked by revelation that never could have entered the mind or heart of humankind.

Drink until you see things!

We must remember, overall, that prophecy is only *one small part* of ecstasy. Ecstatic prophecy is important, but eventually, prophecy, like all the other gifts, will pass away. The goal of ecstasy is not to help you prophesy better, minister better, or see the future. The goal of ecstasy is an abiding intimacy with Jesus.

Ecstasy in the Arts and Sciences

Ultimately, God wants lovers who will invade every sector of society with the colors, sounds, and ideas of Heaven. He wants to permeate our universe with His. Out of the state of ecstasy, the arts and sciences will be unlocked like never before. It was *in a trance* that Peter saw a vision in Acts 10, and visual revelation is usually deposited while in this state of intimate suspension with the divine. Likewise, this state of bliss opens the windows of our soul to think differently, as our intellect and emotions experience freedom from the frustration of the fall.

> *For the creation was subjected to futility, not willingly, but because of Him who subjected it in hope; because the creation itself also will be delivered from the bondage of corruption into the glorious liberty of the children of God. For we know that the whole creation groans and labors with birth pangs together until now* (Romans 8:20-22).

The mind and spiritual senses of man were subjected to futility through Adam's fall, along with all of creation. Your mind was limited to operate at about 10 percent capability when humanity was booted from the Garden of Eden. On your happiest day, you have not experienced 10 percent of the bliss God has intended for you. And your ability to create sounds, music, and colors has not even scratched the surface of its full potential. But in this realm of glory, our mind, will, and emotions begin to taste that glorious liberty of freedom from the frustration of a fallen world. Of course, God had to limit our ability to understand and create, so that we wouldn't destroy ourselves (for example, we could have invented nuclear bombs 6,000 years ago!). But now, as free children of God, our minds and even our artistic/creative abilities are restored in this realm of glorious ecstasy.

Ever notice how the best artists tend to be a little crazy? There is something about stepping outside of ourselves and past the natural limitations of our mind that enable us to access heavenly glory. In that realm of God's creative Spirit, we can pull songs, books, business plans, mechanical inventions, and many more innovations right out of Heaven.

The great composer Handel was in a state of ecstasy when he wrote the *Messiah*. Locking himself away for 24 days and barely eating, his servant finally found him weeping after he wrote the famous Hallelujah Chorus. He said, "I did see all Heaven before me, and the great God Himself."[21]

Handel had pulled this work right out of Heaven. And he brought it right to the streets. He was accused of prostituting the sacred by bringing songs of Scripture into the worldly theatres of his day—but in this Handel was a revolutionary. One newspaper critic asked whether "the Playhouse is a fit Temple...or a company of players fit ministers of God's word."

Self-righteous women of high class, surely possessed by jezebel, would host tea parties or sponsor dueling performances on the days of *Messiah* performances, just to rob Handel of an audience. His critics hired boys to rip down performance posters. Nevertheless, crowds flocked to the performances. They would weep and stand to their feet. A clergyman, William Hanbury, in 1759, said you could not find a dry eye in the entire place during the performance. John Wesley also praised Handel's work. One nobleman commented on how entertaining the piece was, and Handel replied, "My Lord, I should be sorry if I only entertained them; I wished to make them better."[22]

Artists are known to lose themselves in their work. And creativity that supersedes skill comes from a place that is unexplained for most artists. It is said that the great painter and sculptor Michelangelo experienced ecstasies during his artwork. At the age of 60, he would attack a piece of marble, knocking off more chips in a couple hours than could four men who were stronger and younger in age.[23]

Secular artists often pursue demonic trances, through drugs or other means, in order to create outside the parameters of status quo. Consider all the rock stars who are demonically inspired to the degree they can lure multitudes of youth into darkness with them. How much more creativity should we have as Christians, tranced out on the Creator Himself?

Isaac Newton invented the science of mechanics, most of the science of optics and theoretical physics, and he pioneered the understanding of gravitational laws. But did you know that Newton believed the Bible literally, studied it daily, and he wrote more than one million words of notes on his Bible studies? Newton never separated his scientific and theological studies, as he saw them as one in the same. Newton was thoroughly intrigued by the prophets, devoting countless hours to understanding the Book of Revelation and the Book of Daniel. It was during Newton's attempt to figure out the 70 weeks of Daniel that he accidentally *invented* calculus!

Or consider the great scientist Blaise Pascal. He founded probability theory, invented a precursor to the modern computer, and wrote a book on geometry in his teens that modern scientists scarcely believe a boy of his age could have conceived. His work on atmospheric pressure, the equilibrium of fluids, and the science of vacuums was unprecedented. And yet he was such a devout believer and apologist for his faith that he considered math and geometry "mundane" in comparison to the important business of saving souls.

Pascal was not only a Christian, but a radical one, belonging to the Jansenist movement—those shaking prophets who manifested the glory in the streets of France with ecstasies, healings, levitations, and all manner of signs and wonders following!

Pascal understood the bliss of Heaven, and that for worship to be true, God could only be pursued for one reason: the quest for happiness.

> All men seek happiness. This is without exception. Whatever different means they employ, they all tend to this end. … The cause of some going to war, and of others avoiding it, is the same desire in both, attended with different views. The will never takes the least step but to this object. This is the motive of every action of every man, even of those who hang themselves.[24]

Full Blown Rapture

Until now, we have not delineated a difference between *ecstasy* and *rapture*. To prevent confusion, we have used broad terms to digest a basic understanding of mystical prayer. I have said that ecstasy, or rapture, is simply the fourth and highest stage of interior prayer. Most writers and theologians do use the two terms indiscriminately, considering them one in the same. In some schools of thought, however, there are distinctions made between the two.

Raptures are the *highest peaks* of the ecstatic state, which can come on violently, suddenly, and without the person's ability to resist them. Ecstasies on the other hand are generally more tranquil and peaceable. But the distinguishing mark of rapture is this element of suddenness and surprise.

Famed theologian Thomas Aquinas says a rapture is accidentally more than an ecstasy, since it comes on with an aggressive onrush of the divine. He says, "Rapture involves something more than ecstasy, for ecstasy precisely speaking implies a transport out of and beyond oneself, so that a man is removed from his normal well-ordered condition, but rapture entails something of violence."[25]

Theologian Cardinal Bona, in his work, *On the Discerning of Spirits,* holds a similar view, saying:

> This then is the essential difference between ecstasy and rapture. The former estate withdraws the mind from the senses more gently and (as it were) persuasively. The latter more powerfully and not without violence of a kind, so that rapture adds this to ecstasy, namely it catches up the resistless soul with power and might, most rapidly and by divine compulsion sweeping upwards and onwards away from the senses and all things appertaining, so that it is swiftly carried and borne aloft to the enjoyment of the intellectual vision and aflame with the ardent love of heavenly things.[26]

In the writings of Teresa of Avila, ecstasy and rapture are synonymous. For the most part, I hold this same general view. But we could more accurately say that rapture is the *most intense portion* of an ecstasy. This also seems most in line with Teresa's writings, because she spoke of times when sudden transport would come on with a shock, which she could not resist:

> Here there is no possibility of resisting, as there is in union, in which we are on our own ground. Against union, resistance is almost always possible though it costs pain and effort. But rapture is, as a rule, irresistible. Before you can be warned by a thought or help yourself in any way, it comes as a quick and violent shock; you see and feel

this cloud, or this powerful eagle rising and bearing you up on its wings.[27]

We now see that these peaks of rapture, perhaps, are the encounters of short duration, which lasted usually no more than half an hour for Teresa. When we speak of extended ecstasies, we should know that raptures can also occur over longer periods of time, but usually they are intermittent against the backdrop of a general state of ecstasy or union. Extended rapture would likely kill you. Teresa herself died after 14 hours of straight rapture. I do not propose that the rapture killed her, but who am I to say? Teresa herself said, "There are some people who have such poor constitutions that one experience of the prayer of quiet kills them."[28]

Eighteenth century priest and writer Giovanni Scaramelli says that raptures can last for several hours, days, or weeks. But consonant with Teresa, he says they generally last no longer than half an hour at their height, eventually ebbing back to ecstasy. Montague Summers writes in *The Physical Phenomena of Mysticism*, "The fact is that the human soul and body are unable (unless, indeed, miraculously sustained) to stand the sweetly violent influx and onrush of the Divine."[29]

Summers adds, "A rapture cannot be resisted, no, not for a moment, even if the ecstatic be in company with others, or in a public place. It over-whelms and overpowers."[30]

As a young boy growing up in an old-time Pentecostal church, I have clear memories of people bolting around the building, almost uncontrol-lably, when swept into these rapturous states. Mary Magdalen of Pazzi, during her raptures, was so overwhelmed that "she rushed to and fro, up and down the stairs and along the corridors, through the nuns' garth, with inconceivable rapidity, often tearing her habit in her haste, and throwing to one side anything which came in her way," says Summers. He compares her story to Spanish mystic Miguel de Santos, in the 17th century who "when he fell into rapture, often during prayer...ran through the cloisters at wonderful speed uttering loud cries of joy, and darting hither and thither with such celerity that nobody could stay him.... These saints, sublimest mystics both, were literally inebriated with God."

Summers adds that raptures are almost always accompanied by some type of supernatural phenomena such as levitation or other ultra-human activity. He writes, "Many mystical theologians conceive that there cannot be rapture without the manifestation of extraordinary phenomena."[31]

Flight of the Spirit

Yet another term used synonymously with ecstasy and rapture is *flight of the spirit*, but we will narrow our use of the term in this section. *Flight of the spirit* refers specifically to *transport* or *translation*, two terms we outlined earlier when discussing spirit travel (you may want to refer back to the *Lengthening the Silver Cord* section of this chapter). Flight of the spirit deals most explicitly with the travel of the human spirit during ecstasy. Here are a few helpful definitions, both of which are types of spirit flight:

> *Translation* involves *only* the spirit traveling—either to Heaven or to another earthly place. In translation, your physical body stays put.

> *Transport* is a trickier word! A full transportation is when your spirit *and your body* jump geographically together, such as when Philip disappeared from the Gaza road and reappeared in Azotus in Acts 8. It is possible for your physical body to also be taken into Heaven with your spirit.

Understandably, all of these terms get jumbled together to generally describe ecstasy. Except for this brief section, we will continue to use the terms loosely for sake of convenience. My point in clarifying the terms is this: If "rapture" can be deemed the *peak of ecstasy* then these "flights of the spirit" are consequently the *peak of raptures*. In other words, rapture is the highest state of ecstasy, but *flight of the spirit* is the highest state of rapture. Albert Farges says this flight of the spirit—this rapture of raptures—is what the apostle Paul experienced when traveling to the Third Heaven, unknowing as to whether he was in or out of the body:

> The flight of the spirit is a rapture of special intensity which throws the mind into a stupor and a thrill of wonderment. The soul seems to separate itself from the body and to take its flight towards its blessed home; even the body at times follows the movement of the [spirit] and finds itself raised from the earth by means of a divine attraction acting contrary to the laws of gravity. This is the marvelous phenomenon of levitation.... We only mention it here because it is the outward and visible sign of what happens inwardly, when the soul is raised by God to those heights which approach so closely to the beatific vision.[32]

These intense raptures unleash days or weeks of aftershocks. After a tremendous rapture, Teresa of Avila talks about being shattered for days. Off the back of just one intense rapture, I have had weeks of general ecstasy and union, as well as entire shifts that altered my entire natural and spiritual life.

Chapter 12

the supernatural phenomena of ecstasy

W e have already covered a number of common manifestations associated with ecstatic prayer, from immobility and ligature to the ability to receive rapid-fire revelation and heightened spiritual senses. But there are far more demonstrable, outward miracles that accompany raptures—supernatural activity of the most unusual variety.

Among the physical phenomena associated with ecstasy are levitation, glowing auras, supernatural fragrances emitted from the body, miraculous healings, and many other wonders. In ecstasy, "the Lord can 'exalt' the human body to operations above natural abilities, without destroying the body which is being exalted," writes researcher Albert Hebert.[1]

"A mysticism without supernatural phenomena is a starveling. At best it is limited and lopped, however interesting it may prove within its own set bounds. A study of mysticism which ignores so vital a constituent can but be, so to speak, introductory, and who would linger in the narthex when he may approach the altar?" says mystical writer Montague Summers.[2]

Much of what you read in the following chapter can pose severe difficulties for your *unbelief.* The drink of faith requires a great suspension of the human analysis. Be assured as you take this plunge that we are pulling examples from well-documented stories and reputable sources. There is no need for hype when our God is fully capable demonstrating unparalleled marvels. Mystical theologian Herbert Thurston points out the following: "A prejudice against the literature of the supernatural seems to have been created by the uncritical methods of hagiographers (historians of the miraculous). Living themselves in an atmosphere of unquestioning faith, they have accepted and repeated without discrimination all the marvels of which they found any record, and it has rarely occurred to them that the statements of virtuous and well-meaning people are sometimes as untrustworthy as those of unscrupulous romancers."[3]

Our faith must be radically childlike, and yet we also want truth and authenticity when documenting the workings of God. In this chapter, a number of extraordinary phenomena of clear historical repute will be examined. Amazing supernatural abilities come out of the glory realm. When the intoxicating realm of His glory possesses us in trance, we become open vessels to release heavenly activity.

Glowing: The Exastrapto

The act of glowing, or exuding a bright luminescence, is a miracle that sometimes accompanies ecstatics. It is no less than the bright shining shekinah glory that emanated from the face of Moses.

"When Moses came down from Mount Sinai his face shone so brightly that two horns of fire seemed to come from his head. The people were awed, and the Bible says that to hide this radiance Moses had to wear a veil. So also have saints in ecstasy or levitation appeared gloriously radiant," writes Hebert. "St. Philip Neri was often raised in ecstasy and surrounded by light. King Ferdinand I of Naples saw St. Francis of Paola elevated in light when the saint was in the King's palace."[4]

Remember that our Lord Himself was shining with the bright glowing *exastrapto*, the lightning-like visible glistening of the glory that shone both from His face and His clothes in Luke 9 on the Mount of Transfiguration. The Bible even says in the Book of Daniel that the righteous will shine like the stars in the heavens, while Song of Solomon says we will one day shine as bright as the sun (see Dan. 12:3; Song of Sol. 6:10).

Princess Elizabeth of Hungary (1207–1231) would have roses miraculously appear in her apron as she went about bringing food to the poor. Her spiritual director, Father Conrad, told of her raptures of love, "and how her countenance would seem to give forth rays of light after her secret prayers."[5]

One of the most famous glowers, Seraphim of Sarov, an Orthodox Christian monk, said that the very purpose of life is to be filled with the Holy Spirit. At times, Seraphim was witnessed in a transfigured state with his face glowing like the sun in ecstasy.

"Ecstasy is sometimes accompanied by a luminous phenomenon wherein the saint's head is aglow, a light might encompass the entire body, or rays either come toward or proceed from the body. Sometimes called 'luminous effluvia,' it is recounted numerous times in the lives of the saints and has been described and attested by persons of unquestionable integrity," writes researcher Joan Cruz in *Mysteries, Marvels, Miracles: In the Lives of the Saints.*[6]

Some people brightened entire rooms for certain periods of time that rays of light shone from their bodies. Philip Neri, John Ruysbroeck, Gerard Majella, Teresa of Avila, and Ignatius of Loyola are just a few of the people who have emitted luminescence. These manifestations vary in length, but seem to occur only in the state of ecstasy. Montague Summers says it is "a luminous irradiance, not rapid like a flash of light, but steadily shining, bright and clear," and according to Benedict XIV, the miracle usually lasts "of some sensible duration of time."[7]

When we discuss this miracle, we are not merely talking about someone's "glowing personality" or their joyful countenance. This is like a person's body becoming a human light bulb. "Ecstatics have been seen, although more rarely, to light up the whole church or cell during their nocturnal ecstasies," writes Albert Farges.[8]

Consider this interesting case. A blind man, John of St. Samson, lived in a French monastery in the 17th century. Although he did not have the use of his eyes, he was keenly aware of when his physical body would sometimes begin to glow. His close friend, Donatien of St. Nicholas, gives us this eyewitness account:

> In these extraordinary states we often saw his face glowing and radiant with, I know not what kind of luminous ray, which used to be reflected from it. I myself witnessed it with a number of other trustworthy religious. No one can doubt the truth of this since John himself wrote in his Mystical Cabinet that he often experienced this light, which spread from the center of his soul to all his faculties, even to the exterior senses.[9]

Ability to Endure Heat and Cold

A number of believers have been endowed with a supernatural ability to endure extreme heat and cold during raptures. This was a very common occurrence during martyrdoms, when saints were often burned at the stake without effect, or forced into freezing rivers without harm. Even the apostle John was reportedly boiled in oil, yet he walked away from the event without harm.

As for the stories of martyrdoms, these accounts of enduring extreme temperatures usually happened in a state of ecstasy. Christina the Astonishing (1150–1224) would go into wild ecstatic frenzies. Often she would jump into freezing rivers or hide in burning ovens to avoid the smell of "sinful human bodies." Her outlandish behavior was the result of peculiar spiritual sensitivities. Although she was odd, her sanctity was without question and there are firsthand accounts of her life, verifying her miracles.

Like the children of Israel in Babylon—Shadrach, Meshach, and Abed-Nego, who were cast unharmed into the fiery furnace—so have many martyrs in ecstasy been unscathed by flames. One of the first martyrs of the church, Polycarp, in A.D. 155 could not be burned in the fire kindled for him by his persecutors, according to the Christians in Smyrna, who watched his execution. Eventually the men gave up trying to burn him. Instead, they stabbed him with a dagger, and his blood extinguished the flames.

Incendium Amoris

There is another odd manifestation found in some mystics called *incendium amoris*, or the fire of love. In deep ecstasy, many saints have felt a fire of passion burn unnaturally hot within them, so as to require physical cooling. This interior passion somehow produces physiological heat. It is reported that the 20th century stigmatist and sometimes floating mystic Padre Pio's body temperature would occasionally hit 120-125 degrees that would break thermometers.[10] This is humanly impossible.

In *The Physical Phenomena of Mysticism*, Christian researcher Herbert Thurston writes of effects in the lives of the mystics, saying, "when some transport of love took possession of their souls their countenances became inflamed, that they could hardly endure the clothing which seemed to stifle them, and that in the coldest of winter weather they threw open doors and windows, panting for air and half unconsciously seeking...relief...."[11]

Stanislaus Kostka, a 16th-century Jesuit, "was so violently assailed by the love of Our Saviour as often to faint and to suffer spasms in consequence, and he was obliged to apply cloths dipped in cold water to his breast in order to temper the violence of the love he felt," writes Francis de Sales in the *Love of God*. Furthermore, when his superior once found him in a garden, amidst a bitter cold blowing wind, Stanislaus told him simply and straightforwardly, "I am burning, I am burning."[12]

Philip Neri, in the 16th century, often left his garments open from the waist up, even in considerable snowfall. He would also leave open his windows at night in the cold of winter because of the intense heat he felt.[13]

Here is a testimony given of mystic Mary Magdalen of Pazzi in her beatification proceedings from her biographer and confessor Father Cepari:

> Sometimes, overpowered by this excess and abundance of this love, she said, "I can no longer bear so much love, retain it in Thyself"; and through the great and consuming flame of this Divine Love which she felt, she could find no rest, but tore her clothes, went into the garden and tore up the plants, or whatever came to hand. In the midst of winter she could not bear woolen garments, through that fire of love which burned in her breast, but cut and loosened her habit.[14]

Tangible sparks of fire have been seen to emanate from certain mystics at times. We see this recorded among the apostles on Pentecost with flaming tongues of fire resting on their heads as they began to get whacked in the Spirit. But also the Desert Fathers in the third century show examples of manifestations of fire. It also occurs in the life of Philip Neri as sparks shot from his countenance, and in the life of Lutgarde of Aywieres, in the 13th century, when a flame of fire shot right from her mouth, causing a fellow nun to drop in a dead faint.[15]

The actual rise of felt bodily temperature that sometimes accompanies divine love is more than mere sensuality or carnal desire. The intensity of incendium amoris has even scorched the clothing of many saints.

Serafina di Dio was a Carmelite who died near the end of the 17th century. When "rapt in prayer, the community saw her with her face glowing like a red flame and her eyes sparkling fire. 'It burned them if they touched her', and she declared that she was consumed and shriveled with heat, that her blood was as molten lead in her veins.'"[16]

Maria Villani of Naples, in the 17th century, was deemed "'a furnace of love, a furnace thrice-heated.' When she drank cold water a sizzling sound was heard as if the liquid was being poured upon red-hot iron." The physiological heat produced from her spiritual experiences required her to drink about three and a half gallons of water a day.[17]

Some believers' bodies stayed warm for several days after their death, even in the middle of winter. Some were still warm when they were placed in the tomb. Doctors occasionally reported *burning their hands* on their cadavers, forcing them to wait until they cooled down a bit before performing autopsies or preparing them for burial.

Francesca dal Serrone was a Franciscan stigmatist who died at the turn of the 17th century. When she bled from her wounds, the blood was so hot that it cracked the earthenware vessel used to catch it, so that a metal bowl had to be used.[18]

Inedia: Prolonged Fasting Miracles

Under the heavy influence of the glory, a number of ecstatics have experienced miracles of *inedia*, or supernatural, prolonged fasting. There are examples today, too numerous to list, of vibrant churches in Africa and elsewhere in developing nations where believers are undertaking fasts of up to 90 days. Brother Yun of China, in his popular book *The Heavenly Man*, shares about a 74-day fast he undertook while in prison for his faith, even while being tortured. Not only did he abstain from food, but also from water! Afterward, he was immediately clothed in power and led all of his fellow prisoners to Jesus in one fell swoop.[19]

Medically it is impossible to go without water more than four days, without experiencing dehydration and death. But the mystics of the church, especially those who experienced intense ecstasy, have undergone inedia that would be nearly impossible to believe if it were not so well documented. Alexandrina Maria da Costa went from March 27, 1942, until her death on October 13, 1955, with only communion as her food each day. That is more than 13 years! The German mystic and stigmatist Therese Neumann (1898–1962) is perhaps the most amazing modern example. She went *40 years* without food and *more than 35 years* without water, except for communion! Both she and Alexandrina experienced no ill effects from this fasting, nor did their bodies ever eliminate waste. Although Alexandrina was bed-ridden, Therese carried on regular daily activities, and amazingly, was rather plump in size![20]

According to Dr. Imbert-Gourbeyre in his book *La Stigmatisation*, the following persons went without physical nourishment for these respective periods of time:

- Angela of Foligno, 12 years
- Catherine of Siena, 8 years
- Catharine of Racconigi, 10 years
- Domenica dal Paradiso, 20 years
- Rosa Andriani, 28 years
- Dominica Lazzari, 14 years
- Louise Lateau, 14 years
- Elizabeth of Rente, 15 years
- Lydwine, 28 years
- Nicholas von Flue, 20 years

Furthermore in the case of Theresa Neumann, when making her daily communion, she usually did not receive the entire wafer of bread given to most people. When in deep ecstasy, she would eat an entire host, but otherwise, it was not possible for her to swallow more than a small fragment of it—about eighth the size of an ordinary communion wafer.

Understand that there is such grace for these fasts that the person rarely, if ever, desires food. Usually the opposite is true, and the thought of food is repulsive. Some saints would wretch and dry heave at the mere sight of food during these supernatural fasts.

"The Eucharist," said Catherine of Siena, "refreshes me to such an extent that it is impossible for me to desire any kind of corporal nourishment."[21]

Miracles of Sleeplessness

An ability to function without sleep is another miraculous ability that sometimes accompanies the glory. Evan Roberts, the great Welsh revivalist, spent many successive nights deep in prayer, as did Francis Xavier. Xavier, a miracle worker, often levitated in ecstasy, leading an estimated 700,000 to faith in his era. He would spend countless nights in prayer without becoming worn out. The American healing revivalists of the 1940s and '50s, such as Jack Coe, A.A. Allen, and others would often minister at a horrendous pace, going night after night on only a few hours of sleep. This took its toll on some of them, but in the glory realm, it is possible to go at a superhuman pace.

Saints like Peter of Alcantara, who was a friend of Teresa of Avila, operated on less than an hour of sleep a night. Teresa of Avila says he spent *40 years of his life* with no more than an hour and a half of sleep each night.[22] Therese Neumann rarely ever had need of sleep, and Dominican nun Catherine de Ricci slept only an hour a week.[23]

The need for sleep simply vanishes for some mystics. In this respect, it is best to regard this miracle not as a *lack of sleep* per se. "Perhaps one ought to say no *need* for sleep.... This is not insomnia, which brings about a low state of health, depression, and even a settled melancholy," adds Montague Summers.[24]

Catherine of Siena barely slept half an hour every two days, "yet she was never weary, or harassed, or fatigued." Franciscan nun Colette spent an entire year without sleeping. Agatha of the cross, of Spain, who died in the 17th century, did not sleep at all the last eight years of her life.

The Sleeping Preachers

On the other end of the spectrum from sleeplessness, there have been entire movements of believers who did things while they slept! In rural 19th century America, there began to emerge groups of simple, ordinary farmers by day who rose up in the middle of the night to become dynamic preachers—all in the middle of sleep!

These sleeping preachers would sit up in bed and begin to deliver impassioned sermons, with near photographic memory of the Bible, only to wake up the next morning with no recollection of the previous night's events. There were even a sub-group of Amish Mennonites who were formally known as the "Sleeping Preachers Amish." Their group began in the 1870s when a few of them developed this unusual mode of delivering sermons in bed. They called this "spirit preaching." They would fall asleep early in the evening then rise a few hours later in a trance to preach *on the themes of repentance, spiritual renewal or the return to simpler lifestyles.* This phenomenon was also observed among other Christian groups at this time.[25] One of the leading sleeping preachers, John D. Kauffman, started an independent congregation in Illinois in 1907 and the movement spread. Although the practice has been virtually abandoned, there were still nine Sleeping Preachers Amish congregations throughout the Midwest as of 1992.

In 1688, 16-year-old Isabeau Vincent ignited the French prophets of the Cevennes as she began preaching in her sleep. A book in 1815 appeared in London titled *Remarkable Sermons by Rachel Baker, and Pious Ejaculations, Delivered During Sleep*, by Dr. Mitchell, M.D., Dr. Priestly, LL.D., and Dr. Douglass. It tells of a girl born in Pelham, Massachusetts, in 1794 who, at the age of 17, began having trances every evening in her sleep wherein she preached for the span of 45 minutes. She awoke each morning unable to remember anything. It reports that "several hundreds every evening flock to hear this most wonderful preacher, who is instrumental in converting more persons to Christianity, when asleep, than all other ministers together whilst awake."

The book also records a Pennsylvania weaver in 1774 and a 16-year-old English boy in 1759 who both preached in their sleep.[26]

Major Perry, an African American farmer, delivered sermons every night in his sleep for 45 years beginning June 16, 1880. An uneducated farm hand, Perry could neither read nor write, but preached every night in perfect English clearer than his everyday dialect. Soon after falling asleep, he would announce a hymn by number and meter, pray, and announce his text, by book, chapter, and verse. He would read the Scripture, announce a theme, then begin the sermon. Every night he preached a different sermon.

Perry traveled extensively on "sleep tours" and would allow the public to watch him preach as he snoozed every Monday through Thursday. His wife would pull a curtain around his bed in the church or meeting hall where spectators would gather until he fell asleep. Then she would open it up for all to see. Because of skepticism, "while he was preaching, they would twist his hands, hold fire to his skin until it blistered, pinch him until he turned black and blue, do anything they could think of short of high crime to try to break his trance. They never did."

In 1925, Perry died in his sleep in the middle of a sermon.[27]

Walking Through Walls

In the state of ecstasy, we are overcome by the glory to such a degree that at times, persons are capable of penetrating solid objects such as locked doors or other material substances. This has been done by a number of saints, including 17th-century Peruvian saint Martin de Porres and 16th-century nun Rita of Cascia.[28]

After His resurrection, Jesus appeared to His disciples in a closed-door room after apparently walking through the wall (see John 20:26)—yet He had substance because He sat and ate with them. As we are harmonized with the glory realm, the natural body is capable of abilities more common with our future glorified bodies.

Our friend and fellow minister, David Herzog, reports a case in which he and his passengers should have had a collision with another car. But miraculously, their vehicle passed completely *through* the oncoming car and out the other side like light moving through a glass of water. Missionary Heidi Baker, an ecstatic who has planted thousands of churches, shares a similar experience in Mozambique, Africa. Her large vehicle supernaturally passed through an impossibly narrow opening, while she was being chased by gunmen. Later she returned to the spot to measure it, confirming that her vehicle should have been utterly crushed.

There are similar stories of "accidental" miracles of this nature, including cases where certain persons were miraculously uninjured by bullets that somehow passed through them. But saints such as Martin de Porres had so many occurrences of passing through locked doors that he seemed to access the miracle at will.

Of equal interest in this study are those cases of *invisibility* that have marked the lives of some saints. Whether transparency likewise allows them to move through solid objects, that much is not clear. In the relatively modern example of 18th-century wonderworker Gerard Majella, fellow monks were searching for him one day until finally they believed him lost. When he finally showed up for communion, they asked where he had been. He told them he had been in his cell, but they had already searched that small, 10-foot-square room repeatedly. In fact, everyone in the monastery had been looking for him that day. Finally Gerard confessed, "Fearing to be distracted from my [prayer] retreat, I asked Jesus Christ for the grace to become invisible."[29]

Bilocation Miracles

An experience among miracle workers and ecstatics that is almost common throughout history is that of *bilocation*—when a person's body appears in two places at one time. This happened to many great champions of the faith. A bilocation miracle occurred to our friend Jeff Jansen, a minister, who showed up at a Christian conference while he was elsewhere eating with some friends at the same time. During the meeting with these friends, Jeff was eating some supernatural manna that had fallen earlier in a revival meeting. But at the same exact time, he was signing into the conference and greeted about 30 separate people that he knew, simply saying, "Bless you" to them.

Jeff only remembers eating with the couple; however, he says he was intoxicated on the glory at the time and that he *felt like he was two places at once.*

Mary of Agreda was a mystic who spent 46 years of her life in a Spanish convent. Over an 11-year period, Mary made 500 bilocation trips to North America where she was instructed by Jesus to teach the Native American people. There were countless eyewitness reports of her appearing, and she was able to describe in great detail all the things she saw.[30]

"God in His omnipotence may delocalize the material substance, which then by Divine Agency would be rendered capable of receiving definitive, and consequently multiple location," writes theologian Montague Summers, regarding such miracles.[31]

It seems that bilocation, for some, can become a resident gifting to use at will when the Lord leads. The biographer of 13th-century wonderworker Anthony of Padua gives us a startling example. While preaching one Easter Sunday in the Cathedral of Montpellier in front of clergy and a huge crowd, Anthony suddenly remembered he was expected to be elsewhere that day. He had forgotten an appointment to sing mass in the choir of a neighboring monastery. Sinking back into his pulpit, Anthony drew his hood over his head and remained silent for a long time:

> At the moment when he ceased speaking in the cathedral, though all the while visible to the congregation, he appeared in the monastery choir among his brethren and sang his office. At the close of the service he recovered himself in the pulpit of the cathedral and, as his chronicler says, finished his sermon with incomparable eloquence.[32]

During the writing of this book, I had a bilocation experience of my own that occurred on my 31st birthday. Scheduled to visit Ireland for a conference over the summer, I felt that the Lord would have me pull back from the originally planned European itinerary. While I cancelled my own itinerary, we still sent our associate ministers David Vaughan and Justin Abraham to conduct the meetings. While I was at home, part of me longed to be in Ireland, as if I was still supposed to go—although the Lord had clearly told me not to do so.

While David was speaking at the meeting in Ireland on my birthday, he and Justin *felt like I was with them* the entire day. They were even joking, saying, "The spirit of Crowder is with us!"

That day in the meeting, David looked up, surprised to see me standing there, against the wall in the church. He assumed I had come to Ireland as originally planned to surprise them. But then, just as soon as he saw me with his open eyes, I vanished into thin air. He had so clearly seen me that he said something about it to the people there.

Moments later, he looked back, and there I was—again standing against the wall in the very same place David had seen me earlier. At this point, he knew something miraculous was happening. Meanwhile, I was sleeping at home in America. That morning when it occurred, my wife dreamed that we were *planting two seeds*.

How would you like God to enable you to plant two separate seeds at once? Does this explain how God can sometimes tell you to do two things at once? Expect more than just bilocation in these days. Miracles of trilocation (three places at once) and even multilocation (showing up numerous places at once) will be more and more common as the glory of God invades the earth.

Body Elongation

One of the least common but most unusual physical phenomena to accompany ecstasies has been the elongation of the human body. There are few recorded examples of this in the lives of the saints, but there is sufficient record.

Veronica Laparelli, in the 17th century, was known for remarkable ecstasies that would last up to three days in length. She was reported on several occasions by eye-witnesses to have risen from the ground in rapture. In one instance, fellow nun Margherita Cortonesi observed, "when she being in the trance state was reciting her Office alternately with some invisible being, she was observed gradually to stretch out until the length of her throat seemed to be all out of proportion in such a way that she was altogether much taller than usual." To be sure that Laparelli was not rising from the ground again, as she was accustomed to doing at times in ecstasy, the sisters checked her feet to see that they were on the floor. Just after the event occurred, they took a yard stick to measure her. "She was at least a 'span' [ten inches or more] shorter. This we have seen with our own eyes, all of us nuns who were in the chapel."[33]

Similar instances of elongation happened to Laparelli at other times as well. Furthermore, there is the story of Domenica dal Paradiso, whose biography was published by B.M. Borghigiani in 1719. Borghigiani writes:

> Amongst the other remarkable features which have been recorded concerning that intoxication of divine love from which Domenica suffered, one was this, that the spouse of Christ was made to appear a taller woman than she really was. Castiglione, her director, noticed the same thing happen in many other ecstasies, though she returned to her normal stature afterwards, as soon as she was herself again.[34]

It would only be reasonable to assume God can change one's shape in ecstasy, if the demonic realm so clearly illustrates counterfeit behavior. Body elongation and even shape-shifting has long been known to occur by diabolical means among mediums and spiritists. Some have been able to stretch or grow by a foot or more by demonic influence. Shape shifting in particular is a well-documented demonic manifestation, and not just the product of over-imaginative simpletons. Though this is not the forum for a lengthy discussion on the subject, and skeptics will consider it ludicrous, but the existence of *werewolves*, for instance, is very much real. Scholarly studies of documented lycanthropy (transformation into a wolf) have been written by noted secular and religious researchers well into the 20th century. Only the popularization of scientism in recent decades has left the church unaware of these sorts of things. Satanists are well aware of the reality of shape shifting.

Patricia King, a well-respected prophetic minister today, gives testimony of encountering a demonized person during a revival meeting in Europe several years ago. In front of her eyes, the person began to morph into a wolf in a way that is physically impossible to do, apart from supernatural forces.

"This man started to manifest a werewolf spirit. His hair bristled back, as if ears were formed out of his hair. Fangs came down out of his mouth. He got on all fours and started howling like a wolf," said Patricia, who commenced to cast the evil spirit out.[35] Many people pretend these things do not exist, not necessarily from unbelief but because of fear. But do not let these things scare you. The powers of darkness are no match for the power of the Lord. With Christ in you, you have the true source of authority: the raw power of God.

Furthermore, we should remember as a Biblical precedent how the Lord seemed to have a *changed appearance* very often after his resurrection. If the enemy can effect shape-shifting, it is only a counterfeit to the resurrection power available to believers. Jesus was not recognized by the women at the tomb, who mistook Him for a gardener, nor was His appearance realized by the disciples on the road to Emmaus until he revealed Himself to them at the table. Jesus "appeared in a different form" to the two disciples (Mark 16:12).

The Odor of Sanctity, Flowing Oil, and Incorruptibility

Another miraculous occurrence that is quite common and often accompanies ecstasy is the release of supernatural fragrances, traditionally called the *odor of sanctity*. Countless saints throughout history have experienced this, but it happens frequently today. There are numerous accounts of saints in medieval times experiencing heavenly fragrances, but this has also happened regularly in the corporate meetings of modern revivalism all the way back to the Great Awakenings. I cannot count the number of times I have personally encountered it in meetings, prayer, or in daily life.

As a relatively new believer, I once had a dream in which a church leader was anointing various people with fragrant oil. In the dream, we were laughing every time the smell wafted our way, because the fragrance itself had the ability to impart joy. Suddenly, without realizing it, she had placed the oil on my head. I was instantly translated in such a way that I scarcely have terminology to describe it to this very day. In all my studies, I have never found a case like it. I instantly awoke from the dream, but lying there on my bed, I was drenched in this deep fragrance in the natural realm. Not only did the aroma seem to penetrate through my entire body, soul, and spirit, but the fragrance seemed to be life itself, as if it were the very living essence of the Holy Spirit Himself. It was both smell and transformative experience all in one.

Not only have heavenly fragrances emanated from the bodies of devout persons or filled their rooms. In the case of stigmatists, the blood flowing from their hands and feet is often supernaturally aromatic. Even the dead corpses of many great men and women of God have emitted supernaturally sweet smells for years, decades, and centuries after death. Rose, sandalwood, myrrh, verbena, and all manner of delicious floral aromas can come seemingly from nowhere, including the deceased cadavers of pious individuals.

This leads us to discuss yet another strange supernatural phenomenon. Many men and women who spent a lifetime of being infused with the Holy Spirit in ecstasy were somehow unable to decay after death. This miracle of *incorruptibility* is surprisingly well-attested among the faithful. The bodies of some saints have been supernaturally preserved without rotting for literally *hundreds of years*, while many others lasted for months on end without the slightest sign of decomposition. This is no psychosomatic event! There is sometimes the absence of rigidity or rigor mortis (the bodies remain flexible), as well as the inability for the blood to congeal for many years, all without the application of embalming fluids or other natural preservations. The bodies of some saints were cut or punctured years after death, and blood would run in liquefied form, never having dried up. Sometimes flasks of their blood were kept, which never dried for decades and longer.

Obviously, this seems a morbid subject to address, but there are sound theological principles behind it. As previously discussed, the glory of God *preserves*. Humankind's body was never intended for death, had we ever dwelt in the glory of Eden. Even after death, the resident glory on an individual's body can slow the natural processes of corruption. This miracle seems to me a prophetic sign, symbolizing to the world in some small way that the Christian will live forever.

Fragrant oil is also known to pour miraculously from the tombs or bodies of long-departed believers. These are not demonic signs to endorse a "saint cult." These are valid miracles of God, and such manifestations are recorded in the Christian church well back to the second century. Countless persons have received supernatural healing by visiting the dead bodies of powerful saints. I am not sanctioning *relic worship*, nor do I endorse any kind of prayers to the dead, which is spiritism. However, just as the bones of Elisha still carried a tangible, resident anointing powerful enough to raise another man from the dead—so do the relics of dead saints often carry a resident anointing of *Jesus Christ* still latent on their physical matter (see 2 Kings 13:21). Relics are not magical, nor should they ever become an idol. As a point of contact, however, they can function similarly to the laying on of hands in a Charismatic impartation service. Or like the lifeless aprons and handkerchiefs touched to the body of the apostle Paul, they can transfer healing virtue or cast out devils (see Acts 19:12).

Overall, there is no need to look for the living among the dead! You've got all the power of God you need when you invite Jesus into your heart. And there's no need to wait for your death bed for miracle oil to flow! Flowing oil is a common manifestation among many Spirit-filled believers today. Miracle oil flowed from the hands of evangelist A.A. Allen in his famous tent revivals, and it flows from the heads, hands, and Bibles of many others today. In some places, it even flows from the walls and ceiling rafters in copious amounts, such as in the small Puerto Rican church of Pastor Dennis Roja today. We have seen oil flow with our own eyes in some of our own meetings. These types of manifestations are not intrinsically linked to ecstasies, but can often accompany them.

In a meeting in New York, during the writing of this book, we experienced a tremendously intense level of corporate ecstasy during some celebratory meetings with our friend Benjamin Dunn over Easter weekend. At the height of the sessions, we began to notice that a mysterious fluid was dripping copiously from the walls of the church from top to bottom, back to front of the building.

Gold Dust Miracles

Many have seen and heard of the gold dust miracles that are happening so widespread in the Body of Christ today. It is becoming so frequent, it is impossible to document even a fraction of these. It seems that the gold dust begins to come whenever there is a tangible atmosphere of God's glory. And very often, it is passionate praise and worship in an atmosphere of rapture that unlocks these miracles. Our friend Joshua Mills has gained quite a reputation for getting covered in gold dust. It often comes in thick flakes all over his body, his clothes, his Bible, and elsewhere. Joshua has been stopped in airport metal detectors because, unbeknownst to him, the gold dust thickly appeared on his calf underneath his pant leg! I have personally watched Joshua go from zero to covered in a fraction of a second. His focus is continually on worship and intimacy with Jesus. In the bliss of first love, miracles happen.

Joshua has also been covered in blue sapphire dust, silver dust, and other colors. His wife, Janet, has been covered in purple glory dust, and very often rainbow- colored gold appears. This is in addition to the many diamonds and gemstones that have appeared in their meetings. Joshua has also watched as unopened bottles of water turned into real wine on several occasions. At times, wine and oil have both flowed copiously from his hands.

One of the forerunners who brought the gold dust manifestation into popular awareness was the late minister Ruth Ward Heflin. Latin American revivalist Silvania Machado was also well known for the manifestation, as was the late Baptist evangelist Bob Shattles and others. But it seems gold dust is showing up on people just about everywhere we go these days. We see it regularly to varying degrees in our own meetings, as well as those of our friends in ministry.

Creation of Matter: Teeth, Gemstones, and Weight Loss Miracles

Although these types of manifestations do not seem to be happening in the dry, "teach-only" type of prophetic streams, we are beginning to see a phenomenal demonstration of creative miracles in those ministries who are pursuing the deep realms of experiential glory in this hour.

In our own meetings, we have seen the Lord bring an extraordinary release of creative miracles that involve either the creation or destruction of physical matter—something that completely defies the laws of physics. We have seen diamonds and gemstones appear in our meetings. Almost everywhere we go, we see the Lord work instant weight loss miracles, from five pounds up to 30 or 40 pounds at a time, instantly vanishing from bodies.

In terms of dental miracles, it is not uncommon for us to see gold teeth, silver teeth, and even brand-new white teeth appear in mouths. We have even seen dark teeth turn white and crooked teeth turn straight. We have watched diamonds grow, even doubling in size on rings (sometimes when this happens, it breaks the metal prongs). We have seen gemstones turn colors, as the Lord changes the substance and adds value to the stones.

We have even watched physical rain fall in buildings on a number of occasions. We have countless testimonies of metal plates, metal pins, metal rods, and other metal implements dissolving out of people's bodies. And in terms of creative healing miracles, we have watched tumors dissolve before our eyes, dozens and dozens of deaf ears open up, and sight restored to eyes. All of these are genuine, creative miracles. The more our hearts catch aflame for the bliss of Jesus, the more addicted we become to living in the atmosphere of His glory. Miracles cannot help but happen in this place of intimacy.

But it seems the Lord is pulling out all the stops in this hour. He will not be satisfied with just a few gemstones falling. When God shows up, He shows out. At the time of this writing, more than 40 perfectly cut 50-carat gemstones have recently fallen at a church in Coeur D'Alene, Idaho. These have been dropped by angels, and the estimated value on some of these has ranged up to $20 million individually. In addition, there are resident glory portals opening in some locations today, such as the small Puerto Rican church mentioned earlier pastored by Dennis Roja where the supernatural oil flows. In addition to oil and myrrh flowing from the walls, the rafters, and Roja's Bible, there have also been hundreds of large and small gemstones, sequins, and flecks of onyx that have supernaturally appeared. Expect these types of outpourings to cause great controversy in the coming days!

We could write volumes on creative miracles. We have a hunger to demonstrate the phenomenal in this day. The point I hope to make is that there is a correlation between the miraculous and ecstasies. In ecstasy, our heart is aflame with passion, which opens us up to the glory realm. And the glory realm is the realm of wonders.

Gifts of Healing

Gifts of healing frequently accompany ecstatics. Both I and my associates, as healing revivalists, operate in this gift regularly and have seen thousands healed of many sicknesses and infirmities. Although healing may come with the package of mystical prayer, it is not intrinsically connected to it.

It should be said that healing virtue is part of the overall operation of a Spirit-filled lifestyle. Divine encounters and a continual dwelling in the glory always *accelerate* the frequency and intensity of healings. But these experiences are not necessary for healing to occur. Raw faith is sufficient to affect healing. Jesus spent a huge percentage of His public ministry time healing the sick. Anyone in ministry who does not heal the sick is not walking *fully* in the ministry of Jesus. Since gifts of healing, like gifts of prophesy, are not fundamentally linked to mystical prayer, we will not focus heavily on them in this chapter. Besides this, there are many phenomenal teaching resources available through many ministries, including our own, that are helpful in moving into divine healing. I avoid extensive teaching on the subject now, only to make room for the broad panorama of other bizarre physical phenomena of mysticism that get far less coverage in today's church.

Nevertheless, the more time you spend intoxicated in the bliss, the more faith you will receive to heal the sick.

Miracles of Instant Virtue

It is common, in experiences of rapture, to receive one of the greatest graces of all: a download of instant virtue or character. There are countless stories of instant deliverance from drugs, alcohol, marital struggles, anger, jealousy, immoral lifestyles, and all manner of addictions. This is the essence of grace: that we do not fix ourselves! Jesus does it for us through the ministry of His Holy Spirit. By means of pleasure, God causes us to realize that our virtues depend solely upon Him.

So many people feel they need to struggle for years in their own human effort or counseling to overcome their issues. But the Gospel is all about grace. Jesus wants to take care of these things for you in one sweeping stroke of His love. Perhaps you've wrestled for decades with pride, fear, doubt, religion, or other obstacles in your walk with the Lord. Only remember that His name is Jehovah M'Kaddesh, *the Lord who Sanctifies.* He is the one who gives holiness as a gift.

There is sweet, secret nectar that makes holiness attractive and desirable. It is called the *bliss of God.* This is the essence of holiness itself. Many confuse holiness with the outward form of legalism or external religious activities. But holiness is not the absence of sin; *it is the presence of God.* A lot of people think they are in God's will because they have gotten rid of a lot of sin, but emptying out all your bad stuff does God no favors. You can be empty of sin, but still be empty! Don't be empty; instead get full of God! Getting full of God is the only thing that matters, and being filled with the Spirit always produces fruitfulness and wonders.

Virtues have long been imparted to believers very suddenly in the glory. Rapid transformation can take place that would otherwise take years. Even Teresa of Avila speaks of instantaneous *changes in the soul* that take place in union. With every deeper level of the glory we encounter, character faults that have resisted change for years can be suddenly corrected with no industry of our own.

Good character cannot be *earned*. Years of suffering and trials are not the fires that forge Christian virtues. Of course God will use these things if we want to do it the hard way. Virtue, like ecstasies themselves, is a *grace gift*. You have already been made completely virtuous at the cross of Calvary. The more you drink His presence, the more you believe what He has already done. The more you believe, the more virtue you manifest.

"The effect of a Divine Ecstasy results in an increase of holiness and a greater desire for God," writes Montague Summers.[36]

When you try to earn your bliss, you have missed the picture altogether. Christ has cut the covenant of pleasure with us already with His own blood. You have been co-crucified and co-buried with Him. Your old man is *dead*. You cannot earn or strive to put on good character and virtue. Simply believe He has done it for you.

In the same way, we cannot work to enter ecstatic states. "We play no part, as I have said, in bringing a rapture on," says Teresa. "Very often there comes an unexpected desire—I do not know what impels it—and with that desire, which permeates the whole soul in a moment, it begins to become so weary that it rises far above itself and above all creation."[37]

Receive your free gift of grace. Receive that happiness that breeds true sanctity in your life. Sanctification is dependent upon happiness.

"What He chiefly desires for us is eternal happiness, and therefore sanctity," writes mystical theologian R.P. Poulan.[38]

Why earn from God what you already have for free? Again, Teresa says, "In one of these visits, however brief it may be, the Gardener, being as He is the Creator of the water, pours it out without stint; and what the poor soul has not been able to collect in perhaps twenty years of exhausting intellectual effort, the heavenly Gardener gives it in a moment."[39]

The Bloody Bliss

There are rare occasions when the glory comes with such intensity that an ecstatic's body is left worse for wear. This is not a regular occurrence, but usually follows an extreme *encounter* with the Lord or an angel. Physical weakness sometimes follows an intense ecstasy. Teresa of Avila would feel pain in her wrists and throughout her whole body as if her bones were out of joint, even a day later. The miracle-working priest Dominic of Jesus-Mary, in the 17th century, in a more radical case, would have extreme pains, bruised limbs that made it difficult to move, and even vomited blood at times. French Carmelite founder Madame Acarie's biographer writes, "God's onslaughts took her with yet greater impetuosity and with such a violent trembling that it made her bones crack, and wrung from her piercing cries as if she were being stabbed to the heart.... She expected that they would cause her death, so much so that she once told M. Fontaine, her confessor at Pontoise, that on several hundred occasions she had gone to bed not expecting to live in the morning."[40]

I have woken up many a morning after a wild and crazy, radical glory meeting with my bones or feet or some other body part aching terribly. It was like a Holy Ghost hangover. This is simply the *bloody bliss*. The glad price we pay to stay whacked all the time!

Poulan says, "Divine ecstasy is far from being prejudicial to the health." It is imperative that we dispel the common myth that all ecstatic manifestations are painless and comfortable. This is not Disney Land; it is still earth. Some kids gorge themselves at Disney until they vomit. The Second Great Awakening started at Cane Ridge, Kentucky, with thousands of people experiencing wild convulsions, faintings, flailings, and jerkings that lasted for hours and left many people feeling "extreme soreness" afterward. When God moves, human flesh quivers.

This is nothing to fret over—the Lord never forces Himself upon us in a way that is slavishly constricting, as is the norm for the demonic realm.

"Where the Spirit of the Lord is, there is freedom" (2 Cor. 3:17 NIV). But when He shows up, you remember that you are clay.

Any manifestation which causes pain to a believer has, in many pop-deliverance classes, been ruled as a tell-tale sign of the demonic. In a theology of "cast everything out you don't understand," it is considered normative *discernment* to rule out the spiritual benefit of anything that is accompanied by pain. But just because something appears to physically hurt does not mean you have judged it with *spiritual* discernment. We must go to the word of God on this matter. Daniel had an intense encounter with the Lord, which caused him to faint and left him *sick for days* (see Dan. 8:27). John the Beloved fell down *as though he were dead* after seeing the King of glory. This was not an ordinary swoon (see Rev. 1:17). And neither of these men ever fully understood the visions they saw! But they recognized God's hand in it.

As a healing revivalist, I will be the first to say that the glory always brings healing, wholeness, and life to your body, soul, and spirit. But I can also say, paradoxically, that the Lord can do whatever He wants to do! While the general precept is that God always heals and comforts us, there are also deeper realms of glory that incinerate human flesh! Tie a rope to your ankle before you go into the Most Holy Place.

Wounds of Love

One should ask whether it was comfortable for Ezekiel to be bedridden for a year and a half at the Lord's bidding. Do you think a nutritionist would approve of John the Baptist's God-inspired diet of bugs? The point is not to glorify strange activity or suffering, but only to affirm that the movements of the Holy Spirit do not *always* guarantee that a person's physical body will not experience harm or brokenness.

I remember when our associate, David Vaughan, once cracked his rib cage from roaring so violently in worship whilst whacked in the Spirit. All he could do was laugh about it afterward. When angels show up in meetings, people can get thrown around furiously. I cannot count how many heads I have seen bounce off concrete floors during impartation services, where the person felt no pain whatsoever. All sorts of flips and contortions take place in the glory where people *should be injured*, but are protected. Thrown through stacks of metal chairs, bodies crumpled over pews—there is an occasional bruise or bump, sometimes a little blood, but usually God's manifestations do no harm.

In the throes of divine ecstasy, we must also remember that our own soul is still active to a degree, and our own human resistance or involvement in the encounter is usually the reason to blame for difficulties. It is usually the *resistance* to the ligature of bliss that causes injury, not the opposite. We must remember that by *precept*, God does not send affliction. That is the enemy's domain and the legal wages of sin. But our God is not a tame God. We should never limit Him. When we draw close, anything is possible. Be careful!

The Stigmata

Another supernatural phenomenon that accompanies ecstasy, but garners significant controversy in Protestant circles is the *stigmata*. These are the spontaneous manifestation of bloody wounds on a person's hands, feet, forehead or back—similar to the wounds of the crucified Jesus. Stigmata is something we at Sons of Thunder tenderly refer to as *"stiggy!"* There have been more stigmatists over the past century than any other on record. R.P. Poulan estimates that as of 1907, there had been conservatively 321 known stigmatists. Now, a century later, that number has grown to 500. Despite common misperceptions, these occur as much among Protestant believers as Catholic.

Francis of Assisi in the 13th century was the first believer known to carry the stigmata, and there are a number around today, including Charismatic Protestant Lucy Rael, who also operates in a powerful revelatory gift. Fr. Elias is a young Catholic stigmatist in Italy today, and even the great revivalist A.A. Allen would highlight the miracle in his own tent revivals in the 1960s. In addition to the stigmata appearing on some in Allen's miracle services, many people would receive a supernatural mark in the shape of a cross on their foreheads.

Although not a stigmatist, our good friend, Joshua Mills, was recently in a meeting in New Zealand when warm blood dropped into his hand out of thin air. After a while, it turned into deep crimson "glory dust." Many people were physically healed and converted to Christianity at the meeting. Joshua said he received more persecution from critics for this one sign than perhaps any other to date!

There are many "blood miracles" throughout church history. The great miracle worker Francis of Paola once refused to take a chest of gold coins from a wicked king who had exploited the poor for the money. To show that this was literally *blood money*, Francis picked up a gold coin and was able to snap it in half between his fingers. Blood dripped out of the coin miraculously, and the king was instantly repentant.

Without a doubt, blood miracles are simply taboo in Western Protestantism. A lot of misinformation is fed to us by Hollywood—there is even a movie titled *Stigmata*, which incessantly portrays the experience to be demonic and cultish. There should not be pointless division over such a trivial issue. However, I do believe that as we honor the miracles God releases, He is prone to bring more blessing. Why must we always drop the gavel and make a judgment call on things we don't understand? Don't slap a demonic label on everything inexplicable. The bottom line is that miracles are from God when He is glorified, and thousands of people have come to faith through the manifestation of stiggy. This is a most awe-inspiring miracle, and for those who are arrested by it, *love explains all.*

In the case of stigmatists, history shows that all of them were *ecstatics*, meaning they all experienced trances, deep sensations of divine pleasure, and the general bliss of Heaven. Most of them had visions of Christ, revealing Himself to them in His blood-stained garments. There are some stigmatists who did not even receive pain from their wounds. Often a stigmatist's wounds will open and then close again miraculously. Gemma Galgani, who died in 1903, is an example of a modern recipient of these marks of Christ whose wounds would open and close again each week after her ecstasy was over on Friday.[41]

In the case of the 1873 stigmata of Louise Lateau, documented by medical doctors (as are nearly all modern examples), there were no actual *wounds* per se. The blood would flow from unbroken skin. Other stigmatists' hands and feet have been completely perforated all the way through the flesh. This is what occurred with 18th-century stigmatist Maria Francesca delle Cinque Piaghe. Her confessor, Don Paschal Nitti gives this testimony:

> I have seen them, I have touched them, and to say the truth I, as the apostle St. Thomas did, have put in my finger into the wounds through her hands and I have seen that the hole extended right through, for in inserting my finger into the wound it met the thumb which I held underneath on the other side of the hand.[42]

Some have received an *invisible* stiggy. That is, their hands felt the pain of the stigmata, but they never received the actual blood sign. As in the case of Catherine of Siena, some had visible bleeding stigmata, but after requesting the Lord to make the sign invisible, He did so.

I have never encountered an instance of valid stiggy in my studies where there was no *choice* made by the recipient to willingly endure this mark. That is, it has always been a grace gift that could be received or rejected without condemnation. In those cases where stigmatists asked the Lord to remove it, time and again He has obliged.

In 1972, a 10-year-old, Baptist, African-American schoolgirl named Cloretta Robinson received an unexpected, yet painless stigmata. Likewise, a number of housewives, ordinary people and even nominal believers have been recipients of this miracle without a pre-existing history of visions or trances. Some stigmatists were virtually "surprised" by the onset of the miracle, yet their faith was given a tremendous breakthrough when it occurred. Such was the case when Jim Bruse, an assistant priest of a parish just outside Washington, D.C., received his stigmata in 1991, His boss, Fr. Daniel Hamilton, was taken off guard:

> I have now seen Jim Bruse. I know what I see and I'm not given to visions. I have seen his wrists bleed, once the blood was all over the carpet in the rectory....I doubted it all in the beginning. Are you crazy? Holy smoke! Guy who works for me...walks into my office,

goes on about the whole thing. . . . that he has this funny bleeding. And I am sitting here, right at this same desk, looking at him, listening to him, and I'm saying to myself as he's talking and I'm listening to all this crap, "hey, buddy, if you think what you're telling me is true, I'm not going to have you as my assistant much longer. You're whacko."[43]

Bruse experienced what has occasionally happened with other stigmatists: the blood flowing from his wounds in a way that defies gravity: flowing up over the toes, or up the hand supernaturally. There was a smell of roses from the wounds, and while he sometimes felt pain, "along with the pain came these sensations, these beautiful sensations," he said.

On a deeper level, stigmata is an outward manifestation of ecstasy that comes from a spiritual condition called the *wounds of love*, or the *anguish of love*. Jesus sweat blood in Gethsemane. Jacob wrestled with an angel until his leg was injured. Just because a manifestation *hurts* does not mean it is not from God. And on the same token, not everyone is called to carry stiggy. It is not a superior mark of piety.

In the anguish of love, states of pleasure and suffering come in near equal strength. It is possible to experience bliss and suffering both simultaneously, and with great intensity. Most stigmatists have meditated long hours on Christ's passion, and they have been graced with a condition of deep heart-sickness. As Poulan writes:

Something of the same kind is experienced in human love when it is violent. A great sweetness is felt, the lover does not wish to quit the thought of the beloved; he enjoys it. But at the same time he feels his heart torn because of his absence from her, or because of the difficulty of conversing with her freely. There is thus a mingling of joy and of sorrow. So, too, it is possible to have delicious experiences of God and of His love, and to feel at the same time a secret anguish which is nothing else than the thirst for God, kindled by Himself.[44]

Common questions need to be answered to arrive at proper discernment in such cases. Does the subject feel drawn closer to God in these experiences? Does the person want the manifestation to continue, despite the obvious pain, or is it solely an oppressive experience? Remember that any ecstasy can be intense, but generally it is very welcome because it is an *intensity of bliss*. Perhaps the guiding factor is this: is there an essence of God's presence and peace in the midst of perceived suffering?

"The ecstatic suffers, and he not only accepts his pain, but he dominates it, he triumphs over it, he accepts it with enthusiasm. These joyful sentiments are not of the earth," writes Fr. Hamon in 1906. "He interests himself, as though he were in complete health, in the joys and sorrows of others."[45]

Overall, I believe we can accept stigmata as a valid miracle of Jesus, without having to embrace a depressed theology of suffering. The best stigmatist is a happy one!

Stigmata can be accepted as a marvelous and beautiful miracle without assuming the flawed notion that the stigmatist is somehow taking part in the redemptive sufferings of Christ (i.e. they are helping Him to do the job that He already finished on Calvary).

Of those contemplatives who suffer in some supernatural way, Teresa of Avila says:

> They have need that His Majesty should afford them some refreshment, and this not of water, but wine; that so, inebriated with this celestial wine, they may not consider that they suffer, and may be able to endure it.[46]

I have determined in my heart that, if there is a heavier hit of glory on something, I want it—no matter how much it hurts!

Diabolical Stigmata

As with every valid miracle of God, there simultaneously exist demonic counterfeits. Mediums can affect demonic healings. Spiritualists engage unholy trances. Yogis and Eastern religions mimic miracles of ascension (floating off the ground). Psychics offer counterfeit prophecies. In the same way, there do exist cases of *diabolical stigmata*.

There seems to be much warfare, controversy, and counterfeit activity over this particular miracle more than any other. For this reason, many true Christian prophets today get spooked out over it, and some even claim stiggy to be produced by *seducing spirits*. The truth is that some of them are. Levitation, bilocation, gifts of healing—these are all extravagant miracles. But because the visual imagery is so dramatically *Christ-centered* with stigmata, invoking the emotions with such a direct picture of His passion—the enemy will attempt to confuse it as much as possible.

History shows that stigmatists are *intensely prophetic persons* by nature. They are almost always seers. In demonic cases, the same is true (the person has a misplaced call to the seer realm) but instead of listening to God, the source of revelation is mixed up. The diabolical stigmatist is open to dark prophetic forces, often channeling demonic spirits in poltergeist-type manifestations.

In cases of godly, divine stigmata, the person nearly always gets revelation from God. Unfortunately, the church has had poor teaching on the prophetic office for the past 2,000 years, so even a valid stigmatist's revelation has often been delivered in a strange or confusing way. Sometimes the person would speak on behalf of God or angels in a *first person* type of way, but without good protocol or delivery style. This has led to much confusion. Needless to say, there has been a stigma on stiggy!

Ecstasies, fits, and all manner of hysterics tend to accompany the lives of stigmatists. The accounts of many resemble wild, Holy Ghost manifestations. "All true stigmatics have received the wounds of rapture in ecstasy," writes Montague Summers.[47] Others, quite honestly, resemble cases of multiple personality disorder and demonic agitations. Herbert Thurston writes, "Many of them were intensely devout…but in others piety was combined with eccentricities and with apparent dissociations of personality which were strange and not exactly edifying."[48]

These eccentricities are not true for all stigmatists. Capuchin friar Padre Pio, for example, was always "exceptionally calm and composed. There is no bad family history. He himself, with a candid simplicity which evidently made a profound impression upon the rationalist Professor, declared that he had never suffered from any nervous malady. He has never been subject to fainting fits or convulsions or tremors. He sleeps well and is not troubled with dreams."[49]

Demons can scrawl letters, words, and other *dermatography* on people's flesh, like something you would see in a horror movie. This sign does not always come as a mark of piety, by any means. Religious devils are so prone to glorify personal suffering; one must discern clearly whether a person's experience is a valid miracle or a "crucifixion complex" of sorts.

Some critics have claimed that stigmata are produced by the imagination, intense mental concentration, or some other naturalistic, physiological phenomenon. There is no need to waste time refuting such an unscientific argument, which is devoid of *common sense*. The imagination cannot cause the body to perforate itself. Angels and devils can. The body cannot cause such wounds to smell fragrant or glow with light, as many have. This is no routine biological process like digestion, circulation, or ordinary tissue mechanics. Unless the stigmata is fraudulently self-inflicted (and a number have been, for attention, money, or spiritual pride), then the question remains whether the stigmata is divine or diabolical in origin.

"That the divine stigmata could be produced through the force of the emotions acting upon a lively subject is altogether impossible," notes Summers.[50] Hemophilia, a tendency to bleed spontaneously or from injury, has no connection whatsoever here. There are only two types of stigmatization: the holy and the profane. You will know the tree by its fruit.

Transverberation of the Heart

Lots of manifestations are grouped under the blanket term "stigmata," but stigmata generally include the five main wounds of Christ: piercing of the two hands, the feet, and side. A number of stigmatists also receive wounds corresponding to the crown of thorns, the lashes on the back, and abrasions to the shoulder, where Christ carried the cross. Some have cried tears of blood.

I am including separately the manifestation called the *ferita*, also known as the heart wound or the transverberation of the heart. In this case, the heart itself is supernaturally pierced, even as the heart of Jesus was pierced on the cross. Teresa of Avila is by far the most famous recipient of this. In her writings, she tells us that an angel approached her and did this with a fiery-tipped, golden lance.

> The angel appeared to me to be thrusting the spear of fire
> into my heart and piercing my very entrails; when he drew
> it out, he seemed to draw them out also, and left me all on
> fire with a great love of God.[51]

Some days after her death, Teresa's body was opened and her heart removed. There on its side was a large puncture wound, with which she had evidently lived for years. The heart was put on display after her death in 1582 and has remained miraculously incorrupt ever since.

> Transverberation is a piercing "under which condition
> normally the subject would die, since the wound
> (humanly speaking) ought to be mortal."[52]

Veronica Giuliani, in the 18th century, somehow believed that her physical heart had hardened into the likeness of certain shapes: a cross, a crown of thorns, a chalice, three nails, a pillar, seven swords, and certain letters that represented a number of virtues. These were emblems she had long meditated on. She had such a clear vision of this that she would draw small pictures of them for her spiritual directors. Years later, upon her death, her heart was extracted; the images of these objects were actually found on the heart, exactly in the manner she described them in her latest drawings.[53]

This may sound unbelievable, but in comparison with Biblical miracles, it is a mere trifle. A more extraordinary case of stigmatization and ferita were faithfully recorded in the 13th-century life of Lady Helen of Veszprim by her fellow nuns and contemporaries. From her stigmatized hand, a golden budded thread began to appear, which grew into a stalk. Fragrant lilies began to blossom from the end of this golden stem. And from the ferita on her side, another of these gold filaments appeared with white-petaled lily blossoms. Greatly embarrassed and not knowing what to do with these lilies growing from her stiggy, Helen pulled them out, as if by their roots. They remained intact for years after her death. Furthermore, Helen's wounds turned to golden circles, and on certain holy days, her stigmata "shone with a soft radiant glow."[54]

Chapter 13

levitation in ecstasy

There are many more wondrous phenomena that attend Christian mysticism than we could be covered in just one book. Outward manifestations are just one part of ecstatic prayer, but they are valuable for revealing the knowledge of Christ to the outside world. In this chapter, we will discuss one of the most unusual, controversial, and yet surprisingly common ecstatic phenomenon among saints both past and present. It is the occurrence of levitation during raptures.

I have a number of friends who have experienced this manifestation, some more regularly than others. Christian history has a rich tradition of these miracles. Because of the ample stories that abound of this most fantastic feat, and its implicit connection to raptures, I feel it is important to write at length on this subject more than any of the outward marvels previously discussed. Another reason for investing an entire chapter on the topic is because it has been under-studied, if not shrewdly ignored among Protestant Charismatic scholars. While there are reams of books on prophecy, healing, visions, and the like, one would wonder at the prejudice toward levitation. It is surely a most exceptional miracle in its own right, deserving of discussion, and I hope to allay any misgivings here.

The word "levitation" has numerous occultist or demonic inferences for the modern-day church goer. But levitation has a greater heritage at the core of Christianity than in any false religious practice. Other "churchy" terms for this marvel are *miracles of ascension*, or perhaps the *lifting miracle*. Jesus Himself walked on water in Matthew 14, overriding the laws of gravity. Again, He floated from the ground and ascended into Heaven in Luke 24, further illustrating His authority over the physical laws of nature. Because we now have the same Spirit that raised Jesus living in us, He tells us in John 14:12 that "he who believes in Me, the works that I do he will do also; and greater *works* than these he will do, because I go to My Father."

Levitation is one of these greater works that has long attended deep states of ecstasy. "Levitation often accompanies ecstasy. Innumerable saints have been levitated to heights, thus defying the law of gravity. St. Teresa of Avila used to beg her fellow nuns to hold her down so she would not be embarrassed before others. St. John of the Cross twisted bars of an iron grille in a convent as he resisted being drawn upwards. St. Joseph of Cupertino would hover near the ceiling of the chapel, and he 'flew' in the air," writes church historian Albert J. Hebert.[1]

Humankind, though living in the natural world, was never intended to be bound by *physical laws* such as gravity. This is a result of the frustration of all creation that followed Adam's fall from Eden. We now have access again, through the cross, to those same realms of possibility that Adam knew in Garden...and even greater. The fact that *"all things are possible to him who believes"* (Mark 9:23) should be enough biblical precedent for us to move into any manner of unusual sign or wonder. But in terms of flight miracles, we have been given a rich treasure trove of scriptural examples already.

The prophet Ezekiel, in an encounter with the Lord, was pulled up by the hair of his head, suspended between Heaven and earth.

> *He stretched out what looked like a hand and took me by the hair of my head. The Spirit lifted me up between earth and heaven and in visions of God He took me to Jerusalem...* (Ezekiel 8:3 NIV).

Not only was Ezekiel taken to Jerusalem in flight, but there was another instance when he was physically lifted up and taken miles away to Tel Abib, where he was left for seven days.

> *So the Spirit lifted me up and took me away, and I went in bitterness, in the heat of my spirit; but the hand of the Lord was strong upon me. Then I came to the captives at*

Tel Abib, who dwelt by the River Chebar; and I sat where
they sat, and remained there astonished among them seven
days (Ezekiel 3:14-15).

We also read that Enoch, the seventh from Adam, *"walked with God; and*
he was not, for God took him" (Gen. 5:24). Is it possible that God levitated
Enoch right off the face of the planet? It is quite possible. After all, it happened
with Jesus, who floated up to Heaven in sight of a large crowd of people:

He said to them: "It is not for you to know the times or
dates the Father has set by His own authority. But you
will receive power when the Holy Spirit comes on you;
and you will be My witnesses in Jerusalem, and in all
Judea and Samaria, and to the ends of the earth." After
He said this, He was taken up before their very eyes, and
a cloud hid Him from their sight (Acts 1:7-9 NIV).

The prophet Elijah was also lifted supernaturally from the ground:

Then it happened, as they continued on and talked, that
suddenly a chariot of fire appeared with horses of fire, and
separated the two of them; and Elijah went up by a whirl-
wind into heaven (2 Kings 2:11).

Remember that God is the inventor of gravity, and it has no hold except
for when He so chooses. Gravity, like everything else, is *just a word*, spoken
into existence by God at the dawn of creation along with everything else (see
Gen. 1:3). But there is a better Word that came down from Heaven that has
freed us from the frustration of the created universe and enables us to live in
glorious liberty as supernatural sons of the living God! Like it or not, one day
you will levitate! The Scriptures say that we will one day meet Him in the air:

. . . we who are still alive and are left will be caught up together
with them in the clouds to meet the Lord in the air. And so we
will be with the Lord forever (1 Thessalonians 4:17 NIV).

Also, Isaiah 60:8 bids the question, *"Who are these who fly like a cloud, and like doves to their roosts?"* I believe the answer is *you and I.* It is time for the church to arise, *literally,* as we read Isaiah 60:1-2, *"Arise, shine; for your light has come! And the glory of the Lord is risen upon you. For behold, the darkness shall cover the earth, and deep darkness the people; but the Lord will arise over you, and His glory will be seen upon you."*

Exposing the Diabolical

The historical church has nearly always made room for ascension miracles. Unlike today, our forefathers did not lump this miracle in with its demonic counterfeits. Occultist levitation has always been viewed by the traditional church as a cheap, diabolical parody to the real thing. In the Inquisition, for instance, it was never doubted that witches could fly. But their flight was believed only to be an *imitation of the transport of saints.* Let us not kid ourselves: demonic levitation is real and in existence in the world today. A number of Far Eastern religions, for instance, have adherents who float by devious means.

However, as Christians we should never avoid the legitimate, simply because the phony also exists. We must be spearheading such signs and wonders far in advance of the enemy's minions in order to convert the unbeliever and bring in the end-time harvest. The miracle itself may seem strange, but the only relevant question we should ask is this: *Who is your source?* If Jesus is the source of our power (versus satan), then we can truly do anything. Moses worked some pretty creepy miracles. His hand turned leprous; he changed rivers to blood. Imagine turning your stick into a snake in the middle of church! And yet this was the same type of miracle that the sorcerers of Egypt were performing! The God miracles and the demonic miracles looked outwardly similar. But Moses' source was not the same as Pharaoh's diviners. Moses' miracles came from the living God, and his serpent gobbled up all the rest.

In a similar fashion to Moses, expect believers to arise who will challenge sorcerers right in the streets in this hour with the raw power of God. There are popular magicians today who are increasingly flaunting their demonic power right on the streets of New York City on prime time television. Some of their acts are phony, but others are hell-inspired supernatural stuff. Believers like you are about to become so empowered as to lay hands on the floating heads of demonic priests in the marketplace and cast out devils. They will drop to the ground, but *you* will float up!

Modern-day prophet Bobby Conner shares a story that occurred in the middle of a meeting with 600 people. He was preaching in America when a coven of witches marched boldly into the service and stood around the walls of the room. The Lord told Bobby, "I want you to challenge them."

Bobby asked who their leader was, and the head witch told him they had come to shut down the meeting. Bobby said, "Do whatever you're going to do. But I will tell you right now: you cannot hurt me, *but I can hurt you.*"

The witches then commenced to curse and hex Bobby for a few moments. Nothing happened. Then Bobby extended his hand toward the leader. The power of God threw her into the air, and she stuck against the wall screaming. She was suspended so high that her feet were as high as Bobby's head. Then she fell to the floor and began rolling in a seizure, foaming at the mouth. Bobby told them this was the power of Jesus Christ at work. The coven quickly collected themselves and walked out the door. Bobby then called one of them out prophetically by name, "Sarah! God is going to redeem you from this web you've got yourself in." A blonde-haired woman turned to look at him, and then scurried away.

Three days later, this woman came back to the church, no longer wearing her robe, looking pale as a ghost and shaking. Her name was Sarah. Bobby asked where she had been. Then he prophetically began to answer his own question, telling her she had just come from a funeral of an 18-year-old boy who had put a gun in his mouth and shot himself dead. Sarah began screaming for help, and received deliverance that night.[2]

The power of Jesus is greater than any occultist counterfeit. We need not fear edging into spiritualism as we pursue these experiences, as long as our hearts are grounded in intimacy with Jesus Christ. Spiritualists are preoccupied with levitation and other miracles simply because they are searching for truth and spiritual reality—all mankind longs to be clothed with immortality. This is something that we, as the church, have to offer spiritual seekers. It is normal to want these things, as long as we seek them in Christ, rather than deviant sources. As we pursue God's hand of might, we can do great exploits for the Gospel.

Famous Floaters

Levitation is more prevalent than you may realize in the church of God. More than 200 saints in the Catholic church alone have experienced the phenomenon of flight, according to Olivier Leroy's book *Levitation*, written in 1928, in which he estimates an average elevation of about 20 inches. In other cases, unusual heights were recorded. J.J. von Görres, in the 19th century, in his book *Die Christliche Mystik*, spoke of 72 such levitated saints. But there are many more.

I have now heard countless firsthand cases of the nameless, faceless believers who have been pulled up a time or two in their personal devotions, while meditating on their beds, or in private prayer. This miracle is not reserved only for a few spiritually elite "saints." Sainthood is for everyone in Christ. The reason for the profundity of Catholic floaters is simply because the Roman church has a theological and traditional framework for the miracle, and they do not reject it the way Protestants have. And so, Catholic believers have a platform to testify and document cases of ascension, whereas many Protestant denominations would shun someone for this. You would be surprised at the vast numbers of closet floaters out there today. I have met dozens. Here is just a short list of a few famous believers who levitated:

- Dunstan, archbishop of Canterbury (918–988)
- Dominic, Dominican Order founder (1170–1221)
- Francis of Assisi (1186–1226)
- Thomas Aquinas (1226–1274)
- Edmund, archbishop of Canterbury (d. 1242)
- Blessed James of Illyria (d. 1485)
- Savonarola (1452–1498)
- Ignatius Loyola (1491–1556)
- Francis Xavier (1506–1552)
- Philip Neri (1515–1595)
- Peter of Alcantara (1499–1562)

- Joseph of Cupertino (1603–1663)
- Alphonsius Liguori (1696–1787)
- Sister Mary, an Arabian Carmelite nun in Bethlehem circa 1700
- Abbé Claude Dhière (1757–1820)
- Fr. Suarez at Santa Cruz, Argentina in 1911

About one-third of historical recorded cases, prior to this century, are recorded with highly respectable, if not conclusive evidence. The other two-thirds are recorded with less firsthand observation. They are not to be considered *mythical* by any means; however, because of posterior sources in many Middle Ages accounts, and lack of "scientific method" in many examinations, we can hold their stories more loosely. Nevertheless, the *fact* of levitation as an occurrence is absolutely without question.

A number of the reputable Protestant revivalists give reports of levitation occurring in their ministries. Healing revivalist John G. Lake (1870–1935) records the following observation in his diary about a man floating up in the glory during one of his meetings:

> One evening as I was preaching the Spirit of the Lord descended on a man in the front row. It was Dr. E.H. Cantel, a minister from England, London. He remained in a sitting posture, but began rising from the chair; gradually he came down on the chair; and again gradually he began to rise, somewhat higher, then gradually he came down. This was repeated three times. Was it reversal of the law of gravitation? I think not. My own conception is that the soul became so united with the Spirit of God that the attractive power of God was so intense it drew him up.[3]

Another popular revivalist of the 20th century, Ruth Ward Heflin (1940–2000), records an instance of levitation in her book *Golden Glory*:

> In another meeting in January 1999, I was speaking about the gold and the gold started to appear. Prior to that, the

supernatural oil was manifesting. One night we had a visitation of the living creatures while the gold was pouring out. A sister who was present, Audrey was dying with cancer of the liver. The cancer had metastasized and spread to her brain. She looked like death warmed over. In that meeting, when the living creatures came and gold fell, she froze and could not move for forty-five minutes. Then she fell to the floor, slain in the Spirit, and as she was slain in the Spirit she was physically lifted up off the floor by the hand of God, and she physically felt the hand of God touching her liver. She went back to the hospital in Tulsa and her doctor could not believe what he saw. She asked him if he thought she was healed and he said no. Her liver was not healed, he said: she had actually grown a brand-new liver. She has been testifying everywhere since, and everywhere she testifies the gold comes in the meeting.[4]

Levitation Today

In 1995 the Lord gave me a very specific night vision, instructing me that one day entire congregations of believers would float simultaneously from their seats in deep trance. Since that time I have looked forward to the release of this corporate manifestation.

Of the numerous believers alive today who have experienced levitation, most say they feel comfortable speaking to me about it, only because of the historical analysis I put forward in my book *Miracle Workers, Reformers, and the New Mystics*. Of those who are in public ministry, very few care to share about their floating experiences publicly for want of avoiding persecution. Some, like Bobby Conner, have openly shared stories of walking in mid-air, right off a stage platform, to prophesy over someone before returning the ground. Others have floated up during evangelism crusades in the nations. Jamie Galloway, a young revivalist friend, openly shares of nearly 12 levitations in his personal devotions and prayer times.

There are several Christians alive today who have walked on water, just as Jesus did in Matthew 14. This same principle is one of bypassing gravitational forces. Mel Tari, author of *Like a Mighty Wind*, gives us fantastic stories of the Indonesian revival of the 1970s. Mel shared with me how he once walked across the top of a rushing, 30-foot-deep river.

Another of our dear friends, a well-respected minister, has floated from the ground about four times at the date of this initial printing. Three of those were cases of a few inches during public worship, and once, while privately in prayer, he floated from the ground about as high as a coffee table. Another friend, a prominent worship leader in New England, levitated about five feet off his bed. One woman, who helps to head a large, respected apostolic network, once levitated during intercession. And one of our crusade evangelist friends, during the writing of this book, floated off his bed for about an hour in ecstasy.

Others float much more consistently. Most interesting is a minister friend from India who floats from the ground nearly every day during personal meditation. She is the only person I know who can do this almost at will, yet she is deathly afraid to reveal this fact from the pulpit. In fact, I am the first American with which she has ever felt comfortable to discuss it. Despite my pleas to go public with this for the sake of the Gospel, she is under the impression it would do more harm than good, for lack of understanding within the Body of Christ. I believe it is time for the sons of God to be revealed. We cannot be bashful about God's power in this hour, while the world goes to hell in a hand basket. We must boldly appropriate and display the *powers of the age to come*!

Revivalist David Herzog gives a further account of someone floating from the ground during his revival work in France, in his book *Glory Invasion*:

> During a revival we held in Paris, France, in 1998 that lasted six months, we witnessed levitations or being lifted up off the ground. During the first weekend of meetings, the Glory came so strong that I could not even grab the microphone to speak. People suddenly started to wail and weep for souls, and a 15-year-old girl in the back of the room slipped into deep travail and intercession for souls. While she was weeping she was suddenly lifted up 13

centimeters off the ground and then she flipped over, still in the air for a few more seconds, and then slowly came down. Her movements totally surprised some of the people sitting near her who were attending the meeting simply out of curiosity. Immediately after the girl returned to her seat, 13 people ran up to be saved—each one had suicidal tendencies.... For the next six months, four nights a week, souls were saved in each and every meeting, along with miracles, signs and wonders displayed, and believers repented of sin in their lives.[5]

Levitation and Ecstasy

Lifting miracles are intrinsically connected to intense raptures. John of the Cross, when offering communion during Mass, would bite the chalice to keep himself from lifting off the ground in ecstasy—much like a person biting his lip to avoid crying. His teeth marks are still visible on the cup to this day.[6] As these raptures come on, Teresa of Avila tells us it is best not to resist them:

> It seemed to me when I tried to resist that a great force, for which I can find no comparison, was lifting me up from beneath my feet. It came with greater violence than any other spiritual experience, and left me quite shattered.... At other times resistance has been impossible; my soul has been carried away, and usually my head as well, without my being able to prevent it; and sometimes it has affected my whole body, which has been lifted from the ground.[7]

Teresa says of the raptures that, "Very often they seemed to leave my body as light as if it had lost all its weight, and sometimes so light that I barely knew whether my feet were touching the ground."[8] This sense of lightness is most acute when in mid-air.

"When the body is lifted up into the air, it often becomes as light as a feather, so that a breath is enough to set it in motion and to cause it to float like a soap bubble," writes Poulan.[9]

One of the most frequent fliers in church history was Joseph of Cupertino. Joseph, the *Flying Friar*, is credited with the most flights: more than 100 separate ascensions. As we mentioned earlier, he was also known as *The Gaper*, because he stayed tranced out in Third Heaven encounters most of the time as well. He would just hear the name "Jesus" or hear the sound of music playing, and the Gaper would lift off the ground. He once flew up into a tree, perched on a branch, and it quivered no more than if he were a bird.

Joseph was a simple man, and in fact, he was rejected from joining certain monasteries, because they thought he was ignorant. Little did they know that Joseph was always absorbed in trances and ecstasies most of the time. His were some of the most well documented flights, and "his ecstasies and ascensions were witnessed not only by the people and the members of his order, but Pope Urban VIII saw him one day in this state and was intensely astonished."[10]

Joseph once grabbed his confessor by the hand, snatched him from the floor, and began to whirl around with him in mid-air. In another instance, he seized an insane nobleman by the hair of his head who had come to him to be healed. He soared up with the man, let out a shout, and the man came down cured.

The Gaper stayed so whacked, he could not manage to say his office because of the bliss. By the evening, it sometimes happened that Joseph had been standing there all day, trying to finish a sermon, turning over the leaves of his breviary, but unable to speak. There stood the Gaper, having flipped his pages all day, but was struck mute and unable to read them. In the acts of his canonization we read, "It was a miracle that amidst all his ecstasies the saint should have been able to finish his Mass. As soon as he had done so...he flew rather than walked to his cell. Reaching it he uttered a cry, threw himself upon his knees and fell into an ecstasy."[11]

His raptures and levitations so upset the choir, the refectory, and the processions that his superiors would not let him participate in public communion for 35 years. He was confined to lock down. Whenever he took communion publicly, it is written that he would barely touch the floor on his tiptoes for the entire service.

Levitation is so connected with ecstatic prayer, church historians have often termed it *ascensional ecstasy* or *ecstatic flight.* The miracle comes in various forms, besides just floating directly from the ground. Levitation is also a type of *mobile ecstasy*, meaning that supernatural movement is afforded during the trance, rather than the adherent just remaining whacked on the floor in ligature. In the lives of some saints, notes mystical writer Albert Farges, "More rarely, again, they skim the earth or the water rapidly as the swallow flies from the ground: this is *ecstatic progress.*"[12]

The Sudden Power of Flight

When raptures of flight tend to overtake a mystic, they often come on suddenly, and great boldness is needed not to pull away from them. If you have ever experienced God begin to pull you out of your body, then you likewise know the immediate sense of fear that can accompany this act. But when we don't resist, it is pure pleasure.

"You realize, I repeat, and indeed see that you are being carried away you know not where. For although this is delightful, the weakness of our nature makes us afraid at first, and we need a much more determined and courageous spirit than for the previous stages of prayer," writes Teresa, adding that these raptures are violent, yet blissful.[13] Sister Maria Villani, a famous Dominican nun of the 17th century, describes being overtaken by such raptures that caused her to levitate:

> On one occasion when I was in my cell I was conscious of a new experience. I felt myself seized and ravished out of my senses, so powerfully that I found myself lifted up completely by the very soles of my feet, just as the magnet draws up a fragment of iron, but with a gentleness that was marvelous and most delightful. At first I felt much fear, but afterwards I remained in the greatest possible content-ment and joy of spirit. Though I was quite beside myself, still, in spite of that, I knew that I was raised some distance above the earth, my whole body being suspended for a

considerable space of time. Down to last Christmas eve (1618) this happened to me on five different occasions.[14]

The strength that is exerted in these levitations is often phenomenal. It seems that the more one floats, the more pronounced the flights become, enabling them even to lift heavy objects. It is as if the Spirit of Might comes to clothe them. There is a recorded instance of Joseph of Cupertino flying up and lifting a huge cross to the top of the church as if it were a piece of straw, though several men could hardly lift it from the ground by human standards.

"Sometimes the ecstatic develops a considerable strength in his ascents," notes Poulan, adding that Cupertino three separate times seized a companion and pulled him up into flight along with him.[15] There are also examples of the Jansenists of France in the 18th century pulling several people up into the air as they levitated. Some of the Jansenists could not be held down by five or six people as they started to fly. We will discuss their phenomenal acts in a later chapter. Teresa of Avila reports similar instances, when her fellow nuns were unable to keep her down under the influence of gravity:

> I lay on the ground and the sisters came to hold me down,
> but all the same the rapture was observed.[16]

Gerard Majella, the 18th-century wonderworker, was speaking to a prioress at a convent, when falling into an ecstasy, he started to rise. He grabbed a metal grill as if to restrain himself, and the metal bars bent in his hands like wax. In a similar fashion, John of the Cross was lifted so violently that he bent the metal bars on a window, trying to restrain himself. At another time, when Majella was walking with two friends in southeast Italy, they saw him rise into the air and fly rapidly to a distance more than a quarter of a mile.[17]

No Fixed Limit to Height

When our Lord rose near Bethany in Luke 24, He flew away as far as the eye could see. In like fashion, there are no rules restricting us to stay just a few inches from the floor in ascension. The lives of the saints do not seem to indicate a fixed height for levitation. In fact, for a believer, it is possible to not merely *hover* but to *fly*.

Francis of Assisi was witnessed by Brother Leo, his confessor, to rise at times to the height of a man, sometimes as high as the trees and other times so high that he could no longer be seen.[18] Thomas of Cori, in the 18th century, was giving communion when he ascended in ecstasy to the vaulting of the church, still holding the ciborium. After his gradual descent, he continued giving communion to the congregation. And Peter of Alcantara, the 16th-century saint, was once carried up to a great height, far above the trees, with his arms crossed on his chest. As he continued to soar, it is reported that hundreds of small birds gathered around him singing.[19]

One of the strangest stories of this century is that of Padre Pio, the Italian mystic and stigmatist whose life was full of bizarre occurrences. During the World War when a squadron of planes was flying over his town to bomb it, the squadron leader reported seeing a monk, levitating in mid-air over the city. In addition, they reported an inexplicable type of "force field" that prevented them from firing their munitions on the town. The confused commander called the pilots back in, and the mission was abandoned.

After the war, the commander visited this small Italian town and realized it to be the home of famed Padre Pio, whom he recognized perfectly from mid-air encounter. Not only had Padre Pio been flying over the town in levitation, but he was also *bilocating* at the same time (his body showing up two separate places at once). During this entire time, Pio had been interceding heavily for his city that it would be protected during the war. In awe of what had happened, the army commander came to faith.

We should understand that miracles can overlap simultaneously in the glory realm. Just as Padre Pio levitated and bilocated at the same time, so have many believers *glowed* with visible light surrounding their bodies whilst levitating. Sometimes, this heavenly aura is so bright and dazzling that it lights up an entire room.

At the beatification hearings for priest Bernardino Realino in 1621, a high ranking gentleman named Signor Tobias da Ponte gave account on oath of a miracle he witnessed 13 years earlier. Sitting outside of Realino's door, Signor Tobias witnessed the saint floating two and a half feet from the floor, surrounded in bright visible light:

> The thing was so clear, unmistakable and real, that not only do I seem to see it still but I am as certain of it as I am of speaking now, or of seeing the things around me.... I noticed the light coming through the doorway not only once, but twice, thrice, and four times before the shadow of any such idea [of the levitation] occurred to me. And so I began to debate with myself how there could be any fire in the room, since the rays which issued from it could only be caused by a great fire...and so I stood up on purpose and pushing open the door I saw with my own eyes Father Bernardino raised from the ground as unmistakably as I now see [you].[20]

Finally, regarding those levitations of extreme height, I should point out that at the end of the ecstasy, the believer's body always seems to float back to the ground without injury. Furthermore, in the case of the Gaper, it is reported that his clothes were carefully arranged while floating in mid-air, as if an unseen hand was holding his robes together.

Angels of Flight

As with all bizarre miracles, there are angels specifically assigned to enable miracles of levitation during ecstasy. The same is true for bilocation, transportation, luminescence, and all other sorts of supernatural abilities. The role of angels is paramount to the fulfillment of God's word (see Ps. 103:20).

I could share numerous stories of angels that appear to release physical healings, deliverance, bizarre miracles, and even release creative substances such as gemstones in meetings. But throughout the ages, believers have also recognized the role of the angelic in levitation. Fr. K.A. Schmöger gives us the statement of stigmatist Anne Catherine Emmerich (1774–1824), who attributes her levitations to angelic assistance:

When I was doing my work as vestry-nun, I was often lifted up suddenly into the air, and I climbed up and stood on the higher parts of the church, such as windows, sculptured ornaments, jutting stones; I would clean and arrange everything in places where it was humanly impossible. I felt myself lifted and supported in the air, and I was not afraid in the least, for I had been accustomed from a child to being assisted by my guardian angel.[21]

Consider the following German newspaper report from the *Frankfurter Zeitung* on September 8, 1861. Even this secular paper acknowledges an instance of levitation. But note that it occurred when a priest began talking about the angelic:

> ...a Catholic Priest was preaching before his congregation last Sunday in the Church of St. Mary, at Vienna, on the subject of the constant protection of angels over the faithful committed to their charge, and this in words of great exaltation, and with an unction and eloquence which touched profoundly the hearts of numbers of the congregation. Soon after the commencement of the sermon, a girl of about 20 years of age, showed all signs of ecstasy, and soon, her arms crossed upon her bosom, and with her eyes fixed on the preacher, she was seen by the whole congregation to be raised gradually from the floor into the air, and there to rest at an elevation of more than a foot until the end of the sermon. We are assured that the same phenomenon had happened several days previously at the moment of her receiving the communion.[22]

Duration of Ascensions

Although most liftings occur for only a few seconds or minutes, there are considerable accounts of much lengthier levitation. Teresa of Avila tells of ecstasies lasting only a short time, about half an hour tops. But in this, she is speaking of the period of greatest *intensity* of trances when flight may occur. Ecstasies themselves can last for long periods of time.

Thomas of Villanova, a 16th-century priest, was reportedly saying his office on Ascension Day when he was seized by an ecstasy and floated in mid-air, suspended for 12 hours.

Spanish monk Dominic de Jesus-Marie was reportedly raised up to the ceiling of his cell where he remained without any earthly support for a day and a night. On another occasion, there was a skeptic on hand who seized his floating body by the feet and was carried up with him. Frightened by this, he let go and fell to the ground.[23]

Savonarola was a famous moral reformer within the Catholic Church in the 15th century and considered a precursor to Martin Luther. He was critical of the pope and the priestcraft of his day and was eventually sentenced to execution. His biographers write that shortly before he died at the stake, he remained suspended for some time at a considerable height over the floor of his dungeon, absorbed in prayer.[24]

Amidst the regular flights of Joseph of Cupertino, he was once seen to remain suspended in mid-air at the height of the trees for more than two hours in the garden.

Supernatural Heaviness

On the opposite end of levitation, the believer in ecstasy sometimes experiences extreme, supernatural weightedness. Mary Magdalen of Pazzi, for example, would become so heavy in her ecstasies, she could not be moved. Many persons would attempt to budge her, but "when she had recovered the use of her senses, she felt pain in such of her limbs as had been too roughly handled."[25]

This is something I have experienced on a number of occasions in public meetings. I have personally entered intense ecstatic states, and although I am a big man, it has taken more than half a dozen men to lift and move my body to another location. Usually, they are clueless that this is a supernatural heaviness, but they try to fight against the tide anyway, unable to dislodge me.

During impartation services when I am laying hands on people for prayer, I often like to move quickly when the glory is most intense. With bodies hitting the floor in holy chaos, the people assigned to "catch" them can rarely keep up with me. I often have to stop and look for these catchers. I frequently find them several rows away, still trying in vain to move someone's body that was stuck to the carpet with *supernatural heaviness*.

Practice Makes Perfect

I have been around the block enough to know that these kinds of stories provoke people. On one hand, talk of such bizarre miracles irritates religious spirits. On the other hand, they invoke hungry hearts to burn for more of the supernatural.

In today's Charismatic arena, we have learned that spiritual gifts do not always come to us with a lightning bolt on a silver platter. Rather, they usually come through development, training, and a process of maturity over time. Prophets are not born in a day; and even in the Old Testament, they developed their ears to hear the Lord's voice in schools with training. If we are allowed to practice with prophecy and to practice with healing gifts, so does the Lord want us to practice the working of unusual miracles. There is nothing wrong with practicing levitation or moving objects with our words, as long as our motives are rooted in intimacy with Jesus, who is our Source of power.

I don't suggest that we test the Lord by jumping off a building! But we can practice the working of these miracles. If we are not seeing a radical manifestation of signs and wonders in our life, there is a good chance that we are missing out on some deeper levels of faith, intimacy, and His abiding glory. I used to practice levitating by getting in the glory and stepping off the edge of my fireplace!

Having a trance does not mean you become a mindless glory zombie. The nature of the Kingdom is that God wants to enjoy our *participation* with Him! He wants you to choose Him with your free will. Don't just wait for God to possess you and lift you in a vegetative state. Position yourself for the next level! Interact with Him.

I once had a dream in which I was flying. In this dream, I could never leave the ground until I started to *flap my own arms*. Although my arms have no wings or feathers, God wanted me to flap them a little, just to exert my *will* in the matter. I was not working or striving to fly by flapping my arms. It showed that I must *willingly* lean into the experience. Yes, we want to be possessed by God, but not in the hollow, slavish sort of possession that a demoniac knows. We are *love slaves*, compelled by the bliss of His love. We *choose* Him, responsively, just as He first chose us. Exert your will and practice pressing in—not as a work, but as a joyful response of faith!

One of the best ways you can press into these miracles is by ensuring your character is right before God. God is about to give resident miracles to many of His children, like He did with Moses in Exodus 4. At any given time, Moses could work some far-fetched miracles at his own discretion. The spirit of a prophet is subject to a prophet. In terms of levitation, a number of saints could do it *at will*.

It is imperative that we position ourselves in intimacy for this level of power. You will not be able to count the little fishes that jump into your boat when this level of power hits the streets. Francis Xavier, whose missionary efforts brought 700,000 to faith in India and Japan in the 16th century, was known for raising the dead, healing entire villages instantly of plagues, and performing a host of unusual, documented miracles. It was reported that when Xavier took communion, he habitually floated right off the ground in ecstasy.

There is power available today for the end-time revival. Let's position ourselves for it in the bliss.

Aligning the Heart to Fly

With great power comes great responsibility. I think Spiderman said that, but it's true. God wants to literally pour superpowers out on His children, bringing us back to an Adamic level of power, but even greater—the powers of the age to come that are afforded to us through Jesus Christ, the Second Adam!

I think that one of the main reasons God has to keep our abilities limited in this hour is because of our propensity to misuse and abuse the power He wants to give us. God wants you to fly more than you do. It is your birthright. But just because a toddler owns his dad's Lamborghini as his birthright, does not mean he will get the keys until he's mature enough to drive it.

God wants to mature us for power. That does not mean we have to warm a pew for 20 years or get five seminary degrees. Maturity only comes in the place of intimacy. Hunger and purity equal maturity in God's book, and as soon as we step into the place of abandoned hunger for Him, He can entrust us with those things He's been dying to give us. Jesus said the following in Luke 12:48 (NIV):

> *From everyone who has been given much, much will be demanded; and from the one who has been entrusted with much, much more will be asked.*

There is a high standard of responsibility that comes with great gifting. God does not want to start lifting people off the ground who will use the gift to build their own kingdoms. I can already see it coming: Levitations "R" Us Ministries International. God is not looking for superstars, show-offs or insecure people who will use His power to prove themselves. When believers start openly levitating, this is going to be a transferable gift that can be received through impartation, and He wants His whole Body moving in these powers: not just a one-man show.

Furthermore, the Lord does not want us to use these gifts to prove our pet doctrines (whether good ones or bad ones). Nor is He giving the signs to affirm everything we say. These will just be signs that affirm *Him*! I think it is imperative that we stay humble in these matters. If we do, there is a great promise:

> *Humble yourselves in the sight of the Lord, and He will lift you up* (James 4:10).

> *The Lord lifts up the humble; He casts the wicked down to the ground* (Psalm 147:6).

I would encourage you to take these verses literally for a moment. He will *lift you up*!

Positionally, we have all been given the ability to fly at the cross. But the Lord is being cautious with the manifestation of these levels of power, I believe, because once He gives a gift, it is without repentance. He doesn't take it back. It is one thing to see the occasional lift, but an altogether different thing to have a *resident anointing* for flying at will!

If you can't believe in a miracle such as levitation, how will you ever believe in something as far-fetched as Heaven? Wrestling down the spirit of doubt and obtaining the faith for flight is not the only thing that will bring it to pass. Let us get our hearts ready for what God is about to do. There is responsibility. The funniest thing of all is that God's idea of responsibility is far different from ours! God doesn't just want to give us miracles in a practical, purpose-driven way. It is not strictly for *works* of evangelism, with an end product in mind! He doesn't give these gifts just so that we will build a ministry machine. Chiefly, God just wants to play with His kids and give us a taste of the realms of the age to come. How would you like a foretaste of your glorified body, which will fly all the time? Benedict XIV, an 18th-century pope, said the primary reason God grants levitation during ecstasy is to *foreshadow the powers of the age to come*:

> By Divine power the body may be raised on high, not because this has any necessary connection with ecstasy or rapture resulting from a vehement, divine contemplation, but because God...in order to instruct us therein, grants at times to the enraptured this special gift; which gift is a certain imperfect participation of the gift of fleetness, which will be bestowed on glorified bodies.[26]

God will want us to steward such miraculous gifts, but He cannot trust such power to performance oriented people who have a *religious productivity* mindset. He wants us to be more like children. One day, the Lord asked me: "*Son, why do you want to fly?*" I told Him that I wanted it because it will bring in the harvest. If I levitate on the streets, people will get saved by the droves, I said. I also told Him that I wanted it because it would give Him glory. Then I paused for a moment and answered again...

"I want it because it would be fun."

At this, the Lord told me, "*That was your purest answer.*"

The concept of flight produces a childlike wonder in us. This is precious to the Lord. This is our inheritance. Walking in the supernatural is the nature of the Kingdom. Adam was made for this realm, and so were you and I. If you are thinking at best only of the souls you will win—or at worst, the fame and recognition you will achieve—then your motives for this gift still need to be checked. Yes, we need the supernatural for harvest, but our number one goal should just be to enjoy God with this stuff!

Miracles Do Not Equal Intimacy

While discussing so much supernatural phenomena, keep in mind that miracles alone are not an indication of intimacy with the Lord. Nor are they a litmus test for the spirituality of the minister. Deep intimacy will always produced wonders—though not all wonders are an indication of intimacy.

Miracles can come *despite* a lack of intimacy in our lives. Remember the Lord's exhortation, in Matthew 7:22-24:

> *Many will say to Me in that day, "Lord, Lord, have we not prophesied in Your name, cast out demons in Your name, and done many wonders in Your name?" And then I will declare to them, "I never knew you; depart from Me, you who practice lawlessness!"*

Jesus knows everything. The fact that He did not know these wonder-workers means that He did not *know them intimately.* Knowing Him intimately is the only thing that matters. This verse has oft been quoted in an attempt to discourage miracle working in modern ministry, but that is a ridiculous reading of the passage. The issue at stake here are not the miracles, but the condition of the heart. If even a miracle worker can perform signs yet never truly know Jesus, what does that say about the fruitless ones who have never even seen a miracle! If even a wonderworker can miss the big picture, how imperative is it that ordinary believers contend to know Him more!

Jim Jones was the infamous cult leader who led more than 900 followers to drink cyanide-laced punch to their death in Guyana in the

1970s. He is a prime example of a false, miracle-working prophet. Jones claimed to be God. One of the things news agencies will not tell you about Jones—because of the secular disbelief in the supernatural—is that he actually *did* affect the working of miracles. Clearly, Jones' inspiration was demonic. But I have seen videos of him healing the sick, even causing wheelchair-bound persons to come out of their seats. Jones claimed to have raised 40 people from the dead, though the claim is sketchy and documentation for this would be difficult to uncover. Even satan seems to affect a dead-raising miracle in the Book of Revelation, if this were possible (see Rev. 13:3).

The Lord is pouring out such a massive wave of supernatural glory in this hour; we will need greater discernment than ever before to navigate the waters ahead. But discernment is not paranoia or witch hunts. The greatest discernment is not to point out devils and recognize the enemy in every a situation, though that is a part of the equation. The most important thing is to recognize when the *Lord* is truly moving, so we do not miss out on His fullness. The watchmen on the wall had a two-fold responsibility in Old Testament times. They sounded an alarm when they saw the enemy approaching. But this was not their primary task. The greater responsibility was to *watch for the king coming*, so the gates could be opened and the inner chambers prepared for him. Without the King in our camp, we are power-less against the adversary. As we open our hearts to Jesus, we can trust Him to lead us in the way everlasting.

God is going to be doing some things that look absolutely creepy in these times, and if we are not sharp we are going to miss it. When He launches a massive harvest revival among the Goths, the punks, and the hardcore youth, it is going to look like mayhem, but *it will be God*. And at the same time, there are going to be some Jim Joneses on the block who say the right things, dress the part, and even work a few wonders. But they are masquerading as angels of light, while underneath they are wolves in sheep's clothing.

Our discernment models have been good at "pushing the enemy out." But did you know that we have also been pushing the Lord out? It is no less a failure in discernment to "push the Lord out" than it is to let the enemy come traipsing right in. God is about to do the bizarre. He is about to detonate your religious box. Don't shut the door on God in this hour, though He comes in unusual forms. Because in the same stroke, you could be letting in the big bad wolf.

Consequently, it should be noted of Jim Jones that he was described as a "humorless" man, and many friends and acquaintances later recognized this as his fatal flaw.[27] The irony is that being overly serious, paranoid, or fearful of deception can be the very thing that *leads us into deception*. Here is a good rule for discernment: if it's not fun, it's probably not God! Staying in the Kingdom equates to staying in joy. Joy cannot coexist with paranoia or control any more than it can exist with outright lawlessness. As an emerging apostolic movement is at hand, there will be many people barking orders and trying to assert their authority. But true apostles can be determined by their "joy levels." The apostle Paul wrote, "not...that we have dominion over your faith, but are helpers of your joy..." (2 Cor. 1:24 KJV).

Part V

mass glory movements

Chapter 14

the awakening

Throughout the course of history, there have been massive ecstatic movements and glory outbreaks on the streets that have shaped the course of entire societies. When God's presence pierces the thin membrane between His church and the hungry populace outside its four walls, radical transformation has occurred at epidemic proportions.

We have made the case that shaking, ecstatic prophets have been in vogue, and in fact were the norm among many great revivals, whether Protestant or Catholic, both in biblical eras and the church age. Furthermore, there has been no significant movement or denomination that was not somehow birthed apart from wild, outward manifestations, tranced prophetic utterances, swoonings, faintings, or the general *splat* of God coming in to show off His glory.

From feeling a general sense of God's joyful pleasure to the more bone-shaking encounters of His heavy glory, we have seen a wide variety of stages and intermediate ways that the bliss of God can impact our lives and cause supernatural happenings around us. As we embrace this realm of glory, we become channels of blessing—literally gateways of Heaven—spilling out the substance of God everywhere we go.

We are on the cusp of the greatest revival the world has ever seen. It will be the most violent, the most gloriously blissful, and the most visible public demonstration God has ever released on the earth.

It is not an evangelism technique or manmade program that will usher in the end-time harvest. There is a *glory*—God's very presence—that attracts new believers at a colossal scale. Simultaneously, there is a vast increase in harvest angels being released in the earth who help us emanate the fragrant bliss of Heaven, that we might *"diffuse the fragrance of His knowledge in every place...the aroma of life leading to life"* (2 Cor. 2:14-15).

Cultivating the deepest throes of interior, intimate bliss between you and Jesus enables you to one day spill this excess of joy out to the multitudes as a precious aroma. Power is released through the ecstasy of this inner flame that grows to impact the nations. Our secret relationship produces public displays of Heaven.

John Wesley understood this principle. He said, "I set myself on fire and people come to watch me burn." Wesley's own passion in the Secret Place became a vortex of glory that sucked in the masses like a magnet, sweeping the streets with harvest glory.

John Wesley on Fire

The supernatural swirl surrounding the life of Wesley is incredible, though his stories have been clinically suppressed in most contemporary Methodist streams. A number of Methodist scholars have noted how Wesley's biographers found his emphasis on the supernatural to be "embarrassing." Methodist writer Stephen Gunter says that "for two centuries students of the Methodist revival have tended to 'play down' Wesley's emphasis on...miraculous intervention."[1]

Take a moment to picture an early Methodist meeting. They were full of stamping, shouting, weeping, wailing, and people falling to the floor in trances all over the place. These were wild God encounters, and prophetic utterances and visions were taken seriously. It was reported that you could hear the meetings from miles away. In one Methodist meeting in 1807 for instance, Hugh Bourne was speaking to thousands of people on God's judgment, and "many ran away, while others fell upon each other in heaps."[2]

As John Wesley and George Whitefield zipped through their circuit riding routes in America and Britain during the First Great Awakening, it was not uncommon for them to preach 20 times a week to crowds ranging up to 30,000 strong. And this was no sissy preaching. It was loud and brutal. It was soul-winning, heart-wrenching thunder. During both of the Great Awakenings, droves of the population came to Christ and experienced severe spiritual renewal.

Wesley ran his circuit like a mad man. He went through horses like a fish goes through water. He never had a moment to lose. He would preach to thousands, then jump on a horse and ride like lightning to the next town, where more thousands would be gathering for another meeting. He had his routes planned out impeccably and was never late. He would run a horse until it was hot, sweaty, and half dead, then switch it out for another and keep running. Once when he was made to wait for a new horse, he was heard to say, "I have lost ten minutes forever."

Wesley would ride 5,000 miles a year on horseback, clocking in a quarter of a million miles by the end of his life. That is equivalent to circling the globe nine times on a horse. At one point he made 90 miles in the saddle in one day, riding 20 hours straight. As snowdrifts and slippery ice threatened to block him from the saddle, Wesley said, "At least, we can walk twenty miles a day, with our horses in our hands."

Wesley would ride with a book in one hand and the reins in the other. Many times he narrowly escaped death as a horse would stumble and fall on him, or he would have some sort of collision. There are numerous times recorded in his journal where he was miraculously saved from death or healed on the spot after being crushed by a horse. Other times, he would pray for a sick, dying horse, and it would be instantly cured, allowing him to make it to the next town and reap harvest.[3]

Revival is about to come on so strong, so unexpectedly, and on such a massive scale, that the church must be prepared. Like the early disciples calling out for help because of the massive quantity of fish in their nets, we will truly need all hands on deck just to pull them all in. It will be a time of acceleration, running fast, and gathering heaps of fruit. Imagine thousands amassing in parking lots, open fields, municipal parks, and stadiums at the drop of a hat. This will not be gradual. Like dropping a catalyst into a chemical formula, the reaction will explode in an instantly. *And the Lord, whom you seek, will suddenly come to His temple*" (Mal. 3:1). Bodies will be strewn chaotically among the masses as harvest angels brood through the crowds of tens of thousands.

The now and coming revival will be so disproportionate to anything like it in history, the droves of new believers coming into the church will require the participation of the whole Body of Christ. Brand-new believers will be leading home groups. And those who lead a home group today will be pastoring thousands when this thing cracks open. There is a regiment who will tirelessly haul the nets night and day, like Wesley, who will not sleep in the time of harvest (see Prov. 10:5).

Thunderstruck in the Streets

Let us look further at the example of Wesley. Healings were common in his meetings as well, and there was tremendous influence by the Moravians on Wesley's life—a group steeped in supernatural Christianity. John Wesley's view of the miraculous was much like the Orthodox Christian church, which really doesn't delineate a difference between the natural and the supernatural. For the Orthodox, everything is a miracle from God. The earth itself was spoken into existence by Him. To the Orthodox, even a tree or a mountain is evidence of God's handiwork. Supernatural wonders are no more miraculous than the mundane things of life, only *they occur more infrequently*.

Wesley gives numerous accounts of trances and ecstasies experienced by believers and new converts in his meetings. Writing in his journal on April 26, 1739, he simply says, "Immediately one and another and another sunk to the Earth: they dropped on every side as thunderstruck."[4] In another entry, after preaching to thousands in the open air, Wesley notes that "one and another and another was struck to the Earth, exceedingly trembling at the presence of His power."[5]

Wesley considered these manifestations a sign of God's ever-present power. While preaching on the apostles' prayer in Acts 4, for the Lord to stretch forth His hand and perform signs and wonders in the name of Jesus, people began to cry out and fall in Wesley's meeting. He said it was proof that God's hand is "still stretched out to heal, and that signs and wonders are even now wrought by His holy child Jesus."[6]

Five years after these incidents in 1739, Wesley noted in a letter to an acquaintance that the "fits (as you term them) are not left off. They are frequent now, both in Europe and America, among persons newly convinced of sin. I neither forward nor hinder them."[7]

When the Holy Spirit first began to fall in the evangelistic services conducted by Wesley and his brother, Charles, the two were a bit fearful as people began going down under the power. Charles said, "No more of this."

But it was not long afterward that Charles Wesley was approached by one of his contemporaries and scolded for quenching the Spirit. "Charles," he was told, "you have not had any great miracles, not even many conversions, since you discouraged people from going under the power."

At times, the glory came in so rapidly and violently, people were thrown about like an 18th-century Holy Ghost mosh pit, with things getting smashed up left and right. Consider this account from March 3, 1788, in Wesley's journal as he preached in his home church at Bristol:

> About the middle of the discourse, while there was on every side attention (as still) as night, a vehement noise arose, none could tell why, and shot like lightning through the whole congregation. The terror and confusion were inexpressible. You might have imagined it was a city taken by storm. The people rushed upon each other with the utmost violence, the benches were broken in pieces, and nine-tenths of the congregation appeared to be struck with the same panic. In about six minutes the storm ceased almost as suddenly as it rose. And all being calm, I went on without the least interruption. It was the strangest incident of the kind I ever remember, and believe none can account for it without supposing some preternatural influence.[8]

For more than a century, Methodists were known for their loud, ecstatic meetings. Wesley's life was a prophetic blueprint of a new and coming wave of circuit riders—carriers of the glory who will see mass harvest breaking loose on the streets in unprecedented proportions. Violent shakings, droves of converts, and powerful demonstrations of the Kingdom will be displayed in all of Heaven's fury. The multitudes of souls being impacted by the drunken glory on the streets will make the story of Pentecost look like child's play.

Hitting the Streets

There is a *glory movement* taking place in the church today, in which

God is emphasizing His presence above and beyond anything else. Meetings and conferences are no longer just about teachings and giftings, but about the tangible presence of God showing up. The Lord is teaching us how to cultivate a lifestyle in this cloud of glory that is followed by signs, wonders, and harvest. But there is drastic transition about to take place. The glory in the meetings is jumping outside to the streets.

As an itinerant minister myself, I quite honestly get bored in conferences. Although the Lord shows up powerfully with miracles, wonders, and heavy glory—Christians are far too predictable! Experiencing the glory on the streets can be far more exciting. You never know what is going to happen next! Your day could end in hundreds getting saved, miracles on the streets, or even persecution. There is an addiction that comes with *riding the light* out in the margins and the dark places.

For years, the church has talked about *taking it to the streets*. But usually, they have just meant taking a Gospel of *salvation only* to the streets. Obviously the Lord wants to do much more than save souls. He also wants to get people delivered, discipled, healed, and filled with the Spirit. He wants a full *Gospel of the Kingdom* to be released in the marketplace.

Living a Kingdom message is different from just *understanding* Kingdom principles. Even Charismatics who have a revelation of the Kingdom message (perhaps they pray for the sick or prophesy over people, etc.) are often too programmatic, planned, or overly structured in their approach. Teaching about the Kingdom (or even doing Kingdom things) is different than fully embracing the Holy Spirit. The only way to move in the Kingdom is to be completely possessed by the glory.

The Lord wants to powerfully use our gifts to reach the lost through innovative methods like prophetic evangelism, dream interpretation, worship outreaches, healing prayer for the lost, etc. But we *must be careful* that we do not focus on the gifting, as if the techniques or personal revelations will get the job done. Even cool spiritual gifts can become old wineskins when we rely on them too much. Ultimately, we must rely on God's presence beyond any skill or ministry gift. We have discovered that there is another realm that makes evangelism far easier and more fruitful than any manner of gift, outreach technique, or Kingdom revelation. It is simple: *stay in the glory*!

Additionally, with evangelism, we can tend to be too results oriented. We focus on how many souls were saved, instead of just keeping our eyes fixed on the glory. The result is that many people get bored, burned out, or exhausted by evangelism.

Harvest Glory

There is a *harvest glory* being released in this day, which makes evangelism not a task but a delight. We will just float down the street in the presence of God, and the little fishies will jump into our boats! Going to the streets and the marketplace becomes an addiction for those who begin to taste this harvest glory. We long to offer Jesus every delicacy—to give Him the sweet fruit of intimacy, but also the fields of harvest.

I never considered myself an *evangelist*, per se. To this day, I do not feel I am particularly gifted at it. That is not even my main calling from God. I always preferred to stay drunk on God rather than worry about talking to people! Little did I know that all along I was actually choosing the *best thing*. When we love God first, fully and without reservation, only then are we able to be effective in our ministry to other people. All of a sudden, one day I realized that my quest for holy pleasure was spilling out around me, and hundreds of people were getting saved! We don't focus on doing anything—we just get whacked in public.

The key to harvest evangelism is to get blasted in the Spirit and enjoy it! We sometimes bring teams onto the streets with no program or plan in mind. Prophetic evangelism, dream interpretation, and other revelatory-based efforts are wonderful. But when we just get whacked in the Spirit, with bodies falling over, shaking and drinking heavily, it seems that the anointing gets the job done much more easily. Suddenly crowds start to appear, amazed not just at the craziness, but at the obvious fun we are having. Besides that, somehow they *sense the presence of God*. To ride these waves of glory, you cannot have any fear of others, only an enjoyment of God! When we lay down our lives for the bliss, we no longer care about the opinions of others. Seeing the wild and joyful manifestations right in the street, people start to come up to us and say, "Do that to me!"

Here is an example. We once brought a handful of crazies out on the streets for an afternoon of fishing in Bristol, England, which ironically was the home base of John Wesley. The culture of the U.K. may be known for its reserved demeanor, but the people are hungry and the harvest is ripe! We took this small group of ecstatic drinkers with us onto Queen Street and had a Holy Ghost party. Right in the street angels began to yank people around by their arms and legs. Bodies started to hit the pavement, with men and women shaking and convulsing powerfully under the heavy weight of the glory.

It did not take long for a crowd to gather. I felt the Lord say, "Don't think about harvest; think about Me!" The more I stayed focused on the glory of Jesus, the more hammered I got. The more drunk we became, the more people stopped to watch us. We led 30 people to Christ in just an hour and a half because of the crazy drunken bliss in the streets!

The wine of Heaven enables a supernatural boldness and freedom from the fear of man. This joy is the *spirit of a martyr*. You don't have to get killed to have this spirit! But you will get so *blissed* that you don't care if you do! While on the streets in Bristol on this one occasion, I led six teenagers to the Lord simultaneously in one prayer, simply because they wanted to experience what was happening to me! We prayed for a woman in a wheelchair with vertebrae problems, and the fire of God began running up her spine. After a word of knowledge, both she and her daughter received the Lord.

Next, some people came forward for prayer, but when we laid hands on them, they felt God's presence and ran off shrieking! The Spirit of the Fear of the Lord arrested them. A policeman came by to investigate what was going on, seeing all of the dropped and twitching bodies, screams, and laughter. We told Him we were praying for people, but when we asked him if he wanted prayer, he too ran away in fear! Then full of holy boldness, one of the team members chased the policeman down the street for prayer!

Evangelism is not effective if you are dutifully striving to fulfill the Great Commission. Some try to offer the Lord a harvest in immaturity, and they bear little fruit. True maturity is to get possessed by the bliss of the Holy Spirit. Then watch what happens. Joy breaks open the atmosphere. We are matured by the bliss, and when our joy is ripe it explodes out of us in heart-felt devotion for the world to see. If evangelism seems difficult for you—if it still feels like a dry duty—you are probably still doing it out of obligation or striving for acceptance. You may want to stop altogether for a while and just drink the love of Jesus! When you drink enough, it will eventually spill out. It becomes a pent-up fire in your bones! The love will need an escape valve!

Remember that a drunken man will do and say things that a sober man will not. If your sacrifice is a work of duty, you must return to the place of pleasure! Then God will possess you, and the angels do all the work. Harvest will come as an overflowing act of love. We labor in the fields as a blissful byproduct of our unconditional acceptance.

"God wants you to be a lover. And He wants you to be a working lover. Who you are is the lover, and what you do is the work. You are not to be only a worker who struggles to love God. Instead, you are a lover of God," writes Mike Bickle in *The Pleasures of Loving God.*[9] "Being lovers is our very identity. It's who we are. We are lovers of God who happen to work, not the other way around.... God wants us to be relationally oriented first, and achievement oriented second."

Our identity—*lovers of God*—supersedes our actions—fulfilling the Great Commission, etc. Moreover, until we become who we are, we can never fulfill what we've been called to do.

When we get blasted in the love of God, things start to happen around us. Our intimate relationship with God should not be sectioned off from the rest of our lives and cloistered into the prayer closet. God wants to invade the fabric of our lifestyle with the enjoyment of His presence. Actions and fruitfulness are byproducts of a lifestyle of intimacy.

The Great Commission is about to move from a paradigm of work and sacrificial labor to a response of lovesick bridal devotion. There is a place of love that reclines under the apple tree, but there is also an intensity of love that can literally drive us to do great exploits. The apostle Paul said, *"The love of Christ compels us..."* (2 Cor. 5:14). We literally become *love slaves*, compelled and driven by a loving passion that burns in our bones. A love slave bears only the burden of bliss. This slavery has nothing to do with striving to obey God on the chain gang. Instead, you are compelled—you can't help yourself. Your heart is driven by love, inspired by love, and absolutely *enthralled*.

The definition for the word *enthralled* means to be delighted or thoroughly fascinated by something or someone so that your attention becomes completely engaged. It also means to *enslave*: to make somebody a prisoner and claim legal ownership of that person. You have become a slave to joy! A slave to His river of delight.

When you are infected to this degree…when it is real, and not feigned by a religious spirit, then it becomes *contagious*. The world is hungry for pure, abandoned pleasure! Stop striving. Stop twisting people's arms to get saved! Get whacked and just watch the little fishies jump into your boat! Before long, you will be stinking of fish.

Palestinian Pile-ups

Explosions of drunken love are the very things that will win the Islamic world to Christ. Muslim nations are about to be taken in an instant, simply because of outbreaks of joy! These same principles of staying whacked in public are the key to harvesting the hardest nations of all.

At the time of this writing, we took a team of more than 100 crazy Holy Spirit junkies to minister openly in one of the most intense seedbeds of Islamic suicide bombers and terrorists in the world. We traveled to the holy land for an outreach into Bethlehem and especially into a United Nations-secured Palestinian refugee camp. We were able to feed and share the Gospel with more than 500 Muslim girls, as well as pray for hundreds of Palestinian schoolboys. We also brought food—rice, flour, groceries, etc.—to widows and orphans. This was such a volatile area that the Israeli military officials marveled at the fact that someone would return alive.

These are the people who should want to shoot us, but it is difficult to shoot someone who is coming to love on you and bring you food! It is also difficult to shoot at a silly drunken fool who makes you laugh! Jesus has called us to bless our enemies, and it is only the love of God that can radically transform lives!

Because we ministered to orphans and widows, we were able to receive special access from PLO leaders to go right into these camps. This was unprecedented. This area has been one of the most volatile places on the planet in recent years. In fact, the hall in which we met was painted with huge murals, glorifying Islamic suicide bombers. Imagine large colorful paintings of women in burkas throwing hand grenades! But the Lord allowed us to speak to these children and share the love of Christ—even President George Bush had been denied access to speak to these children in past visits.

Our team blazed in, carrying a joyful atmosphere of celebration everywhere we went. None of these people had ever seen such dancing, outward affection, manifestations of the Holy Spirit, and open displays of happiness in worship. We started dropping joy bombs everywhere!

At times, we would have huge pileups of bodies, shaking, twitching, and laughing under the Spirit's power right in public. In one Arab restaurant, the team caused such a loud, obnoxious drunken scene that our associate David Vaughan had to get up and preach to explain that it all came from God. Four of the six Arab workers gave their lives to the Lord on the spot, including the owner of the building who said it was the best day of his life!

What will it look like as the glory jumps from the meetings to the streets? It will be a massive explosion of latter rain in exponential proportions. Not just street preaching or pre-planned outreaches, but signs and wonders on every corner. Not just twisting someone's arm to say a salvation prayer, but leading hundreds and thousands to repentance en masse.

Prophetically I believe we are approaching a threshold in time when the glory of God must be taken from our conference meetings to the marketplace. This is much like the era when the great revivalist George Whitefield left his indoor pulpit and took the Gospel to the open air.

George Whitefield Harvests the Masses

At the start of the Great Awakening, George Whitefield was preaching to crowds of 1,000 people crammed into church buildings. But there were another 2,000 people crowded outside the doors, standing in the church graveyard, straining to hear him. Finally Whitefield said "enough of this," and decided to preach outside in the open streets where the people were.

John Wesley thought Whitefield was off his rocker for leaving the church, but when he saw the fruit, Wesley soon did the same. Before long, crowds of tens of thousands would assemble to receive salvation. I believe that we are about to cross this same threshold in the Western church. As the church encounters supernatural dimensions of love, joy, and miracles, revival will spread so quickly and rapidly that we will have to move our meetings out to the streets. In many towns, the only place large enough to have your meeting will be a spontaneous gathering in the parking lot of grocery stores, or the open fields. There will be no time to set up sound systems, so get ready to preach with a bullhorn!

Whitefield first took to preaching in the open air in Hanham Mount, southeast of Bristol, in one of the worst neighborhoods of the day. Approximately 20,000 poor workers came to hear him, their tears cutting white streaks down their dirty faces and "strong men being moved to hysterical convulsions by [God's] wondrous power."[10] The crowds mushroomed. Regularly, Whitefield had masses of 30,000 people at once cramming in to see him, and at certain times, up to 80,000!

Benjamin Franklin, though not a Christian, describes the effect on the community after Whitefield's preaching in Philadelphia: "It seemed as if all the world were growing religious, so that one could not walk through the town in an evening without hearing psalms sung in different families of every street."[11]

Franklin was a friend of Whitefield and published his journals. However, Franklin was initially skeptical of reports that Whitefield was preaching to crowds of tens of thousands on the streets. Remember that there was no amplification device for his voice, and besides, these numbers were phenomenal. During one of his sermons, Franklin measured the distance that he could walk away from Whitefield until he could no longer hear the preacher's voice in the open air. Then allowing for 2 feet per person around the parameter, Franklin calculated that it *really was possible* for tens of thousands to hear Whitefield preach at once.

Wild manifestations would accompany Whitefield's preaching; however, he was doubtful concerning them. While John Wesley recognized these ecstatic manifestations as a fruit of encountering God, Whitefield criticized Wesley for allowing the phenomena to take place. But before long, manifestations began to happen in his own meetings. Whitefield initially expressed his doubts, saying to Wesley:

I cannot think it right in you to give so much encouragement to those convulsions to which people have been thrown into under your ministry. Were I to do so, how many would cry out every night? I think it is tempting God to require such signs. That there is something of God in it, I doubt not. But the devil I believe does interpose. I think it will encourage the French prophets. It will take people from the written Word and make them depend on visions, convulsions, etc. more than on the promises and precepts of the Gospel.[12]

But John Wesley did not let the story end there. He personally visited Whitefield and had a "sit down" with him, to discuss the issue of manifestations. Here is Wesley's account of the meeting:

Saturday, 7.—I had an opportunity to talk with him of those outward signs which had so often accompanied the inward work of God. I found his objections were chiefly grounded on gross misrepresentations of matter of fact. But the next day he had an opportunity of informing himself better: for no sooner had he begun (in the application of his sermon) to invite all sinners to believe in Christ, than four persons sank down close to him, almost in the same moment. One of them lay without either sense or motion. A second trembled exceedingly. The third had strong convulsions all over his body, but made no noise unless by groans. The fourth, equally convulsed, called upon God with strong cries and tears. From this time, I trust, we shall all suffer God to carry on His own work in the way that pleaseth Him.[13]

It was not long after this that all Heaven exploded on the scene in Whitefield's meetings, for "often as many as 500 would fall in the group and lay prostrate under the power of a single sermon. Many people made demonstrations, and in several instances men who held out against the Spirit's wooing dropped dead during his meetings."[14]

Whitefield's preaching style was loud and dynamic. Preaching extemporaneously, without the use of notes, his arms would flail about in the air, and his voice and expressions were lively and animated. Whitefield had trained as an actor, and his critics cast doubts about his charisma. However, the crowds flocked, and the glory fell.

"He waved his arms, made violent gestures, shouted and danced to the delight of the gathering throngs, who had grown weary of the highbrow, heavily annotated, and gentlemanly styles of preachers from Harvard and Yale," writes author Benjamin Hart. "During a Whitefield sermon, people would shriek, roll on the ground, dissolve into tears, or run wild with religious ecstasy. Even the agnostic Scottish philosopher David Hume once said of Whitefield that it was worth traveling 20 miles to hear him."[15]

These meetings were wild, though not all his listeners were fans. "I was honored with having stones, dirt, rotten eggs, and pieces of dead cats thrown at me," writes Whitefield.[16]

The acting dean of Yale wrote of Whitefield in a letter to a friend in 1741, after he blazed through setting the students aflame with revival:

> *But this new enthusiasm, in consequence of Whitefield's preaching through the country and his disciples', has got great footing in the College [Yale]... Many of the scholars have been possessed of it, and two of this year's candidates were denied their degrees for their disorderly and restless endeavors to propagate it.... We have now prevailing among us the most odd and unaccountable enthusiasm than perhaps obtained in any age or nation. For not only the minds of many people are at once struck with prodigious distresses upon their hearing the hideous outcries of our itinerate preachers, but **even their bodies are frequently in a moment affected with the strangest convulsions and involuntary agitations and cramps, which also have sometimes happened to those who came as mere spectators...** [emphasis mine].[17]*

In the Cambuslang revival outside Glasgow, Scotland in 1742, a large communion celebration was held. It was here that people began falling out in the Spirit by the droves. Whitefield, who was serving some of the tables, was "so filled with the love of God, as to be in a kind of ecstasy."[18] At the next revival service, hundreds fell out in the Spirit, along with manifestations of laughter, prophecy, and groaning.

"Almost as prominent as falling were various bodily movements. Convulsive motions dated at least from early Scottish communions, and after Cane Ridge would become known, collectively and misleadingly, as the 'jerks.' The term concealed the diversity of such motions, including rhythmic dancing. More conventional shouts and groans joined with a near babble of speech, some incoherent, some later distinguished as holy laughter or singing," writes Christian author William DeArteaga in his book, *Quenching the Spirit.*[19]

The power of God's glory resting on Whitefield should not go unnoticed. At times, there was such weightiness; it was like Acts 5, when Ananias and Sapphira had to be dragged out dead from the meeting.

Once when preaching in Yorkshire in 1756, Whitefield stood on a platform erected outside an open window of a church, where he could be heard by those inside as well as the several thousand crowded outside. He read from the text in Hebrews 9:27: "it is appointed for men to die once, but after this the judgment." Suddenly, a "wild, terrifying shriek" came from the audience, as someone instantly dropped dead. One of the ministers pressed through the crowd, and after a moment of confusion, the body was carried away. After a pause, Whitefield, began to loudly read again, *"And as it is appointed for men to die once, but after this the judgment."* Immediately another screech erupted from a different part of the crowd. A second person had dropped dead after hearing Whitefield's words on death and judgment.[20]

The local pastor, Rev. William Grimshaw, pressed through the crowd toward Whitefield, saying that the destroying angel was at hand, "Brother Whitefield, you are standing between the living and the dead!" After that, the mass of people were overwhelmed by his appeal.

The Wildfire Spreads

So impressed with Whitefield's charismatic oratory, lay preacher James Davenport followed him to New York and Philadelphia to learn from the revivalist. Davenport became a radical, picking up Whitefield's delivery style and taking it further. During his meetings, Congregationalist minister Joseph Fish says Davenport allowed "unrestrained liberty to noise and outcry, both of distress and joy, in time of divine service.... promot[ing] both with all his might—by extending his own voice to the highest pitch, together with the most violent agitation of body, even to the distorting of his features and marring his visage."[21]

Davenport was known as a wild man, and he encouraged other lay preachers to spread the revival, in what became known as the Separate Congregationalists. In June 1742, Davenport was arraigned before the Colonial Assembly at Hartford, Connecticut, along with fellow preacher Benjamin Pomeroy, charged with disorderly conduct. They declared Davenport to be under "enthusiastical impressions and impulses, and thereby disturbed in the rational faculties of his mind."

The style of trances and visions experienced by this group of Separate Congregationalists would later be preserved in the worship of the Separate Baptists. These Baptists had people "crying-out under ministry, falling-down as in fits, and awakening in extacies; and both ministers and people resemble [the Congregationalists] in regarding impulses, visions and revelations [*sic*]."[22]

Also regarding Baptist meetings in Virginia, in 1771, observer John Williams wrote, "The Christians (fell) to shouting, sinners trembling and falling down convulsed." And in a following revival, 14 years later, Baptist clergyman John Leland describes "heavenly confusion among the preachers," as well as "celestial discord among the people."[23]

Revival in the Virginia region encompassed the Methodists too, as Wesley appointee Thomas Rankin records in 1776: "Now when the power descended, hundreds fell to the ground, and the house seemed to shake with the presence of God."[24]

In a 1787 Methodist revival, the preachers could not quiet down the congregation enough to speak, amid all the praises and shouting, until finally they gave up. At the height of the noise, eleven rafters broke in the roof, without anyone noticing it amid the commotion. Richard Garrettson, a Virginia Methodist preacher at that time, told of how the noise of the congregation "induced numbers of people to come, so that in places where we used to have but twenty or thirty on a week day, now there will be a thousand, and sometimes more." He added that in the prayer meetings, "five, eight and ten are often converted at one meeting, where there are no Preachers [and] the meetings often hold six or seven hours together."[25]

The Glorious Chaos of Cane Ridge

Thousands of people will again be corporately impacted by God right in the streets as they were during the First Great Awakening. But let us turn our attention now to the glorious chaos that erupted at the birth of the Second Great Awakening. Consider the remarkable event that took place in August of 1801, known as the Cane Ridge Revival. On the sparsely populated frontier of Kentucky, there were an amazing 20,000 people who showed up for this six-day event in the middle of nowhere. Perhaps for the first time in America, falling to the ground in trance was not only normal— it was absolutely par for the course.

The Cane Ridge event involved Baptists, Methodists, Presbyterians, and citizens from all walks of life. In all its drunken, bizarre behavior, literary critic Harold Bloom went so far as to call it "the first Woodstock."[26] A young skeptic, James B. Finley, was among the thousands converted there, and he wrote the following account:

> The noise was like that of Niagara. The vast sea of human beings seemed to be agitated as if by a storm. I counted seven ministers, all preaching on stumps, others in wagons and one standing on a tree which had in falling, lodged against another.... Some of the people were singing, others praying, some crying for mercy in the most piteous accents, while others were shouting most vociferously. While witnessing these scenes, a peculiarly strange sensation such as I had never felt before came over me. My heart beat tumultuously, my knees trembled, my lips quivered and I felt as though I must fall to the ground. A supernatural power seemed to pervade the entire mass of mind there collected.... I stepped up on a log where I

could have a better view of the surging sea of humanity. The scene that had presented itself to my mind was inde-scribable. **At one time I saw at least five hundred swept down in a moment as if a battery of a thousand guns had been opened upon them and then immediately followed shrieks and shouts that rent the very heavens** [emphasis mine].[27]

This was the beginning of the Second Great Awakening.

Observers of the scene confessed their inability to describe it. They said that language could not do it justice. The Rev. Moses Hoge wrote that the people "fall down, cry out, tremble, and not infrequently are affected with convulsive twitchings....Nothing that imagination can paint, can make a stronger impression upon the mind, than one of those scenes. Sinners drop-ping down on every hand, shrieking, groaning, crying for mercy, convulsed; professors praying, agonizing, fainting, falling down in distress for sinners or in raptures of joy!"[28]

While ecstatic manifestations were called "enthusiasms" in the revivals of Jonathan Edwards and John Wesley's day, the coined term for them at the Cane Ridge Revival was the "jerks." This was the name given individu-ally and collectively to the convulsive motions that took place among the people as God's glory descended, as "saints and sinners alike experienced the despair or ecstasy. Such was the noise and disorder that few had opportu-nity to hear any extended sermons. No aerobic exercise could match some of the jerking and dancing and those most exercised reported extreme sore-ness. Those affected, some at the cost of great embarrassment, invariably agreed that what they did was involuntarily."[29] One observer writes:

Their heads would jerk back suddenly, frequently causing them to yelp or make some other involuntary noise... sometimes the head would fly every way so quickly that their features could not be recognised. I have seen their heads fly back and forward so quickly that the hair of females would be made to crack like a carriage whip, but not very loud.[30]

The following is another account from the revival: "…the tumultuous bodily 'exercises' began. Along with the shouting and crying, some began falling. Some experienced only weakened knees or a light head (including Governor James Garrad). Others fell but remained conscious or talkative; a few fell into a deep coma, displaying the symptoms of a grand mal seizure or a type of hysteria."[31]

In another letter from the period, written by Colonel Robert Patterson, of Lexington, he tried, "as well as I am able," to describe the emotion:

> Of all ages, from 8 years and upwards; male and female; rich and poor; the blacks; and of every denomination; those in favour of it, as well as those, at the instant in opposition to it, and railing against it, have instantaneously laid motionless on the ground. Some feel the approaching symptoms by being under deep convictions; their heart swells, their nerves relax, and in an instant they become motionless and speechless, but generally retain their senses [sic].[32]

Patterson said that for some, the manifestations lasted anywhere from "one hour to 24."

Ecstasies in the Holy Fairs

The Cane Ridge revival was, at the time, known as the "Cane Ridge Sacrament," because it was originally a large communion festival. Early Scottish and American Presbyterians had a long tradition of these communion feasts that were marked by wild, ecstatic behavior. These *holy fairs*, as they were called, dated back to at least 1590. They were always known for visions, faintings, and extreme manifestations, though the prevalence of these phenomena were greatly amplified during the Second Great Awakening.

The holy fairs were nearly week-long, seasonal festivals oriented around the Lord's Supper. They were birthed amid the divide between Catholics and Protestants in the 16th century. As Reformers sought to eradicate all holy days from the calendar, for fear of superstitious adherence, early Presbyterians clung to these times as special occasions when God's presence was manifest among them. From these communion seasons, many great revivals erupted in Europe and America.

One of the first great revivals in Scotland was marked by the 1630 sacrament at Shotts. Presbyterian preacher John Livingston, reported a "downpouring of the SPIRIT" at that time, noting how his words had "a strange unusual MOTION on the hearers" with many fainting away and laying on the ground "as if they had been dead."[33] Another report from Presbyterian minister James Glendinning tells of this same revival as it was breaking loose in the 1620s and 1630s in Scotland, noting that many were "stricken, and swoon with the Word—yea, a dozen in one day carried out of doors as dead, so marvelous was the power of God smiting their hearts for sin, condemning and killing." Many of the ministers of this revival were jailed or deported for stirring "up the People to Extasies and Enthusiasms," and were regularly opposed by the government or the Episcopal church— but the communion seasons continued each year, though at times secretly.[34]

The revival at Cambuslang, Scotland in 1742 is perhaps the most well-known of the communion events in the 18th century, leading up to Cane Ridge. Thirty to forty thousand people gathered outside Glasgow for this sacrament. Like Shotts and other Presbyterian communion fairs of that era, it was full of ecstatic activities, trances, falling over, hearing voices, and seeing visions; however, leaders were careful to hide this fact in their histories of the event. Historian Leigh Schmidt writes that "those who edited the Cambuslang manuscripts were especially concerned to minimize this aspect of the saints' piety in order to save revival supporters from charges of enthusiasm and disorder and to reaffirm the rational and scriptural soundness of evangelical spirituality. They thus cut out almost all mention of ecstatic religious experience, such as visions, voices, and trances...."[35]

Schmidt says that the tendency of scholars has been to avoid these manifestations, rather than giving a comprehensive Biblical exegesis for them. By sweeping these exercises under the rug, the church has in effect, handed the task of explanation over to sociologists, psychologists, and satirists. The result is that "those practices have been more often the object of snickers than serious analysis." Historians of the revival such as

Edwin Enzor, Jr., for instance, said that while the jerks, holy laughter, and falling exercises were startling, "they fail to tell the whole story." And William Sweet, a Methodist writer, acknowledged that hundreds were "agitated" with manifestations, but dismissed them "as dubious, to say the least."[36]

"Often considered an embarrassment to those within more sober Protestant circles, these exercises have usually been passed over quickly, euphemistically muted, blamed on emotion-fraught Methodists and Shakers, or simply left aside," adds Schmidt, pointing out that even when historians openly acknowledged the exercises, it was often just to divert attention away from them. "From the mid-nineteenth century through much of the twentieth century, weak-kneed, overwhelmed enthusiasts were regularly hidden away in the closet, attic, or gallery of 'mainstream' Protestant memory."[37]

It seems there is nothing new under the sun. Revival has always produced messy ecstatic behavior, and the institutional critics have always disdained it. Episcopalian critic Thomas Rind questioned "the religious Freaks of the Presbyterian Converts" in 1712, as well as their "Illuminations and Raptures." He spoke of their experiences as "Animal Agitations, luscious Fervours, and amourous Recumbrances."[38]

One of the greatest objections from heresy hunters during the Toronto Renewal of the 1990s centered around one particularly strange manifestation: *barking like a dog.* But Barton Stone, a famous preacher from Tennessee during the Great Revival, reports doing this himself in his own memoirs at a time when he was "seized by the jerks."[39] Furthermore, Second Great Awakening historian Richard McNemar records people manifesting in a similar way nearly 200 years ago, when overwhelmed by God's Spirit, as they "take the position of a canine beast, move about on all fours, growl, snap the teeth, and bark."[40] Some of these ministers, having no other explanation, assumed God was *humbling* the individual. Edward Scribner Ames, a philosopher with the University of Chicago, wrote in 1910 that in revival meetings "many strange extravagances—falling, jerking, jumping, rolling, barking—have occurred."[41]

The bodily contortions and outcries of revivalism in the Second Great Awakening would take the enthusiasm of the Scottish communion feasts to a whole new level. But Presbyterians continued to be prone to such exciting experience. Joseph Thomas, an itinerant preacher, noted of the Presbyterian revivals around 1800, "Here I found the Presbyterians were as noisy and seemed to have as much religion, as any people I had seen," adding "there was much exercise [manifestation] among the people. This exercise consists chiefly in shouting, dancing, jumping, hollowing, laughing...."[42]

James McGready was a minister who spanned the transition from the communion holy fairs to the modern American revivalism that followed Cane Ridge. By 1803, a couple years after Cane Ridge, he noted the continuing ecstatic nature of the communion services. "The exercise at the [communion] tables was indeed a heaven upon earth. Christians at the tables, almost universally, from first to last, were so filled with joy unspeakable, and full of glory, that they might, with propriety, be compared to bottles filled with new wine."[43]

Chapter 15

the new martyrs

The greatest harvest the earth has ever seen is just at hand. And it will largely come through a radical movement of love-crazed, end-times martyrs, whose ecstatic lives will usher in the Last Great Awakening.

Rarely in any theological stream have men and women been able to embrace the paradox of pleasure and suffering, life and death, sorrow and joy. But the spiritual awakening that now broods on the horizon—which will sweep a billion souls into the Kingdom before the return of the Lord—will not come without the shedding of blood. Where there is great victory, there will also be great sacrifice. The good news is that we will not be frowning about it. There is a new wave of martyrs that will come from the Western world, laying down their lives—and most of them will be *laughing*.

There is a bliss we can experience that has driven men and women throughout the ages to offer themselves in sacrifice. The historical account of the martyrs of the church provides us a glimpse of the strongest bubble of glory ever afforded to humankind, right in the midst of their suffering. Are you hungry for the highest level of holy intoxication of them all? I know a secret. . . . Ask for a martyr angel!

In this hour, God is releasing *martyr angels* to those who are craving a deeper level of His bliss. We should understand that these martyr angels are not about death—the death part of the equation is totally negligible. Their chief task is to minister the heaviest imaginable dose of His drunken glory. The delight is literally so good, you can face all manner of persecution, barely even noticing if you die. When the *martyr spirit* comes upon you, there is such a transcending glory you will begin to experience! You don't give a second thought to throwing yourself into harm's way. It is so intense that you will not mind going to North Korea, Saudi Arabia, or any other part of the world where persecution is strongest. You will just see it as a potential bliss-fest! You will no longer care an iota what people think about you, nor fear the opinions of man. You will drink in public, sharing the love of Jesus freely—you will gladly trade in your reputation for these intense raptures.

The beatitudes resonate with this delightful promise of holy pleasure for the persecuted:

> *Yours is the **bliss**, when men shall heap their insults on you and persecute you, and tell every wicked kind of lie about you for My sake* (Matthew 5:11 Barclay).

To talk of death and martyrdom, most Christians miss the point entirely. They get somber or mournful. This is not a fearful thing. The true *spirit of a martyr* is not one of depression, masochism, or religious defeatism. That is a "martyr complex." People who focus on the external death or suffering have entirely missed the internal consolations that a martyr may be experiencing. The true spirit of a martyr is abandoned joy and bliss, such euphoric willingness to sacrifice because of the superior pleasures of the Spirit realm.

One of the greatest mistakes of the church has been to merely pity the martyrs or extol their deeds. Not that this is inherently wrong, but our focus has neglected to realize the utterly tangible elation they experienced during their trials. The hallmark of a true martyr spirit is not depression and agony, but joy and bliss. The apostle Paul spoke of taking "pleasure" when he experienced persecution (2 Cor. 12:10). The new wine is the anesthetic that enables you to bear the cross!

"Christian Hedonism severs the root of self-pity. People don't feel self-pity when suffering is accepted for the sake of joy," writes John Piper, reminding us with the words of Jesus to *"rejoice and be exceedingly glad, for great is your reward in heaven, for so they persecuted the prophets who were before you"* (Matt. 5:12).[1]

Piper says that our utter abandonment to the pleasure of God "is the ax laid to the root of self pity. When we have to suffer on account of Christ, we do not summon up our own resources like heroes. Rather, we become like little children who trust the strength of their father and who want the joy of his reward."

Every great movement throughout church history encountered persecution and martyrdoms. It was quite common in the Reformation. The Anabaptists and Mennonites have detailed histories of their martyrs. But previous to that were the Montanists, the Donatists, and other reform movements who were attacked not strictly for doctrinal differences, but chiefly for the presence of Holy Spirit working in their midst. The French prophets of the Cevennes were slaughtered, like many of the reformers. It would seem from history and the Scriptures that true revival and reform *must* be marked by persecution. Persecution is a manifestation of the Kingdom.

The Holy Ghost Anesthetic

In the early church, martyrs often experienced supernatural ecstasy and drunkenness when they were being killed. They were not masochists; they were Christian hedonists. At times, it seems they had virtual martyr parties! Eusebius writes about some of these early martyrs who would drink themselves to death:

> There were occasions when on a single day a hundred men as well as women and little children were killed, condemned to a succession of ever-changing punishments. No sooner had the first batch been sentenced, than others from every side would jump on to the platform in front of the judge and proclaim themselves Christians. They paid no heed to torture in all its terrifying forms, but undaunted spoke boldly of their devotion to the God of the universe and with joy, laughter and gaiety received the final sentence of death: they sang and sent up hymns of thanksgiving to the God of the universe till their very last breath.[2]

The paradox of the Christian life is this parallel existence of happiness and suffering. Though afflictions come, we need not be aware of them, for Christ bears them for us: we experience all the more ecstasy in the midst of it.

> If ye be reproached for the name of Christ, **happy are ye**;
> for the spirit of glory and of God resteth upon you: on
> their part He is evil spoken of, but on your part He is
> glorified (1 Peter 4:14 KJV).

For so many years I (like many Christians) believed this was a theoretical happiness—Oh, cheer up John! One day in the far, far distant future you will be rewarded for your painful sufferings in Heaven!

Little did I know that I get my bliss—my happiness—amplified *right now* when persecution comes my way. The apostle Paul says that persecution essentially *works for us*. It works up a far, exceeding weight of glory— God's tangible, manifest presence—which is accessible in the present (see 2 Cor. 4:17). There are countless stories of martyrs who felt no pain, experienced no fear, or felt such supernatural, glorious joy during their torture that they could not contain themselves.

In 1597, there were 26 Christians crucified for their faith in Nagasaki, Japan. A number of these were just young boys, but they possessed more courage than even the adults. They were marched a long distance, then given crosses, which they willingly embraced and allowed the executioners to do their jobs. While hanging there, the men and boys sang, prayed, and preached the Gospel. Louis Ibaraki, the youngest of them, was just 12 years old. When they cut off one of his ears, Louis Ibaraki kept singing and laughing. As much as his tortures tried to make him recant, young Louis refused to be talked into apostatizing.

"We have little Louis with us," wrote Fr. Francis Blanco, the night before the martyrdom, "and he is so full of courage and in such high spirits that it astonishes everybody."[3]

One of the earliest recorded martyrdoms was that of Perpetua, in A.D. 203. She was gored and thrown into the air by a wild bull. But Perpetua was in such a trance she did not even know she had been struck. She asked, "Has it started yet?" Perpetua did not even know she was wounded until someone showed her the wound.

Richard Wurmbrand, founder of *The Voice of the Martyrs*, shares a number of stories that highlight the martyrs' joy:

> A missionary, captured by the Chinese communists some years ago, was about to be beheaded. Suddenly, she began to laugh. Her captors asked, "What is so funny about being beheaded?"
>
> "I was just thinking," she replied, "how ridiculous my head would look rolling down the hill!" They let her go. With this sister, love was as strong as death.[4]

Few are aware in the apathetic, Laodicean church of the Western world that there are currently up to 167,000 martyrs dying for their faith each and every year around the globe. This is such a staggering number as to seem unreal. It makes the persecutions of the first three centuries pale in comparison, and yet we speak of martyrdom as if it were a thing of the past or the distant future. We are doped up on Sunday services and Western materialism, while our own brothers and sisters are butchered. Western governments openly ignore the slaughter of Christians by the hundreds and thousands in Asia and Africa.

In decades past, Western nations used their economic muscle as a bargaining chip for human rights and religious freedom in closed countries. Today we sleep. Numbed by moral relativism, our only concern is to open doors of trade with these nations for more sweatshop trinkets and plasma flat screens. Communism and socialism are viewed today merely as *alternative political views*—we have forgotten the horrendously bloody repression such cultic systems have brought upon the saints. On top of it all, we pour billions of dollars into Islamic nations for oil—places that offer the death penalty for converting to Christianity while currently funding the construction of mega-mosques around the globe.

Sadly, there is no government on the planet that does not support persecution against Christians, even if indirectly. The nations of the earth all have bloody hands, and these are desperate times. Until the church awakens, the enemy will continue to rampage. But there has never been any broad sweeping revival on the planet that did not require the spilling of martyrs' blood.

Clearly, there is no such thing as a Christian nation. God's Kingdom is not of this world. Republicans and Democrats alike have bloodguilt. Our war, likewise, is not waged by lobbying, protesting at abortion clinics, or writing enough letters to the editor—though these things are all fine as the Lord leads. The bottom line is this: *"we do not wrestle against flesh and blood, but against principalities, against powers, against the rulers of the darkness of this age* [world], *against spiritual hosts of wickedness in the heavenly* [high] *places"* (Eph. 6:12). A spiritual battle requires spiritual weaponry. And there is no greater weaponry than love. And there is no greater love than the kind that lays down its own life.

Men and women throughout the ages have been compelled to great lengths by this otherworldly love. "Some," says Robanus, "were slain with the sword, some burnt with fire, some scourged with whips, some stabbed with forks of iron, some fastened to the cross or gibbet, some drowned in the sea, some had their skins plucked off, some their tongues cut out, some were stoned to death, some frozen with cold, some starved with hunger, some with their hands cut off, or otherwise dismembered, were left naked to the open shame of the world."[5]

Can a man endure such a thing in his own strength? No. One must be translated out of himself. Let us consider the intensity of Paul's sufferings as he spread the Gospel. We should think of Paul the next time our pansy fears keep us from witnessing to the teenage clerk at the grocery store:

> *Are they servants of Christ? (I am out of my mind to talk like this.) I am more. I have worked much harder, been in prison more frequently, been flogged more severely, and been exposed to death again and again. Five times I received from the Jews the forty lashes minus one. Three times I was beaten with rods, once I was stoned, three times I was shipwrecked, I spent a night and a day in the open sea, I have been constantly on the move. I have been in danger from rivers, in danger from bandits, in danger from my own countrymen, in danger from Gentiles; in danger in the city, in danger in the country, in danger at sea; and in danger from false brothers. I have labored and*

toiled and have often gone without sleep; I have known
hunger and thirst and have often gone without food; I
have been cold and naked. Besides everything else, I face
daily the pressure of my concern for all the churches. Who
is weak, and I do not feel weak? Who is led into sin, and
I do not inwardly burn? (2 Corinthians 11:23-29 NIV).

My intent is not to boast in Paul, any more than he hoped to boast in himself. It is ridiculous to discuss something as noble as martyrdom if we are not willing to make the smaller sacrifices of daily life. Paul said, *"I die daily"* (1 Cor. 15:31). This did not mean he constantly bore some morbid, internal sorrow, as many depressed theologians would have you believe. He was simply talking about the aforementioned dangers that he regularly faced. Physical death was ever before him, because *love and joy* drove him continually into crazy situations where he spent himself—his human life was relentlessly threatened. We often miss the point of this passage: *Paul must have been tanked up on some heavy glory to keep driving him forward.* This was his focus:

Yet indeed I also count all things loss for the excellence of
the knowledge of Christ Jesus my Lord, for whom I have
suffered the loss of all things, and count them as rubbish,
that I may gain Christ (Philippians 3:8).

The Berserkers

One of my favorite analogies to the spirit of a martyr comes not from Christian history, but from secular Viking history—it is the story of the *berserkers.*

You may have heard the U.S. Marine slogan "go berserk!" Our modern term "going berserk" originated with Viking warriors centuries ago. When going to battle in those days, armies would line up and face one another in regimented rows. Standing at the front line of battle was the fiercest place to be. The Vikings had a peculiar but effective strategy. They would take one of their biggest, hulkiest, most menacing guys—the *berserker*—and they would feed him hallucinogenic mushrooms. Next, they would send him hurtling into the enemy's front line...*all by himself.*

This may seem quite crazy, but it was a highly effective strategy. The berserker would become so hopped up on mushrooms, tranced *outside of himself,* that when he slammed his way into the enemy's ranks, his physical body felt nothing. He was a walking juggernaut.

The berserker would take arrows, spears, and swords to his body, but he kept tromping in, crushing his way through the thicket like a mad man—like a psycho Energizer bunny, there was no stopping him! Because his mind and soul were translated away from all the action, he felt no pain, no trauma, and no fear. He just pulverized anyone in his way until he finally ran out of blood and fell over dead.

Although he was just one man—one *crazed* man—the berserker penetrated the enemy's line just enough to afford a *tiny crack* in the formation. The Vikings wasted no time. They rushed in behind him and exploited this small opening in the enemy's front line. Pouring into this breach in the forward ranks, the Vikings decisively penetrated the throng of soldiers. They quickly split the enemy ranks in half, then surrounded and butchered them all.

This one Viking *martyr* made just large enough a crack in the lines for an entire army to sweep in behind him, then divide and conquer. And all of this resulted from one chemically induced trance that pushed him outside his own self! How much more could a single man accomplish who is high on the ecstasy of Heaven?

In a very real sense, the berserker is a prophetic picture of a forerunner who, like the martyr Stephen, is so "hopped up" on the glory, he doesn't even feel the rocks strike him in the head as he lays down his life! He is caught up in the heavens, standing outside of himself, seeing Jesus sit at the right hand of the Father. A martyr who is raptured into the bliss of Heaven runs ahead of the pack and forges a way for the Lord's troops to follow. He freaks out the adversary. He takes no earthly hallucinogens, but his "mushrooms" are of the heavenly variety! They grow under the Tree of Life. He is tripping on Jesus.

I believe we can live this martyr lifestyle. Whether or not our physical body is being persecuted, we can live daily in the heavens to such a degree, we would barely even notice if we were being harmed or mistreated.

We must learn to drink the new wine until we see things! Did you know that the altar is a bar? Jesus wants us to belly up to the altar and drink our lives away.

The early apostles are great examples of those who walked in this martyr glory. When the apostles were brought before the high priest's council in Acts 5 and beaten, they did not seem melancholy about the ordeal; *"they departed from the presence of the council, **rejoicing** that they were counted worthy to suffer shame for His name"* (Acts 5:41).

Consider yet another story of martyr angels at work:

In Armenia, in the fourth century, 40 young believers were sentenced to die for their faith in Sebaste—forced to go naked into a river to freeze to death. A fire was kindled on the shore for anyone who would come out and warm up—if they only denied their faith. The mother of one young martyr helped her child quickly along, saying, "Go, walk with your brethren. Don't linger. Do not arrive in the Lord's presence after them."

One of the believers recanted his faith, coming out of the river. But just as he stepped out of the water, a soldier standing on the river bank saw an angel descend from above holding 40 crowns in his hand. The angel began placing these crowns on the heads of each martyr except for the one who was left over. The soldier on the bank saw that this leftover crown was intended for the young person who recanted. Immediately, the soldier stripped off his own clothes, plunging into the icy water, shouting, "I am coming, angel!" And there, he died with the rest.[6]

> *We must remember that it was for the joy set before Him that Jesus endured the cross* (see Heb. 12:2).

A man named Rogers, who worked alongside reformer and Bible translator William Tyndale, was burned for his faith, though it seemed to cause him no pain. He "died bathing his hands in the flame as though it were cold water."

Lawrence, a deacon from Rome, was put on the gridiron, and with a smile he said, "Turn me, I am roasted on one side." He died without a cry nor a moan of pain.[7]

Pain-killer Glory

Even accidental injuries go unnoticed during ecstasies. Sixteenth-century Jesuit Francis Borgia was lost in contemplative prayer when a wooden column fell upon him, causing a severe wound. But when Francis came out of his trance, he was surprised to find that he was in bed being attended by a doctor, having been carried there by bystanders. He had never felt a thing.

"The insusceptibility of martyrs in the midst of fearful tortures is another most wonderful mystical occurrence. Yet it was frequent," writes mystical author Albert Farges. "Such, in fact, is the ordinary consequence of the ecstatic state: after the first suffering, which very soon passes, the soul is suddenly lifted to the mystical raptures of ecstasy in which the sting of pain is extinguished amidst ineffable spiritual consolations."[8]

A letter from the Church of Smyrna regarding the early martyrdom of Polycarp gives us this account:

> For a great number of martyrs whips, torture, and flames seemed sweet and agreeable. They allowed not a single sigh to escape whilst the blood flowed from all their members, whilst their very bowels were exposed through the gaping wounds in their torn bodies and the onlookers themselves were unable to refrain from tears at such a sight. It is the Lord that watches over their souls and protects them, speaks with them, softens their pains and places before their eyes the heavenly crown which is to reward their patience.[9]

Cyprian, in the sixth century, referred to this wondrous miracle of impassibility when he spoke with the martyr Flavian saying, "The body feels no pain when the soul gives itself wholly to God."[10]

Ecstasies can be triggered in the most gruesome of circumstances. Catherine of Siena had such a devotion to the blood of Jesus, she was sometimes called "Prophetess of the Precious Blood." The mere thought of Calvary's blood would throw her into an ecstasy. Ours is a very bloody faith.

What some would view as grotesque, we hold as most sacred. There is a particularly interesting story in the life of Catherine that is both beautiful and moving, yet on the other hand strikingly morbid. I will give you Montague Summers' account of the execution of young Niccolo Tuldo, a promising 18-year-old Perugian who was unjustly sentenced to death. Catherine accompanied him to the scaffold after his pleadings with her. As she was going to the scaffold, Catherine says, "I felt the sweet fragrance of his blood, and it was a fragrance blended with the odour of my own blood, which I have so often longed to shed for the sake of Jesus my loved one, my spouse." Here is what happened as Catherine went with Niccolo to comfort him at martyrdom:

> "Remember, dear brother mine, the Blood of the Lamb," she murmured. The axe fell. Catherine at the moment saw his soul in the realms of heavenly bliss. In ecstasy she saw Christ her Spouse radiant as the golden sun. In her hands she held the youth's severed head. Her dress was saturated and soaked with his hot streaming blood. And so she passed on her way, still in ecstasy.
>
> "My soul," she says, "was so filled with gentle peace and a calm not of this world, so fragrant was the odour of the blood, that I could not bear to wash off the blood which incarnadined my habit and crimsoned my hands." In her own oratory, to which she had retired, she fell into ecstasy after ecstasy. In some mystic way she was bathed in the blood of Christ, whose love so exhausted and refreshed her that she could only sigh: "O blood! O burning fire! O Love ineffable! O blood!"[11]

Martyr Glory in Yemen

Our own ministry team once had a particularly memorable encounter with *martyr glory* in the nation of Yemen. You may not be aware of it, but Yemen currently ranks at about number five among the most persecuted countries for Christians on the planet. As we walked down the streets and into restaurants, it was amazing to see nearly every man armed to the teeth with swords, scimitars, and AK-47s. Not only are they armed, but 90 percent of the men are addicted to amphetamines. The culture is so rampantly violent; you could literally purchase a Kalashnikov machine gun at the local vegetable market.

Plastered all over the place were photos glorifying the anti-American dictator Saddam Hussein and other extremist Islamic leaders. Yemen is also the home of Islamic terrorist Osama bin Laden. As we drove through the country, passing military checkpoints, our driver always lied and told the police that I was British, simply because Americans are regarded with such hatred.

One day, we had to drive through a treacherous mountain range with sheer cliff drops of more than 3,000 feet, in order to enter a region near the northern civil war zone. Needless to say, this was a very sketchy trip for Westerners.

As we were swerving through the mountains (our driver meanwhile chewing a mouthful of amphetamines—a leaf called "khat"), we suddenly heard the rapid fire of a nearby machine gun. I can honestly say that none of us were gripped by fear or trepidation. Instead, a massive wave of glory came rolling through the car; it was like a swirling, heavenly psychosis. We were utterly blasted. As foolish as it may sound, we could only think about one thing: *"Imagine how much glory we would feel if one of those bullets hit us!"*

There is a drunkenness of faith that enables us to do the impossible. It is absurd in the eyes of the world. St. John of the Cross writes, "May we forget about ourselves. When we are intoxicated by His presence, we will feel that we can do miracles, that we can pass through fire and water, and that we can remain unafraid when thousands of swords are drawn against us. By His grace, we won't fear anymore—neither life nor death, joy nor sorrow. We will be drunk with faith."

The Bliss of Sacrifice

There is a realm of glory that finds supreme joy in the art of sacrifice. The great missionary Hudson Taylor in his later years said, "I never made a sacrifice." Despite all his grueling ordeals on the mission field in China, he was tapping into a deeper vein of ecstasy that quickened him. He said, "Unspeakable joy all day long and every day, was my happy experience. God, even my God, was a living bright reality, and all I had to do was joyful service."[12]

George Mueller established orphanages in England in the 1800s and was known as a man of great faith and sacrifice. He was able to do all his work through one burning inspiration:

> I saw more clearly than ever, that the first great and primary business to which I ought to attend every day was, to have my soul happy in the Lord. The first thing to be concerned about was not how much I might serve the Lord, how I might glorify the Lord; but how I might get my soul into a happy state, and how my inner man might be nourished.[13]

There is such a prevailing spirit of religious masochism, it is nearly impossible to discuss joy and divine bliss without dismantling someone's theology of suffering. I believe the higher truth in the matter is this: rather than fixing our eyes on trials, sufferings, or sacrifices at all—whether we choose them or not—let us fix our eyes on Jesus, the author and perfecter of our faith. As a minister often associated with the present-day "Glory Movement," I am aware that we are sometimes criticized for talking about the glory and the supernatural, but not enough about suffering and cross-bearing. My theology is this: when you are fully focused on the glory, *you won't even be aware of suffering!* You'll carry more crosses than anyone else, but like Hudson Taylor and George Mueller, you won't even realize all that you've done because your soul was in a constantly happy state.

> *Dear friends, do not be surprised at the painful trial you*
> *are suffering, as though something strange were happening*
> *to you* (1 Peter 4:12).

On one hand, we've had a candy-coated Gospel that rejects the concept of suffering altogether. Peter says don't be fooled: *suffering will come.* But on the other hand, we've had a passive, do-nothing Gospel of bend over and take a spanking for nothing. Anytime there's a problem, we assume God must want to teach us a lesson. People spend their entire lives in a downward spiral of depression because they think God is bitter, angry, and out to kill them!

The apostle Peter is clear: why are you guys freaking out because turbulence is coming your way? Nothing strange about that! Get happy because more glory is coming your way! Next, he says:

> *But rejoice to the extent that you partake of Christ's sufferings, that when his glory is revealed, you may also be glad with exceeding joy* (1 Peter 4:13).

Always remember that you are working up a weight of glory in your momentary afflictions. When you focus on the glory, you don't see afflictions. It is all worth the future glory:

> *I consider that our present sufferings are not worth comparing with the glory that will be revealed in us* (Romans 8:18).

Suffering is not God's end goal. If God wanted you to suffer as part of His "Plan A" then Heaven would be full of it. Heaven is not a big torture chamber in the sky. Suffering is not God's perfect will, only a temporary inconvenience until the restoration of all things.

> *For God did not appoint us to suffer wrath but to receive salvation through our Lord Jesus Christ* (1 Thessalonians 5:9).

God's perfect will was to hang out in a garden with naked vegetarians. His primary goal is still to bring Heaven to earth. That's why it is our task to eradicate sickness, disease, sin, and death. We are called to eradicate suffering from the face of the planet.

Remember that most suffering is avoidable through wisdom. We bring most of it down on ourselves. Don't glorify suffering—glorify Christ. The religious spirit wants you to kill yourself. There's no need for that. Don't go looking for crosses to bear. God Himself is quite able to provide you one when necessary.

The Kamikaze Preachers

*When He opened the fifth seal, I saw under the altar the souls of those who had been slain for the word of God and for the testimony which they held. And they **cried with a loud voice**, saying, "How long, O Lord, holy and true, until You judge and avenge our blood on those who dwell on the earth?" Then a white robe was given to each of them; and it was said to them that they should **rest a little while longer, until both the number of their fellow servants and their brethren, who would be killed as they were, was completed** (Revelation 6:9-11).*

History is chock full of accounts wherein persecutors, jailors, and torturers came to faith because of the witness of a martyr in his final moments. Many prison guards, noblemen, and even kings were impressed by the faithfulness of the martyrs in their dying hour. With every dead martyr came dozens of new believers in their place. Tertullian said, "Afflict us, torment us, crucify us—in proportion as we are mowed down, we increase; the blood of Christians is the seed [of the church]." The enemy cannot stop us, because we multiply the more he attacks us.

But the blood of the martyrs throughout history has a *voice*, which is still crying out for vindication to this day. Though their blood brought revival in their respective eras, there has never been a martyr's death which has been *completely* reimbursed. Not a drop of martyr's blood has yet received the full reward it was meant to purchase. Yes, their blood did win regions to Christ. However, the blood of the martyrs is far more potent and mystical to be spent just on the few immediate conversions of their eye witnesses. Not a drop of martyrs' blood has ever been *fully vindicated*, and the harvest of their blood seed has yet to be reaped until the end of the age.

Their blood is still crying out for an end-time generation to step in and reap what they have sown.

The Lord is about to answer the cries of the martyrs. When He does, all Heaven will break loose. The supernatural inheritance they stored up for us will be unlocked, along with the power of this new wave of end-time martyrs that are still being added to their ranks today.

Several years ago, the Lord began speaking to me concerning *the new martyrs.* This will encompass a wave, or movement, of firebrands who will go for the core of Islam and the unreached nations of the world, boldly proclaiming the Gospel in the bliss and power of Heaven. Many of them will be young people from the Western world. These are the ones of whom the Lord spoke who *"overcame* [the enemy] *by the blood of the Lamb and by the word of their testimony; they did not love their lives so much as to shrink from death"* (Rev. 12:11).

There are lots of prophecies about the coming revival generation, but few talk about how bloody it will be. These will burn with a holy zeal like no generation before them.

> *A people come, great and strong, the like of whom has never been; nor will there ever be any such after them, even for many successive generations* (Joel 2:2).

On September 11, 2001, when Islamic suicide bombers destroyed the World Trade Center in New York City, the Lord first began to speak to me about the coming suicide preachers. He also called them *kamikaze* preachers. I was brought into a revelatory encounter where I found myself standing on an aircraft carrier in the Pacific Ocean, apparently in World War II. There I saw a hurling mass of fiery, molten airplane coming down to crash right into us. It was a frightening, unavoidable scenario. The Lord said, "They will freak you out, dude!" Kamikaze means "divine wind." The Lord showed me that these kamikazes will literally "freak out" the enemy, and that many of them will be young people. All of them will burn like shining lamps, and if necessary, will lay down their lives in a blaze of glory.

Like Holy Ghost terrorists, these dread champions will boldly proclaim the Gospel in the toughest environments on the planet. An Islamic suicide bomber would lay down his or her life just to kill a few people in a crowd. So will these fearsome ones stand up in the streets, knowing that an angry crowd could *implode on them*. They will risk being shot, beaten, or stoned, just to save a few souls around them. They will be like living glory bombs, exploding with the love and power of the Holy Spirit. Like Esther, they will say, "If I die, I die." Their only aim is to take a few souls out with them. They are love bombers—exploding not with gunpowder but with joy.

"There is a fire of Divine love. It is this love which burns the believer and can even cause the believer to suffer," writes Christian mystic Michael Molinos. "This intoxicates the believer and puts an insatiable longing within him to be changed into the likeness of his Lord. Therefore, it can be said of love: Divine love is as strong as death, for it kills just as surely as death kills."[14]

The favorite Old Testament book of the mystics and martyrs of the church is by far the Song of Solomon. This book of holy love is the most quoted among those who, entranced by divine intimacy, were compelled to greatest lengths of sacrifice. The love of Christ is by far a love that many waters cannot quench and is stronger than the grave. Those possessed by this passion are the supernatural, unstoppable church. This is not puppet ministry or church bingo night. This is holy terror.

A Movement of Deliverers

There is a generation of deliverers on the rise, whom satan has sought to wipe out—just as he did with the infants of Jesus' day under Herod. Just as he moved through Pharaoh to kill the children of Moses' generation, so has the enemy sought to destroy the youth of the nations in this hour. In the U.S. alone, there have been upward of 47 million abortions since 1973. The enemy has mobilized an effective holocaust of children like never before, with more infants massacred than in the reign of the Roman Empire. The blood of the innocents from indiscriminate slaughter is crying out from the dust like the blood of righteous Abel. This is not a political or social issue; it is a demonic assault of the antichrist spirit intended to wipe out a prophetic generation. It is user-friendly genocide of historic propor-tion, and it is the outright manifestation of the dragon of Revelation 12 seeking to devour the Christ child of our day. But the unstoppable church will give birth to this revival generation, and we will be taken up and given wings to fly to escape the serpent's grasp.

This is all-out war. My contemporaries who should be spearheading revival at my side are not here because they were plucked from the womb. I myself am a post-*Roe v. Wade* child, conceived out of wedlock, and I should also be a statistic. It is a miracle that I exist, being the product of teenage fornication and eight parents—I can empathize with a fatherless generation that has faced relentless assault while the church has slept comfortably on her watch. I am here to prod the lion to wake up. I am not alone.

The unconverted Laodicean "church" of our day is about to be circumcised from the true mystical Body of Christ. Those who will not take a stand will be vomited from His mouth. There is a generation that has known only desperation. Crack babies. Broken homes. Suicidal tendencies. School shootings. This broken generation will be a latter house that carries the greatest glory of all prior ages. In our weakness, His strength will be made known. A generation with nothing to live for is looking for something to die for. Despite the horrendous hand that the two leavens of religion and secularism have dealt them, the Lord has been secretly preparing a martyr generation. To the extent they have been attacked and neglected, so is the extent of their supernatural dependence on the One who delivers them. Their lives they will gladly surrender at the taste of His spiced wine.

One of the greatest revivals we are about to see is going to be sparked among the youth of the Western world—the Goths, the punks, and the head bangers. It is no coincidence that theirs is a culture that glorifies suicide, drugs, and violence. They were made to willingly lay down their lives, to live high on the ecstasies of God and to violently take the Kingdom to the ends of the earth. There is a disenfranchised, disillusioned army just waiting to be rallied. All of their dabbling into wicca, satanism, and the occult merely proves their hunger for the supernatural. What will this generation look like, when they are set ablaze with the truth? Many Christians shudder when they think of the dark, Gothic suicide-pop culture of hardcore music, drugs, and violence. But I can tell you that a generation is being prepared who are willing to die when they've tasted these pleasures of God.

> *And there was war in heaven. Michael and his angels fought against the dragon, and the dragon and his angels fought back. But he was not strong enough, and they lost their place in heaven. The great dragon was hurled down—that ancient serpent called the devil, or Satan, who leads the whole world astray. He was hurled to the earth, and his angels with him.*
>
> *Then I heard a loud voice in heaven say: "Now have come the salvation and the power and the Kingdom of our God, and the authority of His Christ. For the accuser of our brothers, who accuses them before our God day and night, has been hurled down. They overcame him by the blood of the Lamb and by the word of their testimony; they did not love their lives so much as to shrink from death"* (Revelation 12:7-11 NIV).

There is a remnant that will not be devoured by the dragon. Satan is not the only dragon on the block. Did you know that Jesus is also described as a fiery prophetic dragon in a Messianic passage in Isaiah?

> *Do not rejoice, all you of Philistia* [Philistines], *because the rod that struck you is broken* [King Ahaz of Judah]; *for out of the serpent's roots will come forth a viper* [King Hezekiah of Judah], *and its offspring will be a fiery flying serpent* [Jesus] (Isaiah 14:29).

Jesus is the "fiery serpent" Moses lifted up in the desert (see Matt. 3:14; Num. 21:8). And the serpent of Moses gobbled up all the rest. Try standing up in your church next Sunday and saying, "My God is a fire-breathing Dragon!" See how well that one goes over!

Chapter 16

the final wave

There are a people on earth today who are boldly running in to take the land of promise. The age of the wilderness prophets is over. The season has come to possess the land of milk and honey. Mystical experiences, heavenly delights, and an overcoming life of joy will mark a generation that ushers in the last-day harvest with displays of love and power.

The Lord challenged Joshua to be bold and courageous, not to shrink back in fear when he crossed the River Jordan to occupy the land sworn to his forefathers. A new dispensation was at hand. And so the Lord told him:

"Moses Is Dead"

The age of the administrator is over. The age of the generals has come. And God is with us.

Moses was called to manage the children of Israel in their grumbling and unbelief in the desert. Most church leadership has faced a similar task, just keeping the flock together in an arid land—herding sheep in circles around the dry places, yet never arriving anywhere at all.

But now, an awakening is at hand. For Joshua, it was time to aggressively move forward on the offense. It was time to wage war and contend for destiny. Faith was arising in the camp, and God's people were ready to believe Him for what was rightfully theirs: a *good inheritance.*

As Joshua crossed the Jordan, this was not his first trip to the Promise Land. Many years before, he had been there as a scout. Joshua had tasted the big fruit and seen great possibility in those early days—he realized what a sweet prize was ahead of them if they only trusted God. If the people would rise to the occasion, he knew there was a good and fruitful land to be taken. Others were afraid of this new and mystical land. They only saw giants. They did not believe (see Heb. 4).

Like the prophets who have gone before us, Joshua foresaw a future glory in a future land. He foresaw a realm that was only an arm's length away... *if the people could only believe.*

But Joshua is not a scout anymore. Here he is at the River Jordan once again. No longer is he an unwelcome cheerleader, trying to rally a rebellious people to possess what was already given them for free. That stubborn generation has now perished in the desert. *Moses is dead.* A new breed is on the rise.

No, Joshua is not a scout anymore. Now he is a vast and untold army. A swarming multitude of locusts ready to descend like a firestorm on the adversary.

The Glory Revolution

Forerunners have seen what is on the horizon. A few have even tasted the fruit. But there are seasons in the course of history when the swell of the multitudes enter into the land together as one man. It is the sound of a *movement* and the cry of revolution that breaks the back of principalities, overturning strongholds and supplanting wicked dominions.

There are dispensations of God throughout the course of time when the hand of the Almighty moves with untold zeal and fury to showcase His glory to the nations of the earth. These critical junctures have come when the masses could no longer handle their frustration with status quo. The quest for *something more*, the thirst for true nirvana, began to burn like an unquenchable flame within the collective heart of humanity. These were times of *revolution*.

Reformation is not quite the term for such a crossroads. It is insufficient to reform the old, when the old lacked the very substance necessary for societal transformation. The Lord once told prophetic teacher Mike Bickle that He is going to *change the expression of Christianity across the face of the earth in one generation.* This is a radical transition, moving from a shadow of reality to the very substance of those things which are to come.

Moses was never allowed to enter the land of promise.

In his anger at Kadesh, Moses struck the rock with his staff, while God had commanded him only to speak to it (see Num. 20). Moses displayed a sense of God's displeasure with the people, when God was not angry. Let me tell you that a generation that cannot perceive the infinite pleasure of God will be disqualified from this approaching movement. This is a revolution of love, an insurgency of joy.

There is a rising tide, a coming wave. And like Joshua, those who catch the crest of this movement will be like a sharp diamond point driven forward by the limitless strength of Heaven behind them.

The time has come for more than a few prophetic scouts to cross over into ecstasy. It is time for the multitudes to experience the mystical release of bliss and power in the glory realm. Fields and stadiums are about to swell with glory revival, as all of humanity longs to be anchored again in heavenly places. Prophetic teacher Rick Joyner says that this great end-time revival will cause churches of a hundred members to see a thousand new people a week added to their numbers.

"The armies of God in heaven and on earth are mobilizing now. When they march, it will be the most awesome and fearful sight the world has ever seen," says Joyner. "In some places, this army will appear so fast that it will seem to have come out of thin air. Instantly, the greatest spiritual force the world has ever seen will descend upon the earth. To those who are unaware of what is now taking place, it will be like peacefully going to sleep and waking up the next morning to the fact that your entire city, and in some cases, nation, has been occupied by a foreign army. This will be because the army existed right in the midst of the cities without anyone realizing it, including many who are in the army."[1]

Joyner says worship services will break out at truck stops, airports, and wherever people are gathered. Ministers will literally have to hover miraculously over the crowds, just to be heard and to preach the Gospel. Miracles will break out at biblical proportions, and apostolic figures will be followed by news reporters as if they were national politicians, with signs and wonders following.

"Rejoicing is not an adequate word to describe the celebrations that will then break out across the earth," writes Joyner. "The Lord instituted feasting as a primary way to worship Him in the Old Testament. It was feasting before the Lord that I saw breaking out in every city that was touched by this coming move of God. When the Lord is moving, people want to meet all of the time, just as they met in the temple, and then from house to house in the book of Acts. This feasting was the result of a fellowship like has not been known on the earth since the first century church experienced breaking out everywhere. Huge streets were blocked off for spontaneous feasts. There will be large gatherings in parks, stadiums and other public places. There will be many cities where home groups will be meeting on every block, every day."[2]

These spontaneous celebrations that begin to break out will have no clear leader, other than the Lord Himself. Multitudes will begin to gather, singing and worshiping, with anyone speaking or preaching at any given time. As was the original destiny of the nation of ancient Israel, the Lord Himself will be our King. The glory of God will dictate every gathering, every social event, as Joyner describes.

> "The anointing and presence of the Lord were so great that anyone who was presumptuous would be obvious immediately, and they would quickly stop. As the celebrations and rejoicing continued, gift giving and sharing erupted," adds Joyner, relating his vision of this last day outpouring of harvest glory. "Because of this, whole cities were instantly rid of poverty and want."

Large cities will see their crime rates drop to zero, practically overnight, with prostitution, pornography, abortion, and illegal drug use coming to an instant halt.

The Jansenist Convulsionaires

This last-day revival will be like every preceding great awakening combined, super-sized and coupled together with miracles never before seen by the human eye. To catch a shadowy glimpse of the supernatural nature of this coming revival, and the degree of heavenly transport we will corporately experience, we should turn to one more historical example.

One of the largest and most bizarre outbreaks of God's glory on the streets occurred in 18th century Europe between the Reformation and the French Revolution. Out of nowhere, there were literally tens of thousands of people being swept into trances and shaking with wild manifestations in the open air. These radical believers, who couldn't be deemed either Protestant or Catholic, simply became known as the *Jansenists*.

Starting with a prayer meeting at the tomb of one of their leaders, Francois de Paris, at the cemetery of St. Medard in France, the most unusual signs and wonders began to spontaneously erupt, mushrooming into a regional explosion. Secular researcher Michael Talbot writes:

> ...from the beginning, a host of miraculous healings were reported. The ailments thus cured included cancerous tumors, paralysis, deafness, arthritis, rheumatism, ulcerous sores, persistent fevers, prolonged hemorrhaging, and blindness. But this was not all. The mourners also started to experience strange involuntary spasms or convulsions and to undergo the most amazing contortions of their limbs. These seizures quickly proved contagious, spreading like a brush fire until the streets were packed with men, women, and children, all twisting and writhing as if caught up in a surreal enchantment.[3]

It was while they were in this "fitful and trancelike state" that the Jansenists came to be known as the *Convulsionaires*.

The Convulsionaires were a type of reform movement within Catholicism, but they were eventually persecuted severely by both the church and the state. This became such a massive, shaking, ecstatic prophetic movement that it took 3,000 people just to stand on "prayer blanket" duty and cover the flailing women so they didn't become immodest! What a Holy Ghost party this must have been. The most amazing thing is that the streets and cemetery stayed packed, crowded both day and night, as this meeting never ended. It lasted non-stop for *two decades straight*.

Because of intense persecution, few people even know of Jansenism in modern times. Though we hear little of them today, the Jansenist miracles were the talk of Europe for an entire century. In the 1700s, the Jansenists were the buzz of the Western world, as thousands flocked to see them, "including individuals from all social strata and officials from every educational, religious and governmental institution imaginable." They walked in a corporate *harvest glory* that brought multitudes into the Kingdom. The Convulsionaires were so widely known throughout Europe, and their miracles so well documented and verified, that even the skeptical writer Voltaire would not deny their supernatural abilities. Voltaire sarcastically wrote, "God was forbidden, by order of the King, to work any miracles there."[4]

The power of God became so widespread, there were books composed of firsthand, eyewitness accounts of miracles that were four inches thick. Scottish philosopher and critic David Hume even acknowledged the abundance of proof for the Jansenist miracles. One of their investigators, Louis-Basile Carre de Montgeron, a member of the Paris Parliament, published a huge volume in 1737 called *La Verite des Miracles,* giving testimony to the supernatural happenings there.

Interestingly, the Jansenists would enter a trancelike state to work their miracles. There were untold numbers of *creative miracles*, such as decayed limbs being restored. The most hardened atheists were converted at this. Likewise, their persecution became more intense. The Jansenists believed strongly in a Calvinistic type of predestination and preached the necessity of God's grace for salvation. But their miracles did not win them reprieves from the church forever. And this is where the story takes an even more bizarre twist. As their persecutors came to kill them, the Jansenists were suddenly clothed with an *invincibility* that was utterly supernatural. They were able to "endure without harm an almost unimaginable variety of physical tortures. These included severe beatings, blows from both heavy and sharp objects, and strangulation—all with no signs of injury or even the slightest trace of wounds or bruises."[5]

Church history professor Vinson Synan says the following:

> It appears nothing could harm the convulsionaires. They could not be hurt by the blows of metal rods, chains, or timbers. The strongest of men could not choke them.

Some were crucified and afterward showed no trace of wounds. Most mind-boggling of all, they could not even be cut or punctured with knives, swords, or hatchets![6]

The prophet Joel speaks of those in God's army who will be invincible. This is a working of the Spirit of Might, the same that clothed Samson with supernatural ability in the Old Testament and enabled David's mighty men to withstand all manner of battle and warfare. Knives, swords, and hatchets bounced off of the Convulsionaires, as they were left completely unscathed.

In looking at the history of the martyrs, we often saw the presence of ecstasy that numbed the saints from their pain or brought pleasure in the midst of it. But this—what the Jansenists experienced—is an altogether higher level of glory.

Do you believe it is possible to become so invincible in the glory that nothing on earth can stop you?

On top of this all, another most remarkable miracle occurred right in the streets. Jansenist preachers began to levitate, right off the ground, preaching the Gospel to the thousands gathered around them. *This is the most well- documented case of levitation ever recorded in broad daylight in church history.*

"Invulnerability was not the only talent the Jansenists displayed during their seizures," writes Talbot, adding that some could prophesy "and were able to 'discern hidden things.' Others could read even when their eyes were closed and tightly bandaged, and instances of levitation were reported. One of the levitators, an Abbe named Bescherand from Montpellier, was so 'forcibly lifted into the air' during his convulsions that even when the witnesses tried to hold him down they could not succeed in keeping him from raising up off the ground."[7]

What makes these events so unique is that they were observed by countless thousands of observers day and night for a period of many years.

"People of all ranks were compelled to admit the truth of these things. The most celebrated doctors, who had pronounced the incurability of their patients, honourably gave certificates of the fact, and pronounced the cures not only beyond the reach of human aid, but, in many cases, the restoration of injured and decayed members, 'actual creations,'" writes William

Howitt of his Jansenist research. "It may seem to Protestants, hardened by a long course of education against miracles, extraordinary that such miracles should appear at the tomb of a Jansenist. The wind bloweth where it listeth, and God's providence is equally independent, though seldom without a meaning not far to seek."[8]

Reportedly, a Convulsionaire named Miss Thevenet was sometimes "raised seven or eight feet high up to the ceiling, and then could carry two persons pulling down with all their might, three feet above the ground."[9]

One of the female Convulsionaires was bent backward over a stake by her persecutors, in order to put her to death. However, they were unable to make the sharp stake penetrate her body. A 50-pound stone was brought in, and the executioners began pounding it onto her torso, in order to skewer her body onto the spike. Eventually, God's supernatural protection could not be resisted. They gave up the exercise, and the woman walked away without so much as a bruise or a pin-prick.[10]

In Montgeron's book of testimonies, a sharpened point of an iron drill was once pressed to the stomach of a Convulsionaire and pounded so violently with a hammer it seemed "as if it would penetrate through the spine and rupture all the entrails." The person was not punctured, but instead, the Convulsionaire upheld an "expression of perfect rapture," crying, "Oh, that does me good! Courage, brother; strike twice as hard, if you can!"[11]

In another instance, a Convulsionaire nicknamed "la Salamandre" was to be burned over a fiery pit. However, he remained suspended over the fire, levitating for more than nine minutes, covered only in a sheet—which also remained intact and unburned in the midst of the flames. Don't be quick to write these stories off as superstitious legend. Just for a dose of historical perspective, remember that the American colonies were already formed by this time, and the stories of the Jansenists are as well documented as any secular occurrence of the time.

Howitt gives us some further accounts of invincibility:

> One girl, Jane Moulu, in her early twenties, stood with
> her back against a wall, receiving on her stomach 100
> blows of a hammer, weighing 20-30 pounds, adminis-

tered by a very strong man. She said that the hits were not hard enough to do her any damage. One man, after giving her 60 of the blows, was so inefficient, he gave the hammer to a stronger man, who gave her 100 strikes more. In order to test the force of the blows, he tried them against a stone wall, which shattered open to a large hole on the 25th strike.

A large plank was laid atop another female Jansenist, and men piled on top of it, in order to crush her, or at least to suppress her manifestations of shaking. Eyewitnesses say the weight was enough to crush an ox, yet the woman was unscathed.[12]

Among the Jansenists, many reformers began to introduce a sacrament called the *consolamentum*. This was a type of baptismal sacrament that spread among the Albigenses and other branches of Cathars. This was not a baptism of water, but of words, which included the laying on of hands and impartation of spiritual gifts, including the power to bind and loose, absolution, baptismal regeneration, and ordination all in one. *This was considered a baptism of the Holy Spirit.* Historians note instances of ecstatic utterances and speaking in tongues during the consolamentum, but many kept the practice secretly guarded so as not to be accused of witchcraft by the mainstream church.[13]

Spontaneous Waves of Glory

Expect vast explosions of ecstatic experience to invade society again in these days as it did with the Jansenists of old. With supernatural signs and wonders following, this great end-time revival will be ushered in with more glory than any previous move of God. There are already vast numbers of souls coming into the Kingdom all around the world today through the current efforts of the church. With thousands of people simultaneously making decisions for Christ in crusades and evangelism campaigns, huge blocks of the population are being snatched from hell.

We at Sons of Thunder have personally seen thousands come to faith in the nations, and our friends in ministry have seen many more. Crusade evangelism and other events will continue to be an effective means of spreading the Gospel. But one-time events do not produce sustained revival communities for the long haul. The time, planning, and resources involved in hosting large-scale meetings will eventually become unnecessary as *spontaneous waves* of God's glory sweep through regions with no human orchestration or forethought. We will not have time to coordinate major events when full-fledged revival erupts, because God will run ahead of us. *They will just happen.*

Now is not the time to learn how to administer large events. Now is the time to learn how to move in the glory. The days are at hand when we will have to book football stadiums on a day's notice. All pre-planning goes out the window. As mystical miracles such as levitation and other phenomena break out corporately within intimate congregations, these small churches will be so suddenly overfilled on one Sunday that they must meet in their parking lot the next week. Their services will be held in the Wal-Mart parking lot with a bullhorn the following week to contain the crowds, followed by the open fields. An unplanned wildfire will begin to spread from home to home, street corner to street corner.

The coming revival will not be event oriented, nor will it originate in the mind of man. It will not be spearheaded by one man or ministry. No one will have a copyright on it. Streets will be packed with dancing, preaching, and fire, with no one leading the show except God Himself. Entire communities and regions will be spontaneously transformed. True and lasting change will come in mere moments and will affect every sector of society, from politicians, schools, and media to ordinary laborers in the field.

We will see the driest, most barren places suddenly become kindling for this wildfire. A holy fire with a mind of its own. Uncontrollable. Untamed. People throughout the world are hungry for it. When these unseen, unanticipated eruptions of God break loose on the scene, the multitudes will jump headlong into the glory.

Ministry will be completely different under this coming corporate cloud. Preparation is unnecessary and futile when the cloud of His kabod presence comes. The anointing of God does all the work. And do not forget the role of the angels in this hour. *They will be the harvesters*, not you! (See Matthew 13:39.)

When this happens, waves of corporate ecstasy will cover entire city blocks and public squares en masse. We have seen the shadows coming. While preaching in the streets of Africa, we have witnessed scores of people erupt into spontaneous explosions of the joy of the Lord—with laughing, dancing, and shouting—throngs of people literally cheering in the marketplace with unknown numbers coming to Christ. These were not in meetings or crusades where an altar call is expected. These were not conditioned responses. No one taught them how to laugh or faint or explode with joy. They had never been to Toronto. It just happens. This is a real glory that catches like a brush fire, sweeping people up unsuspected and unannounced.

This is already starting in the Western world as well. Our friends now go to football games, amassing crowds in the parking lots with miracles, signs, and wonders. At times, they have nearly taken over the game itself, as there are more people interested in the glory than football. We have other friends who can reach a thousand at a time in a city subway station as they stand under an open Heaven and release miracles. The atmosphere of Heaven is beginning to invade secular venues in this day, overtaking everyone in its path. Now is not the time for ministries to compete, but to build one another up, because we will need everyone strong and available to pull in these massive nets full of new believers.

All over the earth, harvest is coming. The Last Great Awakening is at hand. Revelation 14:15 reads:

> ...another angel came out of the temple, crying with a loud voice to Him who sat on the cloud, "Thrust in Your sickle and reap, for the time has come for You to reap, for the harvest of the earth is ripe."

What is your part to play in this climactic curtain call of the church age? Abide in the glory. Cultivate a secret relationship with the Lord in the intimate place of His bliss. What begins in the Secret Place is eventually revealed in the open. Contend to *belong* to the bliss of God. Only then will the fearsome fire of divine love draw the world to watch you burn.

Lovers will carry their bliss to the extreme. If a man were to give all the wealth of his house for this love, it would be utterly despised. What will this look like—this great and final harvest—this unstoppable church full of glory and power? *Signs and wonders beyond number at a scale not matched by the Book of Exodus.* The concept of reality itself will be challenged at epic proportions. A generation of blazing torches will be fueled by raging joy, limitless strength, and the unquenchable flame of holy love.

Endnotes

Preface

1. C.S. Lewis, *Surprised by Joy: The Shape of My Early Life* (New York: Harcourt Brace Jovanovich, 1986), 140.

2. John Piper, *Desiring God* (Portland: Multnomah Press, 1986).

3. Ibid.

Introduction

1. *John G. Lake: His Life, His Sermons, His Boldness of Faith* (Fort Worth: Kenneth Copeland Publications, 1994), 505.

Chapter 1

1 James A.R. Moffatt, *The Bible: James Moffatt Translation* (San Francisco: Harper Collins, 1922/1994).

2. Joseph H. Thayer, *Thayer's Greek-English Lexicon of the New Testament,* Blue Letter Bible, http://blueletterbible.org/study/misc/thayers .html (accessed Dec. 3, 2006).

3. Ben Campbell Johnson, *The Heart of Paul: A Relational Paraphrase of the New Testament,* Vol. 1 (Waco: Word Books, 1976).

Chapter 2

1. St. John of the Cross, "A Collection of Spiritual Maxims," No. 70.

2. A.W. Tozer, *That Incredible Christian* (Harrisburg, PA: Christian Publications, 1964), 50-52.

3. Mike Bickle, *The Pleasures of Loving God* (Lake Mary: Charisma House, 2000), 126.

4. John Piper, *Desiring God* (Portland: Multnomah Press, 1986).

5. Ibid., 89.

6. Matthew Elliott, *Feel: The Power of Listening to Your Heart* (Tyndale House, 2008), 15.

7. Ibid., 16, 18.

8. John Calvin, *Institutes of the Christian Religion*, translated by Henry Beveridge (Grand Rapids: Eerdmans, 1989).

9. Piper, *Desiring God*, 14.

10. *The Paradise of the Soule*, English translation, including *Of the Union With God* by a Jesuit (1617).

11. Lambert Dolphin, "Yin, Yang, the Tao, and Wholeness" (1991/2007), http://www.ldolphin.org/YinYang.shtml (accessed Mar. 8, 2007).

12. Elliott, *Feel*, 38.

13. Piper, *Desiring God*, 17.

14. Mike Bickle and Deborah Hiebert, *The Seven Longings of the Human Heart* (Kansas City: Forerunner Books, 2006).

15. Jonathan Edwards, "The Spiritual Blessings of the Gospel Represented by a Feast," in *The Works of Jonathan Edwards*, vol. 17, *Sermons and Discourses*, 1723-1729, ed. Kenneth P. Minkema (New Haven, CT: Yale University Press, 1996), 286.

16. Aurelius Augustine, *Confessions*, translated by R.S. Pine-Coffin (New York: Penguin, 1961), 181 (IX.1).

17. M.G. Easton, *Illustrated Bible Dictionary*, 3rd edition (Thomas Nelson, 1897).

18. *The Twentieth Century New Testament: A Translation Into Modern English From the Original Greek* (New York & Chicago: The Fleming H. Revell Co., 1904).

19. Gerrit Verkuyl, *Berkeley Version of the New Testament From the Original Greek With Brief Footnotes* (Berkeley: James J. Gillick and Co., 1945).

Chapter 3

1. Madame Jeanne Guyon, *The Song of the Bride* (New Kensington: Whitaker House, 1997 ed.), 29.

2. Ibid., 30.

3. Robert Wilken and Richard Norris, ed., *The Church's Bible: The Song of Songs Interpreted by Early Christian and Medieval Commentators* (Grand Rapids: William B. Eerdmans Publishing Co., 2003), 190.

4. Richard Francis Weymouth, *The New Testament in Modern Speech* (Cambridge: James Clarke and Co., 1962).

5. Helen Barrett Montgomery, *The Centenary Translation of the New Testament* (Philadelphia: The American Baptist Publication Society, 1924).

6. Charles Bray Williams, *The New Testament: A Translation in the Language of the People* (Chicago: Moody Press, 1950).

7. Joseph Rotherham, *The Emphasized Bible: A New Translation* (London: Bradbury, Agnew, and Co., 1902).

8. C.S. Lovett, *Lovett's Lights on Galatians, Ephesians, Philippians, Colossians, I Thessalonians and II Thessalonians With Rephrased Text* (La Verne, CA: El Camino Press, 1970), 122-123.

9. William Hendriksen, *New Testament Commentary Exposition of Galatians, Ephesians, Philippians, Colossians, and Philemon* (Grand Rapids: Baker Books, 1995), 239.

10. Albert Barnes, *Notes on the New Testament Explanatory and Practical* (Grand Rapids: Baker Book House, 1949).

11. Hendriksen, *New Testament Commentary*, 238, 240.

12. Aurelius Prudentius, *The Hymns of Prudentius*, translated by R. Martin Pope (London: J.M. Dent and Co.) available at http://www.ccel.org (accessed Aug. 4, 2008).

13. John Davidson, *The Odes of Solomon: Mystical Songs From the Time of Jesus* (Bath: Clear Press Limited, 2004), 50.

14. Ibid., 28.

15. Leigh Eric Schmidt, *Holy Fairs: Scotland and the Making of American Revivalism* (Grand Rapids: William B. Eerdmans Publishing Co., 1989/2001), 3, 218-219.

16. Ibid., 199.

17. Ibid., 197.

18. Ibid., 196-197.

19. *A Letter From a Blacksmith to the Ministers and Elders of the Church of Scotland in Which the Manner of Public Worship in That Church Is*

Considered; Its Inconveniences and Defects Pointed Out; and Methods for Removing of Them Humbly Proposed (London: 1759; New Haven: Oliver Steele, 1814), 18-38.

20. C.S. Lewis, *Letters to Malcolm: Chiefly on Prayer* (New York: Harcourt, Brace, and World, 1963), 92-93.

21. Bernard of Clairvaux, *Talks on the Song of Songs*, edited and modernized by Bernard Bangley (Brewster: Paraclete Press, 2002), 86.

22. Hendriksen, *New Testament Commentary,* 239.

23. J.B. Phillips, *The New Testament in Modern English* (The Macmillan Company, 1958).

24. John Chrysostom, "Saint Chrysostom: Homilies on Galatians, Ephesians, Philippians, Colossians, Thessalonians, Timothy, Titus, and Philemon," *A Select Library of the Nicene and Post-Nicene Fathers of the Christian Church*, ed. Philip Schaff, Homily XIX, Vol. XIII (Grand Rapids: William B. Eerdmans Publishing, Co.).

25. Clairvaux, *Talks on the Song of Songs*, 144.

Chapter 4

1 James Strong, *Exhaustive Concordance of the Bible* (Nashville: Abingdon, 1890), Entry *7832.*

2. Stephen Tomkins, *John Wesley: A Biography* (Grand Rapids and Cambridge: William B. Eerdmans Publishing Co., 2003), 90.

3. Paul Murray, "Drinking in the Word: Dominicans and the New Wine of the Gospel," http://www.op.org/international/english/Documents/Articles/murray_drinking.htm (accessed Jan. 23, 2008).

4. John Piper, *Desiring God* (Portland: Multnomah Press, 1986), 141.

5. William Barclay, *The Daily Study Bible* (Louisville: Westminster John Knox Press, 1955/2002).

6. Strong, *Exhaustive Concordance of the Bible,* Entry *3107.*

7. Ibid., Strong Entry *08055.*

8. Heinrich Gesenius, *Gesenius's Hebrew and Chaldee Lexicon to the Old Testament Scriptures*, edited by S.P. Tregelles (London: Samuel Bagster and Sons, 1847/1857).

9. Albert Pietersma and Benjamin Wright, *A New English Translation of the Septuagint* (New York/Oxford: Oxford University Press, 2007).

10. Murray, "Drinking in the Word: Dominicans and the New Wine of the Gospel."

11. Ibid.

12. Ibid.

Chapter 5

1. C.H. Dodd, ed., *The New English Bible* (Oxford and Cambridge: Oxford University Press and Cambridge University Press, 1961).

2. Murray, "Drinking in the Word: Dominicans and the New Wine of the Gospel."

3. Chris Armstrong, "Christian History Corner: 'Tell Billy Graham the Jesus People Love Him.'" *Christianity Today*, Vol. 46 (Dec. 2002).

4. *The Woody Allen Show*, Interview of Rev. Billy Graham by Woody Allen (Sept. 21, 1969).

5. Ronald Enroth, Edward Ericson, and C. Breckinridge Peters, *The Jesus People: Old-Time Religion in the Age of Aquarius* (Grand Rapids: William B. Eerdmans Publishing, 1972), 73.

6. Tim Dickinson, "A Prayer for W: Meet Arthur Blessitt: The Man Who Helped George W. Find Jesus," *Mother Jones* (The Foundation for National Progess, 2005), http://www.motherjones.com/news/outfront/2005/12/prayer_for_w.html (accessed Sept. 3, 2008).

7. Arthur Blessitt with Walter Wagner, *Turned on to Jesus* (Hawthorn Books, 1971).

8. Enroth, Ericson, and Peters, *The Jesus People: Old-Time Religion in the Age of Aquarius,* 164.

9. Robert Lynn Adams and Robert Jon Fox, "Mainlining Jesus: The New Trip," *Society*, Vol. 9, No. 4 (New York: Springer, February 1972).

10. *Philo*, vol. 5, pp. 554-55, translated by F.H. Colson and G.H. Whitaker, "On Dreams."

11. Adam Clarke, "Commentary on Proverbs 9," *The Adam Clarke Commentary* (1832), http://www.studylight.org/com/acc/view.cgi ?book=pr&chapter=009 (accessed Sept. 1, 2008).

12. St. John of the Cross, *A Spiritual Canticle of the Soul and the Bridegroom Christ*, translated by David Lewis, stanza xxv (Wincanton, 1909).

Chapter 6

1. Brother Lawrence, *The Practice of the Presence of God: The Best Rule of a Holy Life* (New York: Fleming H. Revell Co., 1895), 25-26.
2. R.P. Augustin Poulan, *Graces of Interior Prayer* (Reprinted by Kessinger Publishing, 1910), 62.

Chapter 7

1. Thomas Merton, *Seeds of Contemplation* (New York: New Directions Publishing, 1986 ed.), 69.
2. Clement of Alexandria, *The Instructor*, Book II, Ch. IV (A.D. 190).
3. W.E. Buszin, "Luther on Music," *Musical Quarterly*, Vol. 32 (1946), 89.
4. Ibid.
5. "Why Should the Devil Have All the Best Tunes?" (The Salvation Army) http://www1.salvationarmy.org/heritage.nsf/0/ 42d53ced9e c1583080256954004bff3e? OpenDocument (accessed Oct. 1, 2007).
6. John Waller, "Dancing Death," *British Broadcasting Corporation*, http://news.bbc.co.uk/today/hi/today/newsid_7608000/7608874.stm (accessed Sept. 27, 2008).
7. Robert Bartholomew, "Rethinking the Dancing Mania," Committee for Skeptical Inquiry, http://www.csicop.org/si/ 2000-07/dancing-mania.html (accessed Oct. 1, 2007).
8. Ibid.

Chapter 8

1. Jonathan Edwards, "The Distinguishing Marks of the Work of the Spirit of God," *Jonathan Edwards on Revival* (Edinburgh: The Banner

of Truth Trust, 1984), 91.

2. Dr. Barry Chant, "Myths About Jonathan Edwards," *Renewal Journal*, No. 14, http://www.pastornet.net.au/renewal/journal14/ 14c%20Chant.htm (accessed Dec. 10, 2007).

3. Jonathan Edwards, *A Treatise on the Religious Affections* (Edinburgh: Banner of Truth, 1746/1986), 52.

4. Jonathan Edwards, "Personal Narrative," *Jonathan Edwards: Letters and Personal Writings*, edited by George S. Claghorn (New Haven: Yale, 1998), 117.

5. Edwards, *Jonathan Edwards on Revival.*

6. A.A. Allen, *The Price of God's Miracle Working Power* (1950), http://www.netchapel.com (accessed Sept. 30, 2008).

7. John of Ruysbroeck, *Livre des Amants de Dieu*, translated into English as *Reflections From the Mirror of a Mystic*, by Earle Baillie (Thomas Baker, 1905), 57.

8. John of Ruysbroeck, *L'ornement des Noces,* Book II, Ch. 20.

9. Charles Chauncy, *Seasonable Thoughts on the State of Religion in New England* (Boston, 1743; reprint edition Hicksville, NY: Regina Press, 1975), 126-129.

10. Ibid., 94-95.

11. Stanley M. Burgess, "The Pentecostal Tradition," *Christian History & Biography* (Carol Stream, IL: Christianity Today, Inc., April 1, 1998).

12. Charles G. Finney, *The Autobiography of Charles Finney* (Minneapolis: Bethany House, Inc., 1977), 21-22.

13. Francis MacNutt, *The Power to Heal* (Notre Dame, IN: Ave Maria Press, 1977), 200.

14. Gertrude Chambers, *Oswald Chambers: His Life and Work* (London: Simpkin Marshall, Ltd., 1947), 103.

15. "Enthusiasm in Asia: the New Prophecy," *Christian History & Biography*, Issue 9 (Carol Stream, IL: Christianity Today, Inc., Jan. 1, 1986).

16. Ibid.

17. John Wesley, "Journals and Diaries," *The Works of John Wesley*, edited by W. Reginald Ward and Richard P. Heitzenrater, Part III, Vol. 20, 1743–54 (reprinted Nashville: Abingdon, 1991), 356.

18. Burgess, *The Pentecostal Tradition*.

19. Chris Armstrong, "Christian History Corner: Timeline of the Spirit-Gifted," *Christianity Today*, Vol. 46 (Oct. 2002).

20. "Shouting Methodists" (Jesus Army/Jesus Fellowship Church), http://www.jesus.org.uk/ja/mag_revivalfires_methodists.shtml (accessed Oct. 13, 2004). Article source: Hudson, Winthrop. *Encounter* (Winter, 1968, Vol. 29).

21. Ann Taves, *Fits, Trances, and Visions* (Princeton: Princeton University Press, 1999), 92-93.

22. MacNutt, *The Power to Heal*, 198.

23. Ibid., 199.

24. Peter Cartwright, *Autobiography of Peter Cartwright* (New York and Nashville: Abingdon Press, 1956), 68, 88-89, 102-104, 130, 143, 161.

25. Taves, *Fits, Trances, and Visions*, 333.

26. Ibid.

27. "Trance Evangelism: Continuance of Mrs. Woodworth's Meetings at Hartford, Ind." *The Daily Democratic Times* (Lima, Ohio: Feb. 2, 1885), cf. Kenneth Richard Kline-Walczak, *Testimonies of Signs and Wonders, Evangelistic Crusades of Maria Buelah Woodworth-Etter in Moline, Rock Island, Illinois, and Davenport, Iowa in the Years 1902-1903-1907 or Redigging the Wells of Holy Spirit Renewal: Our Forgotten Heritage in the Quad Cities* (2006).

28. "Sister Woodworth Names Her Date for Fort Wayne—Remarkable Scenes at Pendleton," *The Gazette* (Fort Wayne, IN: May 23, 1885), cf. Kline-Walczak, *Testimonies of Signs and Wonders*.

29. "The Rise of Pentecostalism: A Gallery—Setting the Vision. Pentecostalism's Early Leaders Were as Varied as They Were Dynamic." *Christian History & Biography*, Issue 58 (Carol Stream, IL: Christianity Today, Inc., April 1, 1998).

30. Maria Woodworth-Etter, *A Diary of Signs and Wonders* (Tulsa: Harrison House, 1980 ed.).

31. "Said to Be Religion: Strange Scenes at 'Revival Meetings' Held in Indiana," *The New York Times* (New York: Jan. 24, 1885), cf. Kline-Walczak, *Testimonies of Signs and Wonders*.

32. Wayne E. Warner, *The Woman Evangelist: The Life and Times of Charismatic Evangelist Maria B. Woodworth-Etter* (Metuchen, NJ, and London: Scarecrow Press, Inc., 1986), 82, 83, 95.

33. Dean Peck, "Field Notes," and "Alliance Notes," *Christian and Missionary Alliance Weekly* (Aug. 11, 1897), 137.

34. A.W. Tozer, *Worship: The Missing Jewel* (Camp Hill, PA: Christian Publications, 1992), 20-21.

35. Irene E. Lewis, *Life Sketch of Rev. Mary C. Norton: Remarkable Healings on Mission Fields* (Los Angeles: Pilgrim's Mission, Inc., 1954), 27.

36. A.B. Simpson, *Days of Heaven on Earth* (Camp Hill, PA: Christian Publications, 1984).

37. A.B. Simpson, "Simpson's Nyack Diary," cited by Charles W. Nienkirchen, *A.B. Simpson and the Pentecostal Movement* (Peabody, MA: Hendrickson Publishers, 1992), 145.

38. A.W. Tozer, *Wingspread* (Harrisburg, PA: Christian Publications, 1943), 62.

39. Taves, *Fits, Trances, and Visions,* 154.

40. Ibid., 157.

41. Charles G. Finney, *The Autobiography of Charles Finney* (Minneapolis: Bethany House, Inc., 1977).

42. Eifion Evans, *Revival Comes to Wales* (Bryntirion, Bridgend, Wales: Evangelical Press of Wales, 1959, 1967), 70.

43. Leona Choy, *Andrew and Emma Murray: An Intimate Portrait of Their Marriage and Ministry* (Winchester, VA: Golden Morning Publishing, 2000), 85-90.

44. R.A. Torrey, *The Power of Prayer* (Grand Rapids: Zondervan, 1971), 46-47.

45. *Christian and Missionary Alliance Weekly* (Feb. 10, 1906), 84.

46. Hans-Jurgen Goertz, *The Anabaptists* (London and New York: Routledge, 1996), 21.

47. Johann Lorenz Mosheim, *Institutes of Ecclesiastical History, Ancient and Modern: In Four Books*, translated by James Murdock (New York: Harper & Brothers, 1841), 205.

48. "The Anabaptists," *Christian History & Biography*, Issue 5 (Carol Stream, IL: Christianity Today, Inc., 1985).

49. *Revelation and Revolution: Basic Writings of Thomas Muntzer,* translated and edited by Michael G. Baylor (Bethlehem: Lehigh University Press, Bethlehem, 1993), 54-55.

Chapter 9

1. "'Toronto' in the Cevennes" (Jesus Fellowship Church), www .jesus.org.uk/ja/mag_revivalfires_cevennes.shtml (accessed Oct. 13, 2004). Article sources: Henri Bosc, *La Guerre des Cevennes* (1985-1993 reprint); Hillel Schwartz, *The French Prophets* (1980); anon, *The Protestant Prophets With the Accounts of Various Marvels* (1707).

2. Georgia Cosmos, *Huguenot Prophecy and Clandestine Worship in the Eighteenth Century: "The Sacred Theatre of the Cévennes"* (Aldershot and Burlington, VT: Ashgate, 2005).

3. Ibid.

4. Marc Vernous, *A Preservative Against the False Prophets of the Times* (London: 1708), 23-24.

5. Ann Taves, *Fits, Trances, and Visions* (Princeton: Princeton University Press, 1999), 20.

6. Ibid., 192.

7. Lambert Dolphin, "Yin, Yang, the Tao and Wholeness," (1991/2007), http://www.ldolphin.org/YinYang.shtml (accessed Mar. 8, 2007).

8. Albert Farges, *Mystical Phenomena Compared With Their Human and Diabolical Counterfeits,* translated by S.P. Jacques (London: Burns Oats & Washbourne Ltd., 1926), 497.

9. Montague Summers, *The Physical Phenomena of Mysticism* (London: Rider & Co., 1950), 162-163.

10. Teresa of Avila, *The Way of Perfection,* translated by E. Allison Peers (Image Books, 1964 ed.).

11. Ibid.

12. George Barker Stevens, *The Epistles of Paul in Modern English* (Wheaton, IL: Verploegh Editions, 1980 ed.).

Chapter 10

1. This transcript is from Teresa of Avila's beatification proceedings. Cited from Herbert Thurston, *The Physical Phenomena of Mysticism* (Chicago: Henry Regnery, 1952), 12.

2. Clairvaux, *Talks on the Song of Songs,* 3.

3. *Abrege de la doctrine mystique,* quoted by Fr. Meynard and Cited by R.P. Augustin Poulan, *Graces of Interior Prayer* (Reprinted by Kessinger Publishing, 1910), 193.

4. Teresa of Avila, *The Life of Saint Teresa of Avila by Herself* (London: Penguin Group, 1957 ed.), 136.

5. Poulan, *Graces of Interior Prayer,* 143.

6. A valuable source on the life of Sundar Singh is *The Saffron Robe* by Janet Lynn Watson (London: Hodder and Stoughton, 1975).

Chapter 11

1. R.P. Augustin Poulan, *Graces of Interior Prayer* (Reprinted by Kessinger Publishing, 1910) (Citing Cepari, *Vie,* English translation), 166.

2. Ibid.

3. Teresa of Avila, *The Life of Saint Teresa of Avila by Herself* (London: Penguin Group, 1957 ed.).

4. Poulan, *Graces of Interior Prayer,* 179.

5. Albert Farges, *Mystical Phenomena Compared With Their Human and Diabolical Counterfeits,* translated by S.P. Jacques (London: Burns Oats & Washbourne Ltd., 1926), 162-163.

6. Ibid.

7. Ibid., 182.

8. *The Life of St. Philip Neri,* edited by Fr. F.T. Antrobus, Vol. 1 (London: 1902), 145.

9. Montague Summers, *The Physical Phenomena of Mysticism* (London: Rider & Co., 1950), 96.

10. Ibid., 112.

11. Albert J. Hebert, *Saints Who Raised the Dead* (Rockford: Tan Books & Publishers, Inc., 1986), 95.

12. Teresa of Avila, *The Life of Saint Teresa of Avila by Herself,* 136.

13. Teresa of Avila, *Interior Castle* (London: Thomas Baker, 1921 ed.).

14. N. Marion Page, "Akiane: An Interview With a Miracle," *The Independent* (Oct. 2007) http://westsider.org/joomla/index.php?option =com_content&task=view&id=116&Itemid=2 (accessed Oct. 2007).

15. Teresa of Avila, *The Life of Saint Teresa of Avila by Herself,* 142.

16. Ibid.

17. For more than 400 accounts of bizarre dead raising stories throughout history, see Albert J. Hebert's *Saints Who Raised the Dead* (Rockford: Tan Books & Publishers, Inc., 1986).

18. Ibid., 117.

19. Ibid., 151.

20. Teresa of Avila, *Interior Castle*, sixth mansion, ch. 4.

21. Ed Hird, "Rediscovering Handel's Messiah," *Deep Cove Crier* (April 1993), http://www3.telus.net/st_simons/cr9304.htm (accessed July 30, 2007).

22. Ibid., cf. Horatio Townsend *An Account of the Visit of Handel to Dublin* (1852) p. 93, citing Laetitia Matilda Hawkins *Anecdotes, Biographical Sketches and Memoirs,* vol. 1 (1822).

23. George Barton Cutten, *The Psychological Phenomena of Christianity* (New York: C. Scribner's Sons, 1908), 42.

24 W.F. Trotter, *Pascal's Pensees* (New York: E.P. Dutton and Co., 1958), 113.

25. Summers, *The Physical Phenomena of Mysticism*, 103.

26. Ibid.

27. Teresa of Avila, *The Life of Saint Teresa of Avila by Herself,* 136.

28. Teresa of Avila, *Interior Castle*, sixth mansion, ch. 4.

29. Summers, *The Physical Phenomena of Mysticism*, 105.

30. Ibid., 103.

31. Ibid.

32. Farges, *Mystical Phenomena Compared With Their Human and Diabolical Counterfeits,* 169.

Chapter 12

1. Albert J. Hebert, *Saints Who Raised the Dead* (Rockford: Tan Books & Publishers, Inc., 1986), 246.

2. Montague Summers, *The Physical Phenomena of Mysticism* (London: Rider & Co., 1950), 11.

3. Herbert Thurston, *The Physical Phenomena of Mysticism* (Chicago: Henry Regnery, 1952), 1.

4. Ibid., 251.

5. Ibid., 83-84.

6. Joan Carroll Cruz, *Mysteries, Marvels, Miracles: In the Lives of the Saints* (Rockford: Tan Books and Publishers, Inc., 1997), 159.

7. Summers, *The Physical Phenomena of Mysticism*, 62.

8. Albert Farges, *Mystical Phenomena Compared With Their Human and Diabolical Counterfeits*, translated by S.P. Jacques (London: Burns Oats & Washbourne Ltd., 1926), 547.

9. Cruz, *Mysteries, Marvels, Miracles: In the Lives of the Saints*, 167.

10. Ibid., 241.

11. Thurston, *The Physical Phenomena of Mysticism*, 209.

12. Ibid., 209.

13. Cruz, *Mysteries, Marvels, Miracles: In the Lives of the Saints*, 177-178.

14. Ibid., 210.

15. Ibid., 179.

16. Summers, *The Physical Phenomena of Mysticism*, 71.

17. Ibid., 71.

18. Thurston, *The Physical Phenomena of Mysticism*, 221.

19. Brother Yun and Paul Hattaway, *The Heavenly Man* (Michigan: Monarch Books, 2002), 11-12.

20. Hebert, *Saints Who Raised the Dead*, 242-243.

21. Farges, *Mystical Phenomena Compared With Their Human and Diabolical Counterfeits*, 562.

22. Teresa of Avila, *The Life of Saint Teresa of Avila by Herself* (London: Penguin Group, 1957 ed.).

23. Hebert, *Saints Who Raised the Dead*, 243.

24. Summers, *The Physical Phenomena of Mysticism*, 63.

25. "The Amish: History in the U.S. and Canada: 1700 to Now," Ontario Consultants on Religious Tolerance, http://www .religioustolerance.org/amish2.htm (accessed Sept. 12, 2007).

26. Cutten, *The Psychological Phenomena of Christianity*, 58.

27. David Mason, Jr., "The Preacher Who Slept on the Job," http://refugembc.org/Sleeping%20Preacher.htm (accessed Sept. 28, 2007).

28. Hebert, *Saints Who Raised the Dead*, 245.

29. Cruz, *Mysteries, Marvels, Miracles: In the Lives of the Saints*, 208.

30. Ibid., 6-8.

31. Summers, *The Physical Phenomena of Mysticism*, 61.

32. Ibid., 9. Referencing Charles Warren Stoddard, *Saint Anthony, The Wonder Worker of Padua* (Notre Dame, IN: The Ave Maria, 1896; Rockford, IL: TAN, 1971), 56.

33. Thurston, *The Physical Phenomena of Mysticism*, 198.

34. Ibid., 200-201.

35. Extreme Prophetic TV, "Psychics, New Age, and the Occult," Program 10 (2005).

36. Summers, *The Physical Phenomena of Mysticism*, 97.

37. Teresa of Avila, *The Life of Saint Teresa of Avila by Herself*, 139.

38. R.P. Augustin Poulan, *Graces of Interior Prayer* (Reprinted by Kessinger Publishing, 1910) (Citing Cepari, *Vie*, English translation), 158.

39. Teresa of Avila, *The Life of Saint Teresa of Avila by Herself*, 117.

40. Poulan, *Graces of Interior Prayer*, 172.

41. *Life of Gemma Galgani*, translated by A.M. O'Sullivan, O.S.B. (Sands and Co.).

42. Thurston, *The Physical Phenomena of Mysticism*, 56.

43. Ted Harrison, *Stigmata: A Medieval Mystery in a Modern Age* (New York: St. Martin's Press, 1994), 87.

44. Poulan, *Graces of Interior Prayer*, 144-145.

45. Fr. Hamon, *Revue pratique d'Apologetique* (Dec. 15, 1906), 351. Cited in Poulan, *Graces of Interior Prayer*.

46. Teresa of Avila, *The Way of Perfection*, translated by E. Allison Peers (Image Books, 1964 ed.), 53.

47. Summers, *The Physical Phenomena of Mysticism*, 61.

48. Thurston, *The Physical Phenomena of Mysticism*, 205.

49. Ibid., 101.

50. Summers, *The Physical Phenomena of Mysticism*, 127.

51. Teresa of Avila, *The Life of Saint Teresa of Avila by Herself.*

52. Summers, *The Physical Phenomena of Mysticism*, 118.

53. Thurston, *The Physical Phenomena of Mysticism*, 68.

54. Summers, *The Physical Phenomena of Mysticism*, 156-157.

Chapter 13

1. Albert J. Hebert, *Saints Who Raised the Dead* (Rockford: Tan Books & Publishers, Inc., 1986), 243.

2. Extreme Prophetic TV, "Psychics, New Age, and the Occult," Program 10 (2005).

3. *John G. Lake: His Life, His Sermons, His Boldness of Faith* (Fort Worth: Kenneth Copeland Publications, 1994).

4. Ruth Ward Heflin, *Golden Glory: The New Wave of Signs and Wonders* (McDougal Publishing Co., 1999).

5. David Herzog, *Glory Invasion* (Shippensburg, PA: Destiny Image, 2007).

6. Hebert, *Saints Who Raised the Dead*, 248.

7. Teresa of Avila, *The Life of Saint Teresa of Avila by Herself* (London: Penguin Group, 1957 ed.), 137.

8. Ibid., 142.

9. R.P. Augustin Poulan, *Graces of Interior Prayer* (Reprinted by Kessinger Publishing, 1910) (Citing Cepari, *Vie*, English translation), 171.

10. "Levitate," *Encyclopedia of Occultism and Parapsychology* (The Gale Group, Inc, 2001). Cited on *Answers.com*, http://www.answers.com/topic/levitate (accessed Jan. 24, 2008).

11. Poulan, *Graces of Interior Prayer*, 181.

12. Albert Farges, *Mystical Phenomena Compared With Their Human and Diabolical Counterfeits*, translated by S.P. Jacques (London: Burns Oats & Washbourne Ltd., 1926), 536-537.

13. Teresa of Avila, *The Life of Saint Teresa of Avila by Herself*, 137.

14. Herbert Thurston, *The Physical Phenomena of Mysticism* (Chicago: Henry Regnery, 1952), 13.

15. Poulan, *Graces of Interior Prayer*, 170.

16. Teresa of Avila, *The Life of Saint Teresa of Avila by Herself*, 137.

17. Joan Carroll Cruz, *Mysteries, Marvels, Miracles: In the Lives of the Saints* (Rockford: Tan Books and Publishers, Inc., 1997), 23.

18. Poulan, *Graces of Interior Prayer*, 171.

19. "Levitate," *Encyclopedia of Occultism and Parapsychology* (2001).

20. Cruz, *Mysteries, Marvels, Miracles: In the Lives of the Saints*, 22.

21. "Levitate," *Encyclopedia of Occultism and Parapsychology* (2001).

22. Ibid.

23. Ibid.

24. Ibid.

25. Poulan, *Graces of Interior Prayer*, cf. Capari, *Vie.*

26. Ibid.

27. John R. Hall, *Gone From the Promised Land* (New Brunswick: Transaction Publishers, 2004), 45.

Chapter 14

1. Ann Taves, *Fits, Trances, and Visions* (Princeton: Princeton University Press, 1999), 74.

2. "Hugh 'Stoked' up the Old Fire" (Jesus Army/Jesus Fellowship Church), http://www.jesus.org.uk/ja/mag_revivalfires_primitive.shtml (accessed Oct. 13, 2004). Article source: Joseph Ritson, *The Romance of Primitive Methodism* (E. Dolton).

3. John Telford, "The Life of John Wesley," http://wesley.nnu.edu/wesleyan_theology/telford/telford_ch13.htm (accessed Sept. 28, 2007).

4. John Wesley, "Journals and Diaries," *The Works of John Wesley*, edited by W. Reginald Ward and Richard P. Heitzenrater, Vol. 19 (1738–43; reprinted Nashville: Abingdon, 1984), 49-51.

5. Ibid., 60.

6. Ibid., 49.

7. Taves, *Fits, Trances, and Visions* (Citing a letter to Mrs. Elizabeth Hutton in *The Works of John Wesley*, Vol. 26, p. 113), 74.

8. John Wesley, *Journals of John Wesley* (Vol. 4), 419.

9. Mike Bickle, *The Pleasures of Loving God* (Lake Mary: Charisma House, 2000), 47.

10. "George Whitefield," *Wikipedia, The Free Encyclopedia*, http://en.wikipedia.org/wiki/George_Whitefield (accessed Sept. 5, 2007).

11. William De Arteaga, *Quenching the Spirit* (Lake Mary: Charisma House, 1992), 39.

12. Alan Morrison. "True Revival or Apostasy?" http://www .inplainsite.org/html/genuine_revival.html (accessed Sept. 5, 2007).

13. John Wesley, *The Journal of the Rev. John Wesley*, Vol. 1 (London: J. Kershaw, 1827), 201-202.

14. "George Whitefield, 1714–1770, English Evangelist," *Believer's Web*, http://www.believersweb.org/view.cfm?id=94&rc=1&list=multi (accessed Sept. 5, 2007).

15. Benjamin Hart, *Faith and Freedom* (Lewis, Stanley & Associates, 1990), http://www.leaderu.com/orgs/cdf/ff/chap14.html (accessed Sept. 25, 2007).

16. "George Whitefield, 1714–1770, English Evangelist," *Believer's Web*, http://www.believersweb.org/view.cfm?id=94&rc=1&list=multi (accessed Sept. 5, 2007).

17. De Arteaga, *Quenching the Spirit*, 28.

18. Ibid., 56.

19. Ibid., 57.

20. Paul Barker, "George Whitefield," http://www.paulbarker.org/ george_whitefield.html (accessed Sept. 5, 2007), and De Arteaga, *Quenching the Spirit*.

21. Taves, *Fits, Trances, and Visions*, 71.

22. Morgan Edwards, *Materials Towards a History of the Baptists, Vol. 2, 1770–1792* (Danielsville, GA: Heritage Papers, 1984), 90.

23. Taves, *Fits, Trances, and Visions*, 86.

24. Ibid., 87.

25. Ibid., 89-90.

26. Leigh Eric Schmidt, *Holy Fairs: Scotland and the Making of American Revivalism* (Grand Rapids: William B. Eerdmans Publishing Co., 1989/2001).

27. "Revival and Spiritual Awakening," Jeff Ziegler and Jay Rogers, http://forerunner.com/forerunner/X0606_Revival__Spiritual_A.html (accessed July 6, 2007).

28. "Spiritual Awakenings in North America," *Christian History & Biography*, Issue 23 (Carol Stream, IL: Christianity Today, Inc.), 26.

29. Paul Keith Conkin, *Cane Ridge, America's Pentecost* (Madison: The University of Wisconsin Press, 1989), 105.

30. Barry Manuel, "The Pensacola Outpouring: The Father's Blessing for the 90's," http://jmm.aaa.net.au/articles/8955.htm (accessed Sept. 5, 2007).

31. Ibid.

32. Extract of a Letter From Colonel Robert Patterson, of Lexington, Kentucky, to the Rev. Dr. John King, September 25, 1801, http://www.caneridge.org/revival.html (accessed Sept. 5, 2007).

33. Schmidt, *Holy Fairs*, 21.

34. Ibid., 29.

35. Ibid., 146.

36. Ibid., xvii.

37. Ibid., xiv, xvi.

38. Ibid., 170.

39. Ibid., xx.

40. Richard McNemar, *The Kentucky Revival; Or, A Short History of the Late Extraordinary Outpouring of the Spirit of God in the Western States of America* (New York: Jenkins, 1846), 26.

41. Edward Scribner Ames, *The Psychology of Religious Experience* (Boston: Houghton Mifflin, 1910), 261.

42. Joseph Thomas, *The Life, Travels, and Gospel Labors of Eld. Joseph Thomas, More Widely Known as the "White Pilgrim"* (New York: Cummings, 1861), 36, 61, 88.

43. Schmidt, *Holy Fairs*, 64.

Chapter 15

1. John Piper, *Desiring God* (Portland: Multnomah Press, 1986), 222.

2. Eusebius, *The History of the Church* (London: Penguin, 1965), 337-338.

3. Diego R. Yuki, *The Martyrs' Hill Nagasaki* (Nagasaki: 26 Martyrs' Museum, 1979/1993), 9.

4. Richard Wurmbrand, *The Sweetest Song* (Bartlesville: Living Sacrifice Book Company, 1988), 210.

5. John Foxe, *Foxe's Book of Martyrs* (Nashville: Thomas Nelson, 2000 ed.), 1-2.

6. Wurmbrand, *The Sweetest Song*, 206-207.

7. Cutten, *The Psychological Phenomena of Christianity*, 41.

8. Farges, *Mystical Phenomena Compared With Their Human and Diabolical Counterfeits*, 22-23.

9. Ibid.

10. Ibid.

11. Summers, *The Physical Phenomena of Mysticism*, 100.

12. Howard and Geraldine Taylor, *Hudson Taylor's Spiritual Secret* (Chicago: Moody Press, 1932), 30.

13. *Autobiography of George Mueller*, compiled by Fred Bergen (London: J. Nisbet Co., 1906), 152.

14. Michael Molinos, *The Spiritual Guide* (Sargent: Christian Books Publishing House, 1982 ed.), 73.

Chapter 16

1. Rick Joyner, "Revolution," *The Morningstar Prophetic Bulletin*, No. 30 (May 2000).

2. Ibid.

3.. Michael Talbot, *The Holographic Universe* (HarpersCollins, 1991), 129.

4. Ibid., 131.

5. Ibid., 129.

6. Vinson Synan, *The Century of the Holy Spirit* (Nashville: Thomas Nelson, 2001).

7. Talbot, *The Holographic Universe*, 129-131.

8. William Howitt, *The History of the Supernatural in All Ages and Nations: And in All Churches* (University of Michigan Library, reprint 2005), 135.

9. "Levitate," *Encyclopedia of Occultism and Parapsychology* (2001).

10. Talbot, *The Holographic Universe*, 129-131.

11. Synan, *The Century of the Holy Spirit.*

12. Howitt, *The History of the Supernatural in All Ages and Nations: And in All Churches*, 148.

13. "Consolamentum," *Wikipedia, The Free Encyclopedia* (Wikimedia Foundation, Inc.), http://en.wikipedia.org/w/index.php?title =Consolamentum&oldid=149313204 (accessed Jan. 8, 2008).

Ministry
Resources

audio & video resources available from

Books
Miracle Workers, Reformers & The New Mystics

CDs
Bizarre Miracles
The New Martyrs
The Spirit of Burning
The Spirit of the Fear of the Lord

CD Sets
Prophetic School
Fire By Night
Supernatural Encounters
Glory Revolution
Engaging the Seer Realm

Music
Toking the Ghost

DVD Sets
Manifestations of Glory
The Breaker Anointing

More titles available through:

PO Box 2333
Griffin, GA 30224
Phone: 1-866-DIE DAILY
Website: www.TheNewMystics.org

JOHN CROWDER is an itinerant revivalist, ministering in churches, conferences, and events worldwide. He is author of *Miracle Workers, Reformers and the New Mystics* and founder of Sons of Thunder (SOT) Ministries and Publications. John carries a vision to see mystical, supernatural Christianity restored to the church and for revival to burn to the margins of society. SOT currently plants children's homes and hosts evangelism campaigns in developing nations. John, his wife Lily, and their four children find their satisfaction in the simplicity of loving God and demonstrating the finished works of the Cross. They are fascinated by the Glory of God and have witnessed many unusual miracles and manifestations of His power.

Free Weekly Teaching

Stay connected with our ministry by signing up for free, weekly online teachings from John Crowder. Simply visit our Website at www.TheNewMystics.org and enter your e-mail address for our Word of the Week to be automatically sent to you.

How to Book an Engagement

Would you like to request John Crowder or a Sons of Thunder team member to speak at your church or conference in your area? Visit us online or e-mail us at info@thenewmystics.org with the details of your engagement. John and his team will pray regarding your request, and you may expect a prompt confirmation.

Drunken Glory Tours

The Drunken Glory Tour is a traveling love feast, featuring the ministry of John Crowder and Benjamin Dunn. These celebratory events release exuberant impartation in a joyous, playful atmosphere of ecstatic encounter. If you would like join the tour or host a DGT at your church or ministry, visit the tour Website: www.DrunkenGlory.com.

Partner With Us

Thanks to your financial support, we are able to make a tremendous Kingdom impact in the nations. If you would like to link arms with the anointing on our ministry, we would invite you to take a step closer into the Sons of Thunder family by joining us as a regular monthly partner. You will also receive regular teaching gifts and updates by mail. For more information visit our Website: www.TheNewMystics.org.

Additional copies of this book and other
book titles from DESTINY IMAGE are
available at your local bookstore.

Call toll-free: 1-800-722-6774.

Send a request for a catalog to:

Destiny Image® Publishers, Inc.
P.O. Box 310
Shippensburg, PA 17257-0310

*"Speaking to the Purposes of God for this
Generation and for the Generations to Come."*

For a complete list of our titles,
visit us at www.destinyimage.com.